A Concise History of
U.S. Foreign Policy

A Concise History of
U.S. Foreign Policy

Fourth Edition

Joyce P. Kaufman

ROWMAN & LITTLEFIELD
Lanham • Boulder • New York • London

Published by Rowman & Littlefield
A wholly owned subsidiary of
The Rowman & Littlefield Publishing Group, Inc.
4501 Forbes Boulevard, Suite 200, Lanham, Maryland 20706
https://rowman.com

Unit A, Whitacre Mews, 26-34 Stannary Street, London SE11 4AB,
United Kingdom

British Library Cataloguing in Publication Information Available

Library of Congress Cataloging-in-Publication Data
Names: Kaufman, Joyce P., author.
Title: A concise history of U.S. foreign policy / Joyce P. Kaufman.
Other titles: Concise history of US foreign policy | Concise history of United States
    foreign policy
Description: Fourth edition. | Lanham, Maryland : Rowman & Littlefield, 2017. | Includes
    bibliographical references and index.
Identifiers: LCCN 2016048442 (print) | LCCN 2016056731 (ebook) | ISBN
    9781442270442 (cloth : alk. paper) | ISBN 9781442270459 (pbk. : alk. paper) | ISBN
    9781442270466 (electronic)
Subjects: LCSH: United States—Foreign relations.
Classification: LCC E183.7 .K36 2017 (print) | LCC E183.7 (ebook) | DDC 327.73—dc23
LC record available at https://lccn.loc.gov/2016048442

∞ ™ The paper used in this publication meets the minimum requirements of American
National Standard for Information Sciences Permanence of Paper for Printed Library
Materials, ANSI/NISO Z39.48-1992.

Printed in the United States of America

Table of Contents

Preface to the Fourth Edition

As I write this in the summer of 2016, three years after I revised the third edition, I cannot help but marvel at the current state of the world and how much has changed since 2013. While it was clear that the glow from the election of Barack Obama had faded, as we approach another major presidential election his popularity is on the rise again. The Brexit vote raises questions about the future of what had been one of the most stable and important organizations, the EU and also NATO, as well as what globalization really means. Rather than a time of optimism and hope, the summer of 2016 is one of uncertainty and instability as the United States has to react, once again, to major changes in the international system and to ask what those changes will mean to this country and to an incoming president. Rather than a world characterized by integration and cooperation, we once again seem to be facing disintegration and even a possible resurgence of the tensions that characterized the Cold War. There is ongoing instability in the Middle East, even in those countries—Afghanistan and Iraq—that the United States went to war to try to stabilize, calling into question even more the foreign policy decisions of earlier administrations. All of this must be assessed against the rhetoric and rancor of an especially vicious presidential campaign. In short, this is a time of uncertainty.

That said, no U.S. president has the luxury of sitting back and waiting to see what will happen next. Rather, he or she will have to continue to define U.S. foreign policy in a changing world from the moment of taking the oath of office in January. And from that perspective the lessons of the past can help guide the future. Noted foreign policy analyst Walter Russell Mead wrote in his book *Special Providence* that Americans, even those in positions of leadership and responsibility, show a "lack of interest in the history of American foreign policy."[1] And there are many examples of that. At the end of the Spanish-American War, then-President McKinley was persuaded by the "new imperialists" to put a military governor in place in the Philippines over the warnings of the anti-imperialists. The imperialists dismissed the concerns of the anti-imperialists who claimed that the Americans "would be welcomed as liberators."[2] These are virtually the same words used by George W. Bush when he sent the United States into Iraq in 2003, allegedly to protect the United States and its allies against Saddam Hussein and his weapons of mass destruction. In both these cases, the United States in the Philippines and in Iraq, more than one hundred years apart, the results were the same and the naysayers proved to be correct. In the first case, fighting continued in the Philippines until 1916, eighteen years after the United States went into the country. As of this writing in 2016, U.S. troops remain in Iraq thirteen years after they were sent in, and despite the Status of Forces Agreement that was to end U.S. involvement, the country remains unstable and the United States remains involved.

There are lessons to be learned from history, but we need to be willing to learn them. As each president seeks to chart his or her own course, it is often difficult to look at the past. Rather, it is far easier to see each situation as new and unique. But in doing so, the trends of history that could help inform the present tend to be lost. I am a political scientist and I am writing this from that disciplinary perspective. However, this book is historical in focus so that it will be possible to identify the trends, to see what has been continuous and what has changed. I believe that only by understanding these trends is it possible to truly understand the course of U.S. foreign policy and how we got to where we are today.

The fourth edition, like the three that preceded it, is meant to be a concise guide to understanding U.S. foreign policy and therefore it is not meant to be a definitive statement about the topic. As I noted in the prefaces to the previous editions, it can and should be augmented by other readings, including the use of primary source documents. Which documents to use, and how and when to refer to them, is up to each faculty member who chooses to adopt this book. Like earlier editions, this book is meant to be accessible to undergraduates and to anyone else who is interested in learning more about the history and evolution of U.S. foreign policy from the founding of the country to the present.

In writing this book initially and in revising it, I have learned a great deal from the myriad students who have taken this course and others with me at Whittier College, where teaching excellence is a high priority. While my students have learned the substance of the material from me, I have learned how to be a better teacher from them. And I have tried to use my "teacher voice" in writing this so that it would be comprehensible to anyone interested in the topic but who may not have any background on the topic beyond a desire to learn more.

As usual, I am grateful to Susan McEachern, my editor at Rowman & Littlefield and a good friend. While I was not yet ready to revise this book, she was the one who convinced me that it was time and further encouraged me by sending me the various reviews that she had received by faculty who had adopted this book. I thank all of them for their comments, suggestions, and corrections. Also at Rowman & Littlefield thanks go to assistant editor Rebeccah Shumaker, who responded quickly and patiently to all my questions, and Alden Perkins, production editor. I worked with Alden on previous books for Rowman & Littlefield and it was comforting to know that she would be looking over the production of this book as well.

I was fortunate to be able to revise this book in the most peaceful surroundings in the Eastern Sierra where we spend our summers. It would not be possible for me to have the focus necessary to do this writing were I not in a place that allows me to balance my writing and thinking with golf and tennis, activities that are necessary to my well-being in so many ways. My dear friends, both in the Eastern Sierra and in Whittier, have continued to provide a source of inspiration and encouragement. They are the ones to remind me of the need to balance the many aspects of my life that I juggle and are there to help me do so. In Whittier, Elizabeth, Anne, Kathy, and Trish are especially important and our walk-and-talk moments on the golf course are valued. In June Lake, the Divas have provided regular tennis diversions. I have found that being able to walk the golf course with Deborah or have lunch with Francesca after a tennis game provide the perspective that helps me think and gives me the distance necessary to write. The teachers (Judy, Jeanne, Suzanne, and Tookie) have also helped remind me how, before they are students of mine, someone has to teach children the fundamentals. Chuck keeps me laughing with his stories, and Russ reminds me that my tennis really is (and can continue to get) better. Thanks of course to Irene Carlyle, who read an early draft of the revision and provided her usual incisive comments. I owe a special debt to my dear friend from graduate school Lois Vietri, who came to teaching U.S. foreign policy rather late in her academic career but whose questions and approaches are insightful and have really made me think about how best to present some of the materials. I am grateful to all of them and to the countless others who have helped me over the years.

I owe special thanks to my husband, Robert B. Marks, for the ongoing conversations about foreign policy and the state of the world that are far more pleasant when held on our deck in June Lake. Those conversations provide further ideas and refinement to my own thinking. Lest it appear that all we do is have these deep conversations, time walking with Stanton, kayaking, playing golf, and relaxing are also an important part of our lives. And I never forget I how fortunate I am.

Joyce P. Kaufman

Chapter One

Setting the Stage for Understanding U.S. Foreign Policy

What would happen if two schools of thought competed to dominate the making of U.S. foreign policy? One school, led by one of the major political leaders, stressed the importance of a strong relationship between the national government and big business and argued that the country needed to be integrated into the global system, especially the international economy, in terms that were favorable to it. The other school, led by an opposing political leader, stressed that the most important thing for the country would be to remain removed from foreign policy and to concentrate instead on safeguarding the homeland, intervening only when it becomes absolutely necessary. Sound familiar? These sound like arguments made by some of the candidates running for President of the United States in 2016. However, they were the arguments between Alexander Hamilton on the one hand and Thomas Jefferson on the other,[1] put forward when the United States was created. Should the United States be more involved in the world or not? Is it the responsibility of the United States to help spread democracy? When should the United States intervene in the affairs of other countries? These are not new questions, although the answers keep changing as times, circumstances, and the priorities of the presidents and other political leaders change.

This book on American foreign policy draws on basic political science approaches and theories. However, it is difficult to arrive at a practical understanding of U.S. foreign policy and the decisions that have been made without grounding them in history. To integrate the approaches, we will use a historical framework to put the major themes and concepts of U.S. foreign policy into the context of the time at which they were formulated. This requires looking at the various domestic political priorities as well as the international context that helped frame the decisions made, for the two go hand in hand in the making of foreign policy. In addition, this text relies heavily on primary documents in order to explore the ideas as fully as possible, using the words of the authors of those policies. Using primary sources is important since doing so will provide a broader context for understanding the particular policies as they were defined and implemented *at that particular time in U.S. history.* The time and context might change, but each policy set the stage for what followed and therefore must be examined carefully. In an era of Internet technology, finding these documents is relatively easy and provides an accompaniment to this text. [2]

It is important to add a caveat here: most of the references are to the words of the presidents who were the ones charged with making foreign policy, especially in the past. As both the head of state and head of government, the president, as chief executive, defined the direction for the United States as well as serving as the embodiment of the country. In the late 1960s and 1970s, with the war in Vietnam and the increasing assertion of congressional oversight, that balance began to shift, a point that is reflected in this book. However, in charting the direction and course of U.S. foreign policy, there are few better examples than the words of the president to set the context for the policy at the time.

Why is it important to learn about American foreign policy? In other words, who cares? Generally, Americans do not give much thought to foreign policy. They don't make decisions about candidates for office based on the candidates' foreign policy positions unless the country is at war or in a conflict where Americans are dying. In fact, many Americans pay attention to foreign policy only in terms of the value of the dollar against another currency—such as the euro, the yen, or the pound—if they are planning to travel abroad. Some want to know whether a Japanese car is going to cost more or less than it did the last time they bought one or whether there will be a line of cars at the border when they cross into Mexico or Canada.

In fact, most Americans pay little attention to foreign policy unless it appears to affect them directly. But foreign policy *does* affect everyone, not only because of threats of terrorist attacks or the danger of war, but also for far more mundane reasons. Look at the label on the last article of clothing that you bought. Where was it manufactured? In China? Bangladesh? What about your computer—where was it made? When you called the technology helpline because you had a problem with a product, where was that person sitting? Was it in the United States or in India? All of this is possible because of trade, and trade is foreign policy.

Let's look at it another way. Do you know anyone who is out of work because his or her factory closed and the product is now made overseas? Allowing American companies to be based in another country is a foreign policy decision. Do you know someone who came to this country to get an education and then decided to stay because he or she could get a better job here than would be possible back home? The decision about who can enter the country and then stay and work here is a foreign policy decision. In other words, foreign policy is not remote, nor is it important only for diplomats or bureaucrats. Foreign policy can affect everyone.

Most of these foreign policy decisions—what countries to trade with, how many people to allow into the country and from where, whether to allow companies to relocate or outsource—are relatively routine. They become more political, and therefore get more attention, in election years or when something extraordinary happens. We certainly could see that in the run-up to the 2016 presidential election, when the candidates of the two major parties had very different visions for the United States, its role in the world, and even the people within its borders. We will return to this theme in a later chapter with the discussion of U.S. foreign policy today and what the election tells us about the future direction of U.S. foreign policy. The foreign policy decisions that most people know about and follow closely are those that are extraordinary because the stakes appear to be so high. Yet the reality is that many "routine" foreign policy decisions can have a very direct and immediate effect on individual lives.

For example, during the Cuban Missile Crisis in October 1962, Americans were glued to their radios and televisions because of the fear that the world was poised on the brink of nuclear annihilation. (It was only years later we learned how close to truth that was.[3]) The Persian Gulf War of 1991 was a true media event; by the invasion of Iraq in March 2003, reporters were "embedded" with troops in order to quench the public's desire for news about the progress of the war. Furthermore, Americans expected that minute-by-minute account. On the other hand, few people are glued to C-SPAN watching the latest debate on the imposition of steel tariffs. The imposition of that tariff, a decision made by President George W. Bush in March 2002, had important implications for American foreign policy, the relationship of the United States to its allies, and even the price of building or buying a house, something that could affect you or your family. Yet relatively few people followed that discussion or even thought about what it might mean for them.

One could argue that there is little the ordinary citizen can do about foreign policy. Why not simply take the decision-makers' word when they state that U.S. "national interest" is best served by a particular foreign policy decision? As educated citizens, we need to ask what is in *our* national interest. We need to ask *whose* interests are being represented when "national interest" is given as a justification for particular decisions. Before casting a vote on Election Day, everyone should know how to evaluate critically the promises of a politician running for office who claims that she or he will act in the country's "best interest."

Citizens in today's world need to understand that countries are interrelated and that decisions made by one country have implications for decisions made by another. The so-called "Brexit" vote by the United Kingdom in June 2016 to leave the European Union is a case in point. The results of that vote, which was focused on one country's decision, sent shock waves through the international economic system, affected the stock market in the United States, and even raised questions about what it might mean for U.S. security. You cannot ask meaningful questions or make rational decisions unless you know what foreign policy is and what the related concept of *national interest* means. Not everyone will arrive at the same answers and this is a basis for legitimate intellectual debate. Since the results of foreign policy decisions affect each of us, we all have a right—and a responsibility—to ask these questions.

Make no mistake: this is not an easy process. Understanding foreign policy is an inexact science, often with no clear-cut right or wrong answers. Rather, approaching it requires putting many pieces together, looking at the outputs or the decisions that were made, and then trying to understand the various pieces or factors that went into making the decisions and why.

This book will not provide all the answers to understanding U.S. foreign policy. What it will do is provide insights into the components of foreign policy–making that can inform the questions to ask. It will also help point the reader to ways to determine answers to those questions.

INTRODUCTION TO U.S. FOREIGN POLICY

In general, Americans are ahistorical. Most have little knowledge of and little concern with the lessons of history.[4] Yet it is impossible to really understand American foreign policy without putting it into a historical context. To do otherwise means that each generation will have to relearn (and often repeat) the lessons of the past. The point here is that little in American foreign policy really is "new." In most cases the formulation of foreign policy is an ongoing process of assessing and evaluating previous or existing policy in light of changing circumstances. An understanding of why and how certain policies were formulated in the past should help you better understand the conse-quences of current foreign policy decisions for the United States, for other countries, and even for you personally.

Most students of American foreign policy and even many decision-makers tend to look at foreign policy decisions as falling into broad general categories; for example, should the United States be engaged in the world (*internationalism* or *engagement*), or should it remain aloof from the rest of the world (*isolationism* or *unilateralism*[5])? Should U.S. foreign policy be guided by a single overarching adversary, as it was during the Cold War, or should it be based on a broader and less defined set of goals, such as fighting terrorism, as it is today? Is the "war on terror" really different from the fight against communism? Or are they both examples of a conflict against an idea rather than a single country, which is what makes each so difficult to fight? Is it time to stop thinking in terms of a single "threat" and to start thinking about broader threats coming from cyber attacks, for example, or the dangers posed by a depleted environment (human security)? Foreign policy decisions are not made in a vacuum but are the result of a number of factors, both domestic and international, that are taken into account. Moreover, not all factors weigh equally all the time—to be effective, foreign policy must assign different weights to each and reflect changing priorities as well as the context within which they are made.

Changes in foreign policy, at least in theory, should reflect the current needs of the country. Often a country's success in a particular area depends on its abilities to work with actors—countries, nonstate actors, international organizations, and others—outside its borders. The United States, for all its power internationally, is no different. Therefore we can ask: what are the best ways for the United States to engage with these actors to help the country further its national interest? How have these policies changed to reflect a new or different understanding of how best to achieve that national interest? And how has the importance of these actors changed as each has affected the development of U.S. foreign policy?

This approach to foreign policy is not unique to the United States. In fact, each country's foreign policy decisions should be premised on its own priorities and the ways in which actors outside its national border will help it achieve its goals. In the case of the United States, the student of foreign policy can track and document changes in priorities that will provide important insights into the reasons particular foreign policy decisions were made.

In order to really understand any aspect of American foreign policy and the related changing concept of security from the founding of this country through the twenty-first century, the policy must be placed within the framework of both the international situation and domestic priorities. Foreign policy encompasses decisions a country makes that affect actors beyond its own borders. Similarly, the decisions and policies made by other external actors (whether nations, corporations, multinational organizations, etc.) have a direct impact on the United States. Both these components, domestic and international, provide the framework that helps define the context for making foreign policy decisions.

Foreign policy decisions cannot ignore domestic factors that can involve a range of issues, including the economic situation of the country, the "mood" of the people, and the cycle of the political process (i.e., whether or not it is an election year). In fact, foreign policy decisions sometimes appear to be made to distract people from problems within the country. These two components, domestic and international, *both* feed into and affect the foreign policy decisions a country makes. This makes understanding America's foreign policy decisions over time a complex undertaking.

Grasping the general approaches to making policy, along with the assumptions that go with them, are essential to understanding U.S. foreign policy. However, those approaches and assumptions are only starting points. More important to the understanding of U.S. foreign policy is the application of those approaches and assumptions to the realities of the situation. For example, it is possible to look at and define the concept of "isolationism." However, doing so should also lead to questions about the prevailing view of early U.S. foreign policy, such as whether it really was "isolationist" or whether the United States was engaged in the world only in a limited and clearly defined way, which is closer to a "unilateralist" perspective. That series of questions cannot be answered without first defining the terms and then looking at when—and why—the United States adopted and then deviated from a specific foreign policy type or orientation. This exploration should lead to an understanding of why the United States adopted the policy it did and how that policy, put into the context of the time, was designed to help the United States achieve its goals as defined by its own national interest. Only then will it be possible to better understand under what set of circumstances the United States chose to break from that policy and get involved politically and militarily in world affairs. Only by exploring and addressing this range of ideas can you answer the questions posed above and then draw conclusions about the direction of U.S. foreign policy at a particular time in the country's history.

Assessing actual policy against a theoretical type is only one piece of the foreign policy puzzle. When you look at "foreign policy," what you are assessing are *policy outputs*—specifically, the *results* of the policy decisions that were made within the government. Here it is important to make a distinction between the *processes* by which these decisions were made and the actual *decisions*. In most cases, foreign policy decisions are the result of a routine process involving bureaucrats in an executive department (such as State, Defense, Treasury, Commerce, etc.) who make decisions based on what has been done before. The president of the United States or the secretary of the agency sets the priorities, and the bureaucrat implements them.

However, this *implementation* process contrasts with the process of *setting the priorities* that will determine what U.S. foreign policy will be. The actual decision-making and the outputs (i.e., decisions) that result are part of the process performed by those in relatively high-level positions, often under circumstances of crisis or actual conflict, based on their perception of national interest as well as their own priorities and understanding of the political realities.

Here another distinction must be made—that is, the difference between those decisions that are *proactive* versus those that are *reactive*. *Proactive policies* are initiated at a high level (for example, by the president or the secretary of state or defense) and are tied to the creation of a new policy or a dramatic change from an existing one. An example of a proactive policy is the U.S. decision to invade Iraq in March 2003. Here the decision was tied directly to the goals stated in President George W. Bush's "National Security Strategy of the United States," issued in September 2002.[6] This document, which has become known as the "Bush Doctrine," puts forward a new direction for American foreign policy: "defending the United States, the American people and our interests at home and abroad by identifying and destroying the threat *before it reaches our borders*" (emphasis added). In other words, this document states that as part of the foreign policy framework for the Bush administration, the United States will be justified in going to war *preemptively* against any country or group that *potentially* threatens this country or its allies and that it will act alone if necessary. Hence, U.S. foreign policy will be proactive should the country appear to be threatened in any way.

In contrast to a proactive policy, a reactive policy is one where the president and his or her advisors are in a position of having to react to circumstances that were thrust upon them, regardless of what established policy might be. The Cuban Missile Crisis provides a prime example of reactive policy, as does the decision to go to war against Afghanistan in response to the attacks on September 11, 2001. In the case of the Cuban Missile Crisis, no matter how carefully President John F. Kennedy and his advisors outlined what their foreign policy priorities should be, such as fighting communism or aiding developing countries, reacting to the information about the missiles in Cuba pushed that emergency to the top of the policy agenda. It also put the United States into a position of responding to circumstances that were initiated by other countries, rather than planning for what the president hoped would happen or would have liked to see occur. In other words, the United States was forced to *respond* in some way.

Similarly, despite warnings about a possible terrorist attack, the government could not expect or plan for the specific events of September 11. Therefore, those events put the Bush administration into the position of deciding what policies to pursue to *respond* to that crisis. These examples stand in contrast to the decision to invade Iraq in March 2003. In that case, the United States initiated the foreign policy decision, choosing when, where, and how to act. In other words, in the case of the invasion of Iraq, the United States did not respond to events thrust upon it (reactive) but took the initiative (proactive) based on alleged evidence of weapons of mass destruction.[7] Knowing the difference between these terms is important to understanding how and why particular foreign policy decisions were and are made. In addition, these cases are examples of how circumstances dictate that decisions be made quickly, with incomplete or even incorrect information. Yet decisions must be made, and those decisions have important ramifications for future policies.

Understanding foreign policy also requires seeing the broader domestic context within which foreign policy decisions are made. For example, an understanding of the Cold War (roughly from 1947 until the collapse of the Soviet Union in 1991) would not be complete without knowledge of the role played by Senator Joseph McCarthy and the "Red Scare" in the 1950s here at home. The Cold War pitted the United States and its generally democratic allies against the Soviet Union and other Communist countries. McCarthyism, with its desire to ferret out Communists within the United States, fit well within and took advantage of the larger Cold War framework. At the same time, domestically, McCarthy fueled the fear of this ideological enemy, which contributed to public support for foreign policy decisions made during that time.

The role of this short text is not to examine all aspects of U.S. foreign policy decision-making; rather, it is to look at the ideological and political framework of those who made the decisions, and to see the ways in which their approach or understanding guided the decisions they made. For example, the change in U.S. foreign policy surrounding the Spanish-American War in 1898 can be attributed in part to the influence of Theodore Roosevelt and his desire to be more aggressive internationally, as well as to President William McKinley's reluctance to resist the growing pressure from the media and public to take action. Similarly, the decision to get involved in World War I in 1917 is partly the result of President Woodrow Wilson's deeply held commitment to the ideals of democracy and his belief that the war could be fought as "the war to end all wars" and "the war to make the world safe for democracy." In retrospect, we can look at these idealistic pronouncements and wonder how any leader could ever have believed them to be true. But in the context of the time, they framed the foreign policy decisions that were made, and many of the Wilsonian ideals continue to influence U.S. foreign policy today.[8] Further, at the time, they provided a rallying cry that garnered the support of the American public.

What does this tell us about what we need to know in order to understand U.S. foreign policy? First, it suggests that it is critical to understand the theoretical assumptions (for example, whether to remain unilateralist or to engage internationally) that influenced the decisions made. Second, it tells us that it is important to assess the actual decisions made against the theoretical assumptions or constructs that influenced them. Third, it indicates that it is necessary to look at the context (international and domestic) within which foreign policy decisions were made. Based on this information and a critical assessment of reality versus theory, it will be possible to draw conclusions that allow for a better understanding of U.S. foreign policy.

To start the process, we will begin by delving into the world of theory. Specifically, what is foreign policy and where does it come from?

WHAT IS FOREIGN POLICY?

Foreign policy refers to those decisions, made within a country, that are affected by and that in turn affect entities outside the country. Initially, foreign policy (and most of international relations in general) pertained to the interaction of nation-states, as those were the primary actors. Hence, foreign policy generally refers to decisions made by one country or nation-state that directly affect another. One of the major changes seen in the recent past is that foreign policy is no longer just about relations between countries. In our current globalized world, foreign policy now includes a country's relationships with a range of actors, including those that exist outside traditional state borders. These might include organizations that are made up of nation-states, such as the United Nations, the European Union, or NATO. It could include multinational corporations (MNCs), such as Walmart, that end up influencing the policies of the country within which they are housed.[9] It might include stateless actors, such as the Palestinians, that act as political entities to influence the policies of other countries. It might include nonstate actors, such as Al Qaeda or ISIS, that exist outside the boundaries of any established country but influence the foreign policy decisions of other countries. Or it might include nongovernmental organizations (NGOs), such as the Sierra Club or Amnesty International, that increasingly play a role in getting policy issues onto the agenda for international discussion.

The presence of actors that exist outside the traditional nation-state has further complicated the foreign policy process. Generally, countries transmit their policy decisions from one to another through recognized diplomatic channels, whether the head of state, an ambassador, a secretary of state or a foreign minister, or through an established bureaucracy. But the actors mentioned above, especially nonstate actors and stateless peoples, typically do not have such channels or representatives, thereby raising questions about how policy decisions will be transmitted or policy requests made. In some cases, heads of state do not want to meet with representatives of some of these actors because they fear that doing so will grant legitimacy—that is, give the nonstate actors the same status that a country has. However, ignoring these actors or uncertainty about how to deal with them does not mean that they do not have a critical role to play in influencing the foreign policy decisions of a state, even a major power like the United States.

National Interest

Foreign policy decisions are made based on *national interest*. But what does that mean? Exactly what is "national interest"? There are a number of theoretical approaches to guide our understanding of this concept.

Different policy-makers are influenced by their own perspectives, which help frame the policy decisions that they make. If foreign policy involves those decisions that are made within a country that are affected by and in turn affect actors and decisions made outside its borders, it is also important to understand some broad theoretical approaches that decision-makers have used to understand those interactions. These broad theoretical areas of focus have influenced the decisions made by different presidents and other policy-makers. So when we talk about Wilson as an "idealist" or Nixon as a "realist," we need to understand what that really means.

The Realist Perspective

In general, relations between countries are the basis of foreign policy. One of the major schools of thought about understanding these relations is the *realist school*, which assumes that nation-states (i.e., countries) are the primary actors in world politics and that each will act in a way that allows it to pursue its key interests or "national interests."

The realist perspective is characterized by the central role that *power* plays, where power is the ability of one actor to influence the behavior of another. Power can be defined in a number of ways, all pertaining to influencing the outcome of a decision.

According to Joseph Nye, a political scientist as well as policy-maker, power can be defined simply as "hard" or "soft." *Hard power* includes both economic and military strength that is used to induce others to change their position. In contrast, *soft power* involves persuading others to do what you want through co-option or cooperation, rather than coercion. Soft power relies on values rather than might.[10] On the other hand, Walter Russell Meade divides power into four types: sharp (military), sticky (economic), sweet (culture and ideals), and hegemonic. Sharp, sticky, and sweet together contribute to hegemonic in that they come together and the result is greater than the sum of its parts.[11]

The application of hard or sharp power is at the core of the realist perspective. In general, since its emergence as an imperial power in the nineteenth century, the United States has relied heavily on military power in order to get its way. If the realist perspective assumes that the nation-state is the primary actor in the international system and that it will act in a rational way (to maximize benefits and minimize costs), then states will act to maximize their own power by wielding military or economic might as necessary. At the heart of realist decision-making is the notion that "statesmen think and act in terms of interest defined as power"[12] and that it is in the country's best interest to continue to accrue power using whatever means available.

The United States' decision to provoke a war with Mexico in 1846 and to respond militarily to the explosion of the Maine in the harbor in Havana, Cuba, in 1898 are two early examples of realist foreign policy decision-making. Later, in the twentieth century, President Nixon and Henry Kissinger, who served first as national security advisor and then as secretary of state, are both seen as quintessential realist decision-makers, using the threat of military force when necessary, but also knowing how to play one actor (the Soviet Union) against another (China) to the advantage of the United States. Values and moral principles do not play a major role in realist thinking. Rather, the main goal is getting and using power in the belief that power is equated with security.

In the realist perspective, most critical are what are known as "*core interests*,"[13] those that involve the protection and continuation of the state and its people. These tie directly to a country's security and become the central core of any state's national interest. Only when the country's security can be assured can the government make decisions about other aspects of the country. For example, concern about global warming, while important, becomes a far lower priority in the face of a direct military threat.

Liberal/Idealist Perspective

Another major approach to relations between countries is the *liberal* or *idealist school*, which looks at countries as part of a collective body where security is best achieved if countries work together rather than in competition. In contrast to realism, the contemporary idealist or liberal perspective is based on values and on the importance of peoples' and nations' working together cooperatively. *Liberalism* (not to be confused with the political notions of "liberal" or "conservative") grows from the idealist stress on what unites people and countries and leads directly to the creation and growth of international organizations, such as the United Nations. This perspective, in turn, stresses the importance of countries' working together in pursuit of common goals for the betterment of all. Advocacy of free trade policies is another example of the application of this theoretical perspective since the assumption is that all countries will benefit from this form of economic cooperation. The use of soft or sweet power becomes an important element in this tradition, as it is tied to policies rooted in cooperation. The idealist/liberal perspective gained increasing credibility as a framework for foreign policy with the end of the Cold War and the spread of capitalist economics and democracy through the countries that had been part of the so-called "Eastern Bloc."

The foreign policies advocated by Woodrow Wilson are perhaps the clearest application of this approach in American foreign policy. From Wilson's decision to enter World War I, justified in part by the need to make the world safe for democracy, to his advocacy for an organization, the League of Nations, that would bring all countries together to thwart expansionist tendencies of other countries, his foreign policy was steeped in idealism. George W. Bush, with his emphasis on the belief of the importance of spreading the values of freedom and democracy, is a more recent example of this way of thinking.

Underlying the goals of the idealist/liberal approach to foreign policy is the idea that the country's security and national interests are better served by working *with* other countries than by trying to compete with or overpower them.

Feminist Perspectives

Another approach to foreign policy and international relations grew out of the *feminist critique*, which advocates the need to look not only at who made policy and why (generally men who followed the realist approach), but also at the impact of those decisions on the people who were most affected and often had the least access to the decision-makers: women and children. And, as feminist writers point out, women have been an important—if unacknowledged—part of U.S. foreign policy. [14]

The *feminist perspective* argues that those who make foreign policy decisions are largely men who have different interests from the groups affected by U.S. policy, especially when the policy decision is to do nothing. (It is important to remember that doing nothing is a policy decision in and of itself.) It focuses more on understanding who has the power and how that power is used rather than on the processes by which decisions are made. The feminist perspective would remind us of the importance of understanding the impact of decisions on all people and of the ways in which gender might influence our understanding of foreign policy decisions. [15]

When we look at the characteristics generally associated with foreign policy, we see that they are the traits that we tend to think of as masculine: power, military might, strength, and coercion, to name but a few. In contrast, the notions of cooperation and peace, which are typically associated with women and are seen as feminine, are perceived as less important in ensuring a country's security. However, in order to get a more complete understanding of U.S. foreign policy, we need to look at the world through "gender-sensitive lenses." In doing so, we can see that women are an important part of the foreign policy picture, even though they are often obscured by the prominence of men, and that foreign policy is neither necessarily masculine nor feminine. Rather, it is about making decisions perceived to be in the best interest of the country.

The emergence of women as prominent foreign policy decision-makers both in the United States and in other countries has made it clear that women are as capable of making tough decisions as men. In the United States, former Secretary of State Hillary Clinton became the first woman to run for president supported by a major political party; Madeleine Albright and Condoleezza Rice are also examples of women who rose to hold the critical position of secretary of state. Before them, women like Margaret Thatcher in England, Indira Gandhi in India, and Golda Meir in Israel, and now Theresa May in England all became prime ministers in their respective countries. However, it is also important to bear in mind that many of the qualities ascribed to these women were masculine in character (ambitious, ruthless, hardheaded, "hawk" versus dove) and not necessarily seen as positive qualities for women to have.

Security and the Concept of Threat

Regardless of which theoretical approach you take—realist, idealist/liberal, feminist—achieving the country's security is paramount. Inherent in the concept of security is also the notion of threat—that is, anything that endangers a country's core interests, people, or territory. Although this generally refers to physical danger, the concept of threat is far broader and can apply to anything that can harm or interfere with the way of life, ideals, philosophy, ideology, or economy of the country. During the Cold War the primary threat coming from communism was far more than the fear of military attack; communism was also seen as a danger to the democratic ideals and capitalist market economy on which the United States was founded. More recently, the concept of threat has been broadened further to refer to the dangers posed by environmental degradation, the spread of disease, and human rights abuses—all of which run counter to the ideals that are considered important to the United States.

One test of national interest and core values is whether the threat is important enough to go to war about. Would the American public support the decision to deploy U.S. troops against the perceived threat? Clearly, in the face of armed attack on the country, such as the Japanese attack on Pearl Harbor on December 7, 1941, or the terrorist attacks on September 11, 2001, there was little debate about whether a military response was appropriate. But what about the case of human rights abuses abroad, such as those that have taken place in Rwanda or Bosnia or Sudan? More recently, questions have arisen about what, if any, role the United States should play in the bloody civil war in Syria, in which approximately 500,000, many of whom were civilians, were killed in the first five years of the war—with little indication of a peaceful resolution in sight. Because protecting basic human rights is a central value dear to the United States, should the United States use its military might to help those whose rights are being abused or who are fighting against an autocratic and repressive dictator? These are much harder questions to answer, and the response can be debated. Some people believe that the United States has a moral responsibility to intervene in those cases. Others believe that fighting against human rights abuses in foreign countries is not in our national interest because it does not affect this country directly. Therefore, they conclude, the United States should not get involved. Because of the need for public support for military intervention, the resulting foreign policy decision as to whether or when to intervene in such cases is an example of the ways in which international and domestic factors coincide.

As the one who sets the foreign policy priorities, it is up to the president to make the case for (military) intervention as being in the national interest, and it is the president who is held accountable by the public. Former assistant secretary of state for democracy, human rights, and labor John Shattuck, notes that in these cases, "strong public support is unlikely until the president has stimulated it by cogently explaining that the redefinition of U.S. national interests includes the prevention of human rights and humanitarian disasters that might destabilize the world."[16] In other words, while it is easy to make the case for war in the event of direct attack on the country or on U.S. citizens, it is far more difficult to explain why it is necessary or in the national interest to get involved in a country on the other side of the world to prevent human rights abuses or humanitarian catastrophe. If the president believes that such intervention is necessary, it will fall on him or her, as the leader of the country, to clearly explain why Americans will be put in harm's way.

A corollary is that once the president makes the decision to intervene militarily, the public must see results, or support for that effort will wane over time. For example, in 2003 President Bush took his case to Congress and the public and received the support necessary to go to war against Iraq. However, by June 2005, two years after the war was declared "over," with combat troops still fighting and no known exit strategy, public support started to decline.[17] By April 2008, as the presidential campaign was heating up, according to a Pew poll, 52 percent of Americans believed that the war (in Iraq) was going not too well or not at all well, and 57 percent believed that the war had been the wrong decision.[18] Regardless of initial support for the war effort, over time and with little end in sight, support started to wane.

Another element of the concept of threat is tied directly to the ways in which the nation perceives its own power and capabilities as well as its perception of the power and capabilities of an adversary. A nation will pursue a foreign policy that it believes will increase its own security and diminish the threat. This suggests that many foreign policy decisions are tied to intangibles, such as perceptions. For example, it is possible to quantify one country's military might, such as the number of fighter aircraft, aircraft carriers, tanks, and troops. But what should also go into this equation (and is much harder to measure) is the nation's willingness to use those capabilities, that is, its *credibility*. This is an intangible but very real factor when one country is trying to determine whether other countries represent a threat or, conversely, how it can protect itself from a threat. Most will agree that a country with no military force or with a military that could easily be overpowered poses little direct threat to the United States. But what about a country such as North Korea or Iran, both of which are believed to be developing nuclear weapons? Each of those countries can be perceived as a threat because of the fear that it might use those weapons. Thus, a country's credibility enters into the foreign policy equation, and perceptions directly affect the making of foreign policy, where credibility is based on the belief that a country has weapons and is willing to use them to achieve its foreign policy goals.

FOREIGN POLICY ORIENTATIONS

How does a country pursue its national interest? Countries have various foreign policy options or orientations available to them. The particular option that the decision-makers choose to pursue assumes a number of things: that they know or have formulated what is in the national interest; that the decision-makers will then make decisions that are tied to or that will further the national interest; and that the first priority will be to ensure the country's security and that of its people.

We will look at a number of foreign policy orientations in this book: *unilateralism, neutrality, isolationism*, and *engagement*. As you will see, one of the ways in which the United States became engaged internationally was by becoming an *imperialist* power, that is, by extending its reach globally. But it did so initially under the umbrella of unilateralism. This apparent contradiction will be explained in more detail in chapter 2. It is important to remember that foreign policy orientations are generalizations or theoretical types and that few countries pursue any one in its purest form. Rather, the application of the particular policy will be a function of the country and its goals *at a given time*.

The United States has predominantly pursued two of these orientations in its history—unilateralism and engagement—although it was isolationist in the period between the two world wars. The United States initially declared neutrality to try to avoid involvement in World Wars I and II, unsuccessfully it turns out.

Of these orientations, *neutrality* is the only one that has a very specific meaning within the international system. When a nation pursues a policy of neutrality, it chooses *not* to engage in any military, political, or security alliances. In other words, it remains apart from any aspect of the international system that would require it to take sides or get involved militarily. Because of its unique status, a country that is neutral is generally willing to accept specific roles and responsibilities within the international system. Often such a country—Switzerland is a classic example of this—is used as the site for various international negotiations so that no one country in the negotiation has the "home team advantage." Switzerland, moreover, is an international banking center because it is considered "safe." A declaration of neutrality also means that other countries will (or should) respect that position and not invade or attack a neutral nation.

The declaration of neutrality became especially important during the Cold War, when states did not want to be put into a position of having to take sides between the United States and its allies and the Soviet Union and its allies. In fact, a group of countries, primarily smaller developing ones, further assured this special relationship by creating their own bloc called the "neutral non-aligned" (NNA) countries. At the height of the Cold War, led by Egypt under Nasser, Yugoslavia under Tito, and Indonesia under Sukarno, this group of countries met in 1961 to create an organization that would combat colonialism and also assure political and military/security independence for their states. In addition to protecting their countries' national interest by allowing them to remain outside the U.S. and Soviet orbits, these countries also worked together to further a common agenda that would benefit them, including economic cooperation and growth. Many of these countries were very successful at playing the two sides off against each other in order to get economic aid and assistance; both Tito and Nasser were masters at this political maneuvering, for example.

Unilateralism and Isolationism

In the early years of the United States, the prevailing foreign policy was one of unilateralism,[19] which gave the United States freedom to engage with other countries economically while also protecting it by keeping it out of any formal alliances or agreements. This "policy of aloofness" or political detachment from international affairs was advocated by Thomas Jefferson, George Washington's secretary of state, who saw this as "the best way to preserve and develop the nation as a free people."[20] This approach was consistent with that advocated by other founders of the country. In his often-quoted farewell address as president, George Washington warned the leaders of the new country to "steer clear of permanent alliances with any portion of the foreign world." He asked the country why we should "entangle our peace and prosperity in the toils of European ambition, rivalship, interest, humor, or caprice."[21] And John Adams, the second president, wrote in a letter in 1805 of the principles in foreign affairs that he advocated and followed as president and specifically, that "we should make no treaties of alliance with any European power; that we should consent to none but treaties of commerce; that we should separate ourselves, as far as possible and as long as possible, from all European politics and wars."[22]

What did the policy of unilateralism really mean for the United States? Here, again, it is important to think about national interests *within the context of the United States at that time.* When the United States was founded, the highest priority was to grow from within. As a new country, the greatest need was to pay attention to internal priorities, including political stability and economic independence, and the best way to do that, according to the founders of the country, was to remain outside the framework of European wars. Instead, the emphasis would be on economic strength through trade and commerce. This emphasis was essential to the growth and expansion of the country.

Europe in the eighteenth century was in a constant struggle for power, with France and England especially vying for prominence. America's founders warned the future leaders of the United States that it would not be in the national interest to get involved with those struggles, but rather it would be in the country's interest to stay clear of them. Yet "the evidence suggests that the U.S. economy was at least as dependent on foreign trade in 1790 as it was two hundred years later,"[23] and much of that trade, and in fact the U.S. economic system, "was inextricably bound up in the British economic system."[24] Hence, while the United States in its early years remained removed from the politics and wars of Europe, it was linked directly to Europe economically.

Pursuing a foreign policy of unilateralism allowed the United States to pick and choose when, where, and how to be involved with other countries, which was what allowed it to grow. Unilateralism provided the framework for geographic expansion through what would become known as America's "manifest destiny," and it allowed the country to strengthen economically through trade and, eventually, industrialization. And as U.S. trade and commerce grew, a military (especially a navy) was needed to protect U.S. interests. In short, unilateralism allowed the United States to become a "great power" or some would say an imperialist power, by the end of the nineteenth century.[25]

Engagement/Internationalism

The other major policy orientation that the United States pursued was one of *engagement*, or *internationalism*, which has characterized U.S. foreign policy from 1945 to the present. Internationalism deals with the decision to become actively engaged in all aspects of international relations, including the military and political alliances that the United States shunned prior to

World War II. Again, the critical question is why the U.S. decision-makers chose to pursue that course of action. How and why was it in the best interest or national interest of the United States to become involved militarily and politically as well as economically?

An important point is that involvement internationally has both a cooperative and a conflictual component, with a country sometimes pursuing both at the same time. For example, during the Cold War, although the United States and the Soviet Union were major adversaries, they were also trading partners, at least since 1972, because this served the best interests of both countries economically.[26] And while the Bush administration labeled North Korea an "axis of evil" country, under the terms of an agreement signed between the United States and North Korea in 1994, the United States sent fuel to that country.[27]

THEORY AND CONTEXT

As we have seen above, over the course of its history, the United States has pursued two major foreign policy orientations at different points, first unilateralism and then a policy of internationalism or active engagement in the international system, although at different periods it also was either neutral or isolationist, albeit briefly. Deciding which one to pursue and why, and when and why to break from that particular pattern, was tied to what was perceived to be in the national interest of the United States at various points. It is important to note that each of these approaches represents an ideal type and, as we will see, the actual application of each policy was not nearly as pure.

In order to understand which approach the United States opted for and why, it is necessary to place the particular policy into the context of the period during which it was made. American foreign policy is the result of a number of often-competing priorities and issues, as well as the result of the perspectives of the people who make policy. Therefore, it is important to explore when and why the United States broke from its policy of unilateralism. We must also examine why U.S. policies since the end of the Cold War have been different from those pursued during the Cold War, although all could be termed "internationalist," though for different reasons. In other words, understanding U.S. foreign policy is tied to an understanding of history and the context within which decisions were made—both domestic and international.

Fully understanding and appreciating American foreign policy (or that of any country) requires looking within the nation to see who makes policy and speaks for the nation. Generally, the more developed and democratic the country, the more complex the foreign policy decision-making apparatus. In the United States, policy is generally formulated by the executive branch—

specifically, the president, his advisors such as the assistant to the president for national security (the national security advisor), and the secretaries of state and defense, although other components of the executive branch (the bureaucracy) weigh in as well. Other actors, such as Congress, play a role, although a less direct one. The media plays both a direct role, through the stories it covers and how it covers them, and an indirect one, as a vehicle through which the public gets its information. But the power of these other groups to influence policy outcomes diminishes the farther they get from the president and the members of the executive branch.[28] Knowing who makes policy and the relationships these various actors have to one another is a critical part of understanding the process of making foreign policy.

IDENTIFYING THEMES

Thus far, we have identified a number of themes that characterize and explain U.S. foreign policy. We can look at the policies based on how involved the United States was with other countries and the extent of that involvement (unilateralism or isolationism versus internationalism or engagement). We can look at who made the policies and the competing role of the president versus Congress. We can ask who influenced the policies and who are affected by them, both domestic and international actors. And we can ask how U.S. foreign policy at different points in time reflects changes from previous policies and, if there are changes, why these occurred.

One of the points raised in reviewing the history and evolution of U.S. foreign policy is that while the broad shifts might be startling (e.g., unilateralism to engagement), on closer examination hints of those changes actually existed before they were implemented. This, too, is important to note. For example, the ideological battles between democracy and communism following World War II in many ways were extensions of the fight for the spread of democracy advocated by Woodrow Wilson. Hence, as the United States moved into the Cold War, it was possible to hear echoes of earlier ideas about the primacy of democracy and about the need to "make the world safe for democracy." What was different during the Cold War was the fact that military and political engagement in support of those ideals became the norm rather than an exception.

As we explore the evolution of U.S. foreign policy, we will keep returning to these themes in order to place the foreign policy decisions into a broader context for understanding.

WHO MAKES FOREIGN POLICY, AND
WHY ARE PARTICULAR DECISIONS MADE?

The Constitution of the United States laid out a framework for making U.S. foreign policy. Like many other decisions made in the early years of this country, the particular approach built into this document was designed to limit the power of any one branch and to ensure that the system of checks and balances would be applied.[29]

The Actors

The executive branch, headed by the president, and the legislative branch, Congress, are the two parts of the government that have been given most of the responsibility for making—and for implementing—foreign policy. Although the judicial branch, the courts, is usually not considered part of the foreign policy process, it does get involved when a particular law is in dispute, and it has been used to interpret the Constitution in order to clarify the relationship between the other two branches on a range of issues.[30] However, this does not happen very often.

In the early years of the country especially, with a relatively weak and part-time Congress, it is not surprising that the executive branch, primarily the president, set the foreign policy priorities. It was assumed at the time that only the president could look at what was in the national interest and then give the orders necessary for that policy to be implemented. More important, it was also assumed that only the president represented the country as a whole. In an era before cell phones, faxes, and Internet, the primary means of communication was through letters and direct conversation. Hence, in order to get information relevant to this country's foreign policy, the president had to rely on information supplied by U.S. diplomats and emissaries who traveled and lived abroad, as well as information from other countries' diplomats who served as the representatives of their countries here. It was the job of these officials to relay information back through the State Department, where the secretary of state could inform and advise the president, who could then make decisions.

Because the means of communication were slow, decisions could be made more deliberately. Crises did not escalate overnight, nor did circumstances change by the minute. Rather, there was an established international order, and the primary shifting that took place was over the relative power that different countries had within that order.

In the late eighteenth century, the United States was a relatively new country compared to the European nations such as Britain or France, or to the Asian nations of Japan and China. Fearing what would happen if the country got involved with those countries, the founders decided that the highest priority for the United States was to establish itself as a nation and to stay removed from those others politically and militarily.

Over time, circumstances changed. Among the most significant in the making of U.S. foreign policy was the growth of the executive branch following World War II, and subsequently the assertion of congressional power into foreign policy decision-making. Later chapters will explore the various changes and the reasons for them; however, a brief overview will help set the stage for what will follow.

Shifting Balance of Power

As the United States grew as a nation, so did U.S. relations with different parts of the world. With more involvement internationally came questions about the wisdom of the decisions that were made and whether the president really did speak in the best interest of the country as a whole or whether he represented a particular group, such as business interests. As a result of such questions and the political pressure that came with them, Congress became more assertive in accepting the role it was given in the Constitution to balance the power of the president. Perhaps one of the first assertions of congressional prerogative came after World War I, when the Republican majority in the Senate opposed the creation of the League of Nations advocated by President Wilson. Where Wilson saw this organization as one way to avoid war in the future, the Senate feared the opposite—that being a member of the League would guarantee U.S. involvement in future wars outside the country.

This example illustrates different interpretations of national interest that resulted in a clash between the two branches and shows the tension that the Constitution created when it assigned foreign policy powers to two branches, albeit different powers, but in the same arena. Specifically, Article II, Section 2 of the Constitution grants to the president the power to make treaties, but "with the Advice and Consent of the Senate . . . provided two thirds of the Senators present concur."[31] In the case of the League of Nations, because the Senate did not concur, the legislative branch prevailed.

There are other areas where the power of the two branches at best overlap or at worst conflict. One of the most dramatic has to do with the decision to go to war. Here, too, the Constitution builds in ambiguities. Article II, Section 2 states, "The President shall be Commander in Chief of the Army and Navy of the United States."[32] But Article I, Section 8 states very clearly, "The Congress shall have Power . . . To declare War."[33]

Shortly after Pearl Harbor was bombed on December 7, 1941, President Franklin D. Roosevelt went to Congress to ask that body to declare war against Japan, and Congress complied. Subsequently, the authority of the president to take the United States to war (or even what "war" meant) grew increasingly murky. President Harry Truman did not ask for a declaration of war when the United States went into Korea in 1950. Instead, he issued a statement noting that he had ordered "United States air and sea forces to give the Korean Government troops cover and support," under the auspices of and in response to a request by the United Nations.[34] When President Lyndon Johnson wanted to escalate military operations in Vietnam—which was termed a "limited war" rather than a formal "war"—he did not seek a declaration of war. Instead, he asked that Congress pass a resolution allowing him "to take all necessary measures," thereby giving him a blank check to do whatever *he* deemed necessary to prosecute that war. It can be argued that when Congress did so, it abrogated its responsibilities under the Constitution. Subsequently, Congress sought to return the balance by reversing the Tonkin Gulf Resolution in 1971 and then by passing the War Powers Resolution two years later.

The passage of the War Powers Resolution in 1973 was a clear assertion of congressional authority. Congress also designed this act to ensure that the power of the president to take the country into an undeclared war was balanced by the congressional oversight guaranteed in the Constitution. However, since that resolution was passed, its constitutionality has been questioned, and presidents have found ways to either work outside its strictures or to skirt them. Both Presidents George H. W. Bush and George W. Bush asked Congress to support their decisions to send U.S. troops to fight in the Middle East—in the first case, the Persian Gulf War of 1991, and in the second case, the "war on terror" (against Afghanistan and also Iraq). In both cases, they used the Tonkin Gulf Resolution of 1964 as a model to secure open-ended support for the action rather than requesting a formal declaration of war.[35] Given the brevity of the 1991 Persian Gulf War, the wisdom of congressional approval was not debated subsequently, although it passed initially only by a narrow margin.

That stands in contrast to the case of George W. Bush and the war with Iraq that started in 2003. The longer the conflict continued and as more information became available that made it clear there were no weapons of mass destruction (the original rationale for that war), the more public support dwindled. Waning public support for that war suggests that, in the future, members of Congress undoubtedly will raise questions about the wisdom of voting for open-ended support as they are pressured by their constituents and respond to public opinion.[36]

Note that the issue of Iraq came up in the presidential election of 2008, although it was not a factor in the election of 2012. It returned in 2016 because as senator, Hillary Clinton had supported the decision to go to war, a point that was made repeatedly by Republican candidate Donald Trump as an example of her questionable judgment.

President Bill Clinton did not go to Congress to request approval to send troops to Haiti in 1993, nor for U.S. involvement in Bosnia in 1994 and in Kosovo in 1999. In the case of Haiti, Clinton argued that as commander in chief he possessed the authority to send U.S. forces as needed; in the case of the Balkans, he claimed that these were NATO missions (as opposed to U.S. military actions) and that therefore the United States was obliged to participate under the terms of the NATO treaty.

The point here is that tensions do exist between the two branches regarding the conduct of U.S. foreign policy and especially the commitment of troops. Those tensions are exacerbated by domestic political issues, including public (and therefore congressional) support for the mission.

Role of Economics

Despite the claims of pursuing a unilateralist or isolationist foreign policy in the early years of U.S. history, successive presidents made decisions to get involved with various parts of the world. This happened incrementally, first by establishing a "sphere of influence" in the Western Hemisphere (i.e., the Monroe Doctrine and the Roosevelt Corollary), and then by expanding that sphere to encompass more countries, such as Japan and China, in which the United States had economic and business interests.

An important point here, and it is one that can be seen throughout this brief exploration of American foreign policy, is that very often the decision to expand U.S. involvement with different parts of the world was made for economic reasons. In some cases it was to protect business interests, such as the case of U.S. investments in Cuba before the Spanish-American War; in some cases to expand trading opportunities, as was the case with U.S. expansion into Japan in 1853 and China at the end of the nineteenth century. In other cases it was with a desire to increase access to foreign capital and investment, which drove much of America's relations with Britain. The bottom line is that economic motives and the need to protect U.S. businesses often drive foreign policy decisions. These decisions were (and are) made by the president based on his or her perception of national interest.

Another constant in reviewing the history of U.S. foreign policy is that once the United States started to get involved with a particular part of the world, it did not retreat from that area as it became more involved with other parts. U.S. involvement in different parts of the world can be seen as an inverse pyramid, starting with a narrow base, where involvement was limited to a small number of countries in the early years, growing to a very broad platform at the top by the 1960s, as the United States was involved directly on every continent in some way.

Role of Domestic Politics and Factors

That brings us to the next important generalization about making and under-standing American foreign policy—the role that domestic politics and other domestic factors (economic, social, etc.) play. An examination of the history of U.S. foreign policy illustrates clearly the role of domestic politics. Support at home for Cold War foreign policy was increased by Senator Joseph McCarthy and his "Red Scare." Conversely, the decision to pull out of Vietnam was accelerated by an American public that was withdrawing its support for the war and was also losing its faith in the government because of the then-breaking Watergate scandal.

Many African Americans in this country are concerned about and question why the United States has not been more involved with Africa, especially given the genocides that took place in Rwanda in the 1990s and in Darfur in Sudan starting in 2004, and given President Obama's family history. Here, too, the easy answer lies, at least in part, with domestic politics. The United States claims that it has (or had) no vital national interest in these regions. More important, despite pressure from the Congressional Black Caucus and the commitment of then–Secretaries of State Colin Powell and Condoleezza Rice to pay more attention to Africa, the reality is that there has not been a critical voting bloc or a powerful domestic political voice for that position, at least when weighed against the voices of those who oppose deploying U.S. forces in distant lands for humanitarian reasons that are not clearly linked to U.S. national interests. President Obama's first visit to Africa in June 2013 suggested that perhaps this would change, especially in light of China's growing interest in the continent, but to date, the reality is that little has changed.

As noted above, economic factors play a major role in influencing the direction of foreign policy decisions. They are often spurred by business interests that are important to the political process as well as the economic well-being of the country. Big business especially tends to have ties to the political system, through lobbies, campaign contributions, and the interrelationship of business and foreign policy/security through what President Dwight Eisenhower called the "military-industrial complex."[37] Hence, U.S. involvement in many parts of the world has often been tied directly to the need to protect economic and U.S. business interests abroad as well as resources such as oil.

WHO IS AFFECTED BY U.S. FOREIGN POLICY DECISIONS?

This brings us to the next logical question: who is affected by U.S. foreign policy decisions? The most obvious answer to this question is those countries with which the United States is involved. But people at home are affected as well. Another category to consider is the least powerful, or the powerless—specifically those who have least access to policy-makers but who are often affected by their decisions. Each of these is explored briefly below.

Impact of U.S. Foreign Policy Decisions on Other Countries

Since foreign policy is a continuous process where a decision made by one country directly affects the decisions made by another, any change in existing policy will have an important and perhaps long-standing impact on other countries. A good example of this is the U.S. relationship to its European allies. Joined together through NATO, the United States and the countries of Europe have remained allies because it was in all their interests to do so. Despite rocky periods, such as French President DeGaulle's decision to remove France from the military structure of NATO in 1966 or many of the European countries' negative responses to the war in Iraq, the alliance has been able to function as a whole. In fact, after September 11, it was the Europeans, not the United States, who requested invoking Article 5, the collective defense clause, of the NATO treaty in order to allow for a unified NATO response.[38] The Bush administration's decision to go to war against Iraq in March 2003 without UN Security Council approval put it at odds with some of its NATO allies. While some NATO members, such as Great Britain and Poland, supported the United States, others—most notably France and Germany—were outspoken in their objections to this decision.[39] Nonetheless, they all remained allies, bound together by common interests.

Another example is the Cold War, which was premised on competition between the United States and the Soviet Union. The United States based its early Cold War policies on assumptions about Soviet military capabilities and, specifically, the ways in which they lagged behind those of the United States. When the USSR tested an atomic weapon in 1949 and then launched *Sputnik* in 1957, the United States had to rethink its own policies, including the need to accelerate some of its weapons programs. This led to an arms race that was one of the major factors that contributed to the economic bankruptcy and collapse of the Soviet Union, although many years later.

This leads to another important conclusion: foreign policy decisions often have unintended consequences. No matter how carefully foreign policy decisions are analyzed and assessed, not all results can be anticipated. It also means that decisions are made based on assumptions and information available at the time. It is only later, as more information becomes available, that the full range of options (and dangers) becomes clear. This often puts the United States, or potentially any country, into a position of making policies that are reactive rather than proactive.

Domestic Constituencies

The American public is directly affected by foreign policy decisions, although different groups are affected in different ways. Foreign policy decisions can affect each of us, whether we are aware of it or not. The *Wall Street Journal* published an article on August 11, 2004, titled "Sticker Shock at the Lumberyard." The article, which is subheaded "Remodeling Gets Costlier as Price of Wood Surges; Impact of China and Iraq," is a good example of the ways in which foreign policy decisions have an impact on "ordinary" Americans.[40] Although it was written more than a decade ago, the point still holds that in a globalized world, decisions made by one country can have a direct effect on the domestic public here in the United States.

An increase in the price of lumber can be attributed to a number of domestic factors, such as a housing boom in the United States that increased the demand for lumber. Foreign policy comes into this as well: a building boom in China has increased demand, a 27 percent tariff on lumber imported from Canada (which supplies 30 percent of all U.S. lumber), and a weak dollar that makes imports more costly all mean that Americans are feeling the impact on their pocketbooks. Those who are remodeling or renovating a house, doing any home improvement, or buying a new house will be paying more for lumber than they would have one year earlier.

Almost every group in this country has some representative who is looking out for and advocating for its interests. Virtually every type of business and labor organization has a lobbying group that represents it in Washington, as do special interest groups that have been formed to advocate for policy areas they care about, such as the environment. Even foreign governments have interest groups to represent their point of view. The goal of these various groups is to make sure that policies enacted by the president and Congress will not harm and ideally will help the constituencies they represent.

However, the success of these groups to influence policy decisions will vary, depending on who is in office, how broad their constituency is, and the amount of access that they actually have. For example, under the Clinton administration, environmental groups were extremely successful in advocating for protection of natural wilderness areas and for policies and agreements to protect the environment, such as the Kyoto Protocol. Part of the reason for their success was a president who was sympathetic to their cause and a vice president who was actively committed to improving the environment. In contrast, the administration of George W. Bush, which was tied more closely to business interests, reversed many of the Clinton administration policies to allow logging and road building in national forests, a position the Bush administration justified on the basis of domestic economic priorities. Shortly after taking office, the Obama administration again reversed many of the Bush administration decisions on the environment and, addressing issues pertaining to greenhouse gasses and other environmental issues, shored up his legacy as a strong advocate for the Paris Climate Change Agreement passed in December 2015. Given the rhetoric of the 2016 presidential election campaign, it remains to be seen whether these environmental policies will again be reversed by the Trump administration, or whether the United States will comply with this major climate change agreement.

Clearly, each administration responds to a different set of needs, priorities, perception of national interest, and interest groups, and the resultant policies have a direct impact on different groups of Americans. In addition to politicizing the issue domestically, changes in policy send confusing and ambiguous signals to other countries that are trying to make their own policies based, in part, on what the United States is doing. Hence, under a Bush presidency, the countries that worked with the United States to reach agreement in Kyoto had to form a new coalition, recognizing the fact that they likely would have to move forward without U.S. help or support.

The "Powerless": The Feminist Perspective

As noted above, in asking "who is affected by policies," the feminist critique becomes especially important. The feminist critique argues that often those who are most affected by decisions are the ones who are the least powerful and, therefore, with little direct access to those who make the decisions. Who represents the interests of these groups? And is protecting these groups, whose interests fall under the broad category of "human rights" and "humanitarian interests," for example, a valid basis for making foreign policy? Are they tied to U.S. "national interest"?

The case of the Vietnam War is instructive when we look at the groups that are both affected by policy decisions and also most powerless to do anything about them. The "peace movement" grew from a small fringe group in the early days of the war to become all-encompassing. While many in this country still supported the war, the violent actions at Kent State University in May 1970, in response to what was seen as the illegal bombing of Cambodia, which was neutral in the conflict, galvanized members of the "silent majority," some of whom later joined with students to protest the war. The term "silent majority" was coined by Richard Nixon in a speech he made in November 1969 in which he hoped to reach out for the support of those Americans who were not protesting the war but had remained silent. Ultimately, though, even many in that group became vocal opponents of the war. Clearly, male students had the greatest stake in the outcome, as they were the ones being drafted to fight and die in Vietnam, but they were also generally removed from the formal political process as they were unable to vote. By 1968 the voices of public opinion were loud enough to keep Lyndon Johnson from running for reelection and were strong enough to persuade Nixon that he needed to find a way out of the war. Furthermore, pressure by the public to give more voice to those who would fight a war resulted in the passage in 1971 of the Twenty-Sixth Amendment to the Constitution, which lowered the voting age to eighteen from twenty-one.[41]

SETTING THE STAGE

This chapter introduced some important concepts about American foreign policy that will help frame the approach taken throughout this book. It also laid out some basic questions about the foreign policy process, including asking who makes these decisions and why. However, this introduction to the theories and concepts is just the starting point—now we have to apply them.

The next seven chapters use a historical approach to U.S. foreign policy and break the more than two centuries of American history into six parts. Chapter 2 looks at a rather long period, from the founding of the country until just after World War I, years in which U.S. foreign policy was largely tied to the concept of unilateralism. We start with a review of why that particular approach was chosen in the context of international politics in the eighteenth and nineteenth centuries, as well as within the context of domestic priorities. But in order to really understand this concept, it is important to explore the circumstances under which the United States broke from that orientation and chose to get involved in international affairs, and why those decisions were made, as well as who made them. In many ways, exploring those exceptional cases, such as the Spanish-American War, provides insights into the foreign policy process.

Chapter 3 looks at the period from the end of World War I through World War II. While spanning only twenty-five years, this was a difficult period for the United States, which had to deal with economic depression as well as expansionist countries such as Japan and Germany. As both of these countries started to conquer others, calling into question the viability of the League of Nations and the concept of "collective security," the United States had to make some tough decisions about whether to intervene in world affairs, and when.

Chapter 4 explores the period in which the Cold War dominated U.S. foreign policy, from the end of World War II until the election of Ronald Reagan in 1980. The policies of the United States, as one of two superpowers, also directly affected the course of international politics. This was a period characterized by the active engagement of the United States with the international system and the creation of a foreign policy and defense bureaucracy that could support the changing role for the United States. All of U.S. foreign policy during this period was designed with an eye toward containing communism, which influenced not only U.S. policies, but relationships with other countries as the United States built its system of alliances. As we will see, the United States became involved with different parts of the world—from Europe and parts of Asia to the Middle East and Africa—but did not retreat from any. Therefore, within a few decades after World War II, the United States was involved on virtually every continent. And along with the expansion of political and military ties came broadened economic ones.

Chapter 5 looks at the period beyond the Cold War, starting with the administration of Ronald Reagan (1981–1989), which marked the beginning of the end of the Cold War, and going through the administrations of George H. W. Bush (1989–1993) and Bill Clinton (1993–2001). During this period the Soviet Union collapsed, and democratic movements swept the countries of Eastern Europe. While these changes brought with them a sense of euphoria, as the United States and forces of democracy triumphed over communism, they also brought new challenges that were largely unforeseen, such as increased civil wars and ethnic strife, and the growth of terrorism. What made these events especially difficult for the United States was that the entire foreign policy/national security apparatus to that point was tied to the old Cold War structure and so was not appropriate to or adequate for meeting these new threats. Not only was a rethinking of foreign policy necessary on the part of the decision-makers, but it also required an articulation of the new or revised concepts to the American public at a time when their attention was focused inward ("it's the economy, stupid"). To many students of American foreign policy, the result has been a muddled and unfocused policy that puts the United States in the position of responding to the latest challenge rather than proactively pursuing policies deemed to be in the national interest.

Chapter 6 focuses on the administration of George W. Bush. It begins with the contested election of 2000 and ends with the election of 2008. Despite the course that the Bush administration appeared to be on when coming into office, everything changed with the events of September 11, 2001. How that administration responded to the attacks that day and the resultant changes in U.S. foreign policy are the focus of this chapter. Included here are some recent analyses about the Bush administration policy decisions and what they have meant for Obama and future presidents.

Chapter 7 addresses the Obama administration and the challenges that the next president will face virtually as soon as he takes office in January 2017. The chapter begins with the changes proposed by the Obama administration in his first term and details what was—and was not—accomplished during his eight years in office, which will have an impact on his legacy. It will address the threats that emerged during those eight years as opposed to the proactive policies that Obama initially outlined for his administration, and what these mean for his successor.

Chapter 8 concludes the volume by returning to the basic questions raised in this book with an eye toward answering them in light of what you have learned thus far. It will focus on the changing nature of the threat, U.S. relations with its allies, the wars in Iraq and Afghanistan, and how the United States can address all these in a way that will allow it to regain its role as global leader—if that is the intention. All of these will be framed within the context of a changing economic situation especially given the uncertainties of "Brexit."

The goal of this book is not to pass judgment about the wisdom or "rightness" or "wrongness" of any single foreign policy decision as much as it is to provide the tools for understanding those decisions in the context of the time at which they were made and with the information available then.

Chapter Two

Unilateralism to Engagement

The Founding to the End of World War I, 1777–1920

In 2016, an unlikely musical, *Hamilton*, based on a biography of Alexander Hamilton, won eleven Tony awards and was breaking box-office records on Broadway. According to an interview with *Hamilton*'s creator and star, Lin-Manuel Miranda, "[T]he show, almost entirely sung-through, transforms esoteric Cabinet debates between Jefferson and Hamilton into riveting, delirious rap battles."[1] Why is this such an engaging topic? Surely the music and theatrics are terrific, but ultimately it was the story that captured Miranda's attention. And that battle between Jefferson and Hamilton resulted in a two-hundred-year journey that has taken the United States along a range of different paths, from unilateralism/isolationism to active engagement in the international system. This chapter will explore the foundations of this journey.

The early years of U.S. foreign policy were defined by those men (and they were all men) who believed that the nation's highest priority should be to look inward and build a stable and prosperous country removed from the affairs (and wars) of Europe. This did not mean that the United States would not have overseas involvements. Rather, it meant that foreign policy decisions would involve choosing when, where, and how to get involved with other countries while at the same time building its own.

The first chapter of this book outlined a number of foreign policy orientations, including unilateralism. This policy presumed that the United States would remain removed from the political and military affairs of the rest of the world but would be engaged in limited ways and in areas of its choosing. This chapter will explore the policy of unilateralism (as opposed to isolationism) to describe how the leaders of the United States chose when, where, and how to be involved internationally and how those decisions allowed the country to grow into a great power by the end of the nineteenth century.

We will begin by looking at the perception of national interest at the time that this country was created, and why the founders believed that being removed politically and militarily (i.e., "aloof") from other countries was in the national interest. Nonetheless, as we will see, the country broke from this policy at various points in its early history. Understanding when and why the United States deviated from this policy will give you a better understanding of the foreign policy process as well as the ways in which domestic priorities affected the definition of "national interest" when applied to U.S. foreign policy. It will also give you an understanding of why knowledge of the past can provide insight into the direction that U.S. foreign policy ended up taking at various points in time.

THE BEGINNING

Starting in 1776 the newly independent United States of America had to develop policies and processes for governing domestically and for setting priorities internationally (foreign policy). Much of what the founders of the country did was simply react to (and against) what they had seen in England, especially the tyranny of the monarch. However, they were not in agreement on how to create a new governmental structure that would replace the monarchy they had known and that was the norm at the time.

Creating a Foreign Policy Framework

The Articles of Confederation, drafted in 1777 and ratified in 1781, created a loose union of sovereign states and was the first attempt to frame a new form of government. Given the priorities in the 1770s, the Articles "were designed primarily to facilitate a unified approach to foreign policy and national defense,"[2] with Congress given primary responsibility for speaking on behalf of the whole. In contrast, domestic priorities rested with each of the states. Although the Articles of Confederation failed for a number of reasons, the idea of the country speaking with a single voice on foreign policy remained an important concept that would continue through the evolution of the government to its present form. However, the voice would shift from Congress to the president, although the power for making foreign policy would be divided between the executive (the president) and the legislative branches (Congress).

A Continental Congress convened in Philadelphia in 1787 specifically to revise the Articles of Confederation. The goal was to create a strong central government that would have responsibility for the domestic affairs of the nation (as opposed to the states) and would speak on behalf of the country on foreign affairs. As embodied in the new Constitution, power in foreign policy would be vested in both a president and Congress, with each given certain tasks to ensure that there would be checks and balances. For example, while the president would be the commander in chief of the armed forces, it would be up to Congress to declare war. While the president, as head of state, could negotiate treaties with foreign governments, two-thirds of the Senate must concur through its "advice and consent" function before the treaty would be ratified and could go into effect. In this way the founders believed the national interest of the country would be served because no one person or organization within the government could become too strong.

The Constitution also specified the powers that would be given to the states as well as to each branch of the federal government, and it reflected many of the divisions that existed within the young country. As is the case today, there were divisions between the rural areas and the cities, between those Americans who were educated and well traveled and those who were not, between the farmers and the merchants, and between those who lived on the coast and those who were inland. Those divisions also reflected the differences in how each of the groups viewed the world beyond the borders of the United States. Even with these differences, the primary view of the founders at that time was that the president was "the general Guardian of the National interests."[3] Generally, this has not changed; what has ebbed and flowed is the relationship and relative power of the president versus Congress to make foreign policy. This "push-pull" has often led to tensions between the two branches. The sometimes difficult relationship between the branches, as well as the reasons for the tensions, became more apparent during the Cold War and will be explored in more detail in later chapters.

Beware of Entangling Alliances

The first three presidents of the United States—George Washington, John Adams, and Thomas Jefferson—were wary of foreign involvement that could wreck the young country. Yet each also brought to his position an understanding of the world beyond the United States, as well as the dangers of involvement in foreign wars. Washington was the first commander in chief and, as a general, saw the havoc wrought by war. Adams came to the office with a diplomatic background, as did Jefferson. Each of them feared what would happen if the United States got too involved in the wars of Europe at the expense of "domestic tranquility."[4]

In many ways the primary dispute over U.S. foreign policy and the definition of national interest was between Alexander Hamilton, the first secretary of the treasury, and Thomas Jefferson, the first secretary of state. Hamilton laid out many of his ideas on foreign policy in *The Federalist Papers*, written with James Madison and John Jay between October 1787 and July 1788.

Hamilton believed that the United States needed the capabilities to develop into an important power, with a critical role to be played by an alliance of the government and commerce (business). Because of his emphasis on commerce, he advocated for a navy that could protect America's interests on the high seas, and he wrote of the importance of an army to make sure the United States could withstand the dangers surrounding it, from "British settlements" to "the savage tribes on our Western frontier [who] ought to be regarded as our natural enemies"[5] In Federalist Number 41, Madison affirmed what Hamilton had said and also noted the importance of ensuring "security against foreign danger" as one of the most important powers granted to the new American union.[6]

Jefferson saw the world differently. Rather than using limited U.S. resources to create a military, he emphasized trading with other countries and negotiating commercial treaties that would be in U.S. interests. While he allowed that the United States might need a small navy to protect its commercial interests, his priority was in securing the country's place in North America. The Louisiana Purchase of 1803 and the acquisition of the port of New Orleans resulted from Jefferson's desire to promote commerce. The decision to acquire this territory began a pattern of growth and expansion of the United States that would continue for the next fifty years and, ironically, would be aided directly by the decision to build a navy, as advocated by Hamilton.

The primary rivalry for "great power" status in Europe at that time was between France and Britain, each of which was building its empire, sometimes at the expense of the other. Although Spain, the Netherlands, and Portugal had also established themselves as colonial powers in the "New World" by that time, each of the first three U.S. presidents saw France and Britain as the primary threats; however, they did not agree on which was the greater one. What was clear was that the dangers of getting involved in foreign wars or in any rivalry among the major European powers had the possibility of creating a real threat to the homeland.

Despite these dangers, in 1778 the United States entered into an alliance with France, Britain's primary rival. Using realist political thinking, the early founders saw this alliance as a critical balance to the power of Britain, against which the United States was fighting for its independence. Ultimately, relations between the United States and France soured, with some of the early Federalists calling for war against France. From 1796 until 1800 the French claimed the right to seize any ships potentially bound for their enemy (Britain) and seized more than three hundred U.S. vessels. In 1800 the United States and France negotiated a treaty to end this "quasi-war." The United States agreed to drop all claims against France "in exchange for abrogation of the Franco-American Alliance of 1778."[7] This early alliance made clear to the United States the risks of involvement with the major European powers.

On September 17, 1796, George Washington delivered his Farewell Address to the nation upon his retirement after serving two terms as president. This address laid out his perspective on U.S. foreign policy based on his reading of the priorities at the time and the dangers that seemed to threaten the young country. The address contains much detail regarding Washington's understanding of the world at that time and what it meant for the United States. For example, he advised the United States to "observe good faith and justice toward all nations. Cultivate peace and harmony with all." He told the country that "nothing is more essential than that permanent, inveterate antipathies against particular nations and passionate attachments for others should be excluded, and that in place of them just and amicable feelings toward all should be cultivated."[8] In other words, it would be in the best interest of the United States to deal with all countries equally and fairly and in a positive way.

Washington also said, "The great rule of conduct for us in regard to foreign nations is, in extending our commercial relations to have with them *as little political connection as possible*" (emphasis added). Thus, he cautioned that while it is important to trade with other countries, the United States could do so while also remaining politically removed from them, the very definition of "unilateralist" policy. And he warned that "Europe has a set of primary interests which to us have none or a very remote relation. Hence, she [Europe] must be engaged in frequent controversies, the causes of which are essentially foreign to our concerns."[9] Given the dangers and warnings that Washington laid out, it is logical he would then advocate "our policy to steer clear of permanent alliances," which John Adams, the second president, agreed with.

Consistent with the belief that a strong executive should set foreign policy priorities and speak for the country, these men defined the path the United States would take in foreign policy for more than the next century. Initially, at least, the United States remained removed from European politics and did not enter into formal alliances; instead, the goal was to strengthen the country economically by *trading* with those countries. This policy of limited involvement, and the decision to become involved with other countries when and where the United States chose to, became the basis for the U.S. policy of *unilateralism*.

MANIFEST DESTINY, THE MONROE DOCTRINE, AND WESTWARD EXPANSION

The death of Alexander Hamilton in 1804 meant his voice regarding the direction of U.S. foreign policy was stilled, although his influence and ideas remained important. What guided U.S. foreign policy in the 1800s was the notion of "manifest destiny," or "the belief that it was the destiny of the United States to spread across the continent." Further, "Manifest destiny embodied the conviction that Americans had a higher purpose to serve in the world than others. Theirs was not only a special privilege, but also a special charge: *to protect liberty and to promote freedom*" (emphasis added).[10] Examining manifest destiny from that perspective—that higher ideals were central to the founding of the country and it was the role of the United States to serve and promote them—makes it possible to identify a pattern of idealism and also expansionism, even imperialism, that provided the framework for foreign policy, including the justification for the breaks from the policies of unilateralism and sometimes isolationism that predominated from the founding until World War II.[11]

It is important to remember that most of North America had been colonized by European countries by the end of the eighteenth century. Consequently, if the United States was to expand further, it had two options: it could deal with those countries in a way that could be cooperative (e.g., negotiating treaties) or in a way that could lead to conflict. There seems to be an inherent contradiction between the policies of manifest destiny and expansion versus the policies of unilateralism. On the one hand, the United States had no desire to get involved politically with Europe. On the other hand, if it was to grow and expand, the United States had to engage in various ways with the same European powers that had already colonized parts of the continent and that could, potentially, threaten the United States. Didn't that mean breaking from a policy that was unilateralist or even isolationist?

What made the desire for expansion compatible with the overall doctrine of unilateralism was the belief that the United States was not engaging in political alliances or in European politics or wars but was simply protecting itself and fulfilling its mission—its "destiny"—to expand across the continent. Hence, the U.S. conquest of North America did not seem to contradict what Washington had warned of or the course that he and Adams had set. Domestically, by the early 1800s the young nation became more stable as a democracy with the assurance that the processes and structures of government that had been embodied in the Constitution worked. Events in Europe further helped the United States pursue its manifest destiny. As the United States began its march westward while building an economy based on trade and commerce, Europe was fighting the Napoleonic Wars. The end of those wars in 1815 marked a change in the politics of Europe as alliances and the power balance shifted. What had been the Spanish empire in the New World started to disintegrate as Argentina, Bolivia, and Chile gained their independence from Spain. Meanwhile the United States negotiated with Spain to purchase Florida, which was ceded to the United States in 1819. In 1822 the Monroe administration extended diplomatic recognition to the newly independent Latin American republics of Argentina, Chile, Colombia, Mexico, and Peru.

In Europe, the usual intrigues were ongoing, with suggestions that France and Spain were aligning with Russia, Prussia, and Austria to wage war on the new republics in Latin America in order to help Spain regain its territory. In response, Britain proposed that the United States join it to ward off French and Spanish aggression in the New World. What is of note is that the British foreign minister, George Canning, proposed that the United States and Britain issue a joint declaration in opposition to further European intervention in the Americas. This option was considered by Monroe, who sought advice about the wisdom of this union. He contacted former presidents Thomas Jefferson and James Madison and both affirmed the importance of this joint declaration. However, Secretary of State John Quincy Adams, who was skeptical about British intentions, argued that the interests of the United States would be better served by a unilateral declaration. Monroe ultimately agreed with Adams and on December 2, 1823, he delivered an address to Congress that defined the U.S. position: the United States would continue to stay removed from European affairs but, in turn, the European powers were expected to stay out of the New World, which the United States declared was within its own sphere of influence.

"Our policy in regard to Europe, which was adopted at an early stage of the wars which have so long agitated that corner of the globe, nevertheless remains the same, which is, not to interfere in the internal concerns of any of its powers," Monroe said. "It is impossible that the allied powers should extend their political system to any portion of either continent without endangering our peace and happiness; nor can anyone believe that our southern brethren, if left to themselves, would adopt it of their own accord. It is equally impossible, therefore, that we should behold such interposition in any form of indifference."[12]

With the Monroe Doctrine the United States reiterated its promise not to interfere in European politics. In turn, the Americas were no longer open to European colonization. The only country that now had claim on the continent was the United States.

Continued Expansion

The Monroe Doctrine made clear the intentions of the United States to continue to expand on its own continent. Over the subsequent decades, the country did so by annexing Texas (which had won independence from Mexico) in 1845, acquiring the Oregon territories from the United Kingdom in 1846, and expanding into the western part of the country (which is now California, Nevada, Arizona, and parts of Utah and Colorado) in 1848 (see figure 2.1). Not all of this was done peacefully. Rather, the United States gained some of that territory as a direct result of war. It is clear that U.S. national interest and priorities at the time were best served by ensuring that the United States was no longer surrounded by foreign powers and by asserting primacy over its own lands, even if that meant war. This framework was to guide U.S. foreign policy throughout the nineteenth century and well into the twentieth.

Consistent with the notion that the president defined the national interest, when James K. Polk became president in 1844, he made it clear that he would accelerate the policy of territorial expansion toward the west. One of the prizes was the Mexican territory of California, with its known port of San Francisco. The other area Polk wanted was the Oregon territory, held by Britain. In the latter case, Polk was willing to negotiate with Britain, building on negotiations started earlier by John Quincy Adams. In June 1846, the British proposed a treaty that Polk accepted and sent to the Senate, which ratified it by a vote of 41 to 14. Despite Polk's claim of "Fifty-four forty or fight," suggesting the territorial lines that would be ideal, he was willing to compromise with a border at the forty-ninth parallel rather than risk the domestic political battles and costs of war with Britain.

Unlike parts of the Oregon territory, which were described by then–Secretary of State James Buchanan as "wholly unfit for agriculture & incapable of sustaining any considerable population"[13] (and thereby worth giving up), California was seen as worth fighting for. Initially Polk tried negotiating with Mexico to persuade the country to sell California to the United States. When that failed, Polk resorted to the use of hard power and ordered troops to the Rio Grande, the border area, where they quickly engaged with Mexican forces. Congress responded to the clash between U.S. and Mexican forces by endorsing Polk's request for a declaration of war in May 1846.

Military historian T. Harry Williams describes the Mexican-American War this way: "The Mexican War has always occupied an ambiguous position in the national historical consciousness. Depending on the prevailing mood of intellectuals and historians, it has been denounced as a wicked war of aggression against a weaker neighbor or justified as an inevitable phase in the expansion [of the United States]." He also describes this war as "significant because of the number of 'firsts' associated with it. It was the first overseas war. . . . It was also America's first successful offensive war, the first in which the strategic objectives were laid out with some clarity before hostilities were joined, and the first to be conducted with a large measure of technical proficiency and with relative efficiency. Finally, it was the first war in which the president really acted as commander in chief."[14]

Although it was controversial, the Mexican-American War (1846–1848) was important to the growth of the United States, a priority at that time, and was seen by the leaders of the country as necessary to secure parts of the

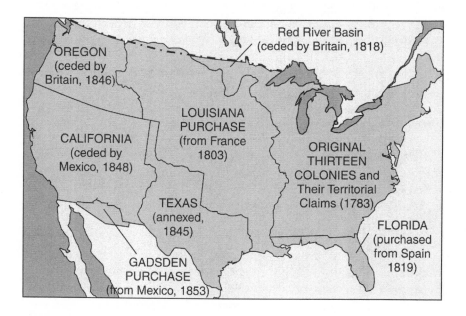

Figure 2.1.   U.S. Westward Expansion

hemisphere that the United States claimed as its own. Despite its large cost to the United States (more than 5,800 Americans killed or wounded in battle, 11,000 soldiers dead from disease, and a financial cost estimated at more than $75 million), the United States acquired approximately 500,000 miles of territory.[15] At the end of the war, U.S. territory extended from the Atlantic Ocean to the Pacific and included the areas now known as Nevada and California, both of which had gold and silver deposits. The promise of wealth from gold and silver helped fuel the westward movement of the population that was necessary to the growth of the country. The acquisition of California also meant that the United States had ports on both coasts, which helped further the goals of increasing trade and commerce.

During the period from December 1845 through the end of the Mexican-American War in 1848, "the United States had grown by about 1.2 million square miles, or about 64 percent."[16] How was this expansion possible? Who paid for the purchase of these new lands or to finance these wars? How could the United States assure the security of this ever-expanding country?

In many ways, the answers to these questions can be found in the concept of what we now call *globalization*, which linked the United States to other countries economically, even as it stayed removed politically. As Walter Russell Mead has argued, "Economically the United States was more dependent on the rest of the world in the nineteenth century than it was during much of the Cold War." In fact, the United States took seriously the need for commerce and trade and depended on foreign investment to provide the funding to sustain much of this growth westward that was seen as critical to the national interest.[17] The only alternative would have been to raise taxes, and that was unpalatable politically. To some Americans this foreign investment was a cause of controversy or resentment, and they were concerned about the influence these investors might have on U.S. policy. But there was little that they could do about it.

The decision to trade with and secure investments from other countries, especially Europe, while positioning itself in the Western Hemisphere is the essence of the early U.S. policy of unilateralism. Pursuing this policy allowed the United States to achieve what it had defined as its national interest, its "manifest destiny," while simultaneously protecting it from the intrigues of Europe.

As the United States expanded westward in the mid-nineteenth century, it also was starting to make a mark internationally. With the Atlantic and Caribbean claimed by Europe and the Atlantic waters nearly exhausted by European whalers, the American whaling trade needed other waters to explore. After 1848, when U.S. territory extended to the Pacific, it was only natural that the United States looked in that direction for trade and commerce that would allow it to compete with Europe economically. In 1853, U.S. Commodore Matthew Perry arrived in Japan, a country then untouched by the West. He offered Japan a choice: trade with the United States peacefully, or run the risk of war. When he returned early in 1854 with a fleet of ships, Japan granted the United States the right to use the Japanese ports of Shimoda and Hakodate, and by 1856 the United States negotiated a trade treaty with Japan. Japan soon extended similar terms to the European countries of France, Britain, the Netherlands, and Russia, but it was U.S. ambition that opened the country to the West.

The U.S. venture into Japan was an example of the growing power of its navy, initially created to protect U.S. commercial interests but also to be used as an instrument of policy. Here, too, we see one of the apparent contradictions of the policy of unilateralism—that is, the growing U.S. presence globally: "During the period of American innocence and isolation, the United States had forces stationed on or near every major continent in the world; its navy was active in virtually every ocean, its troops saw combat on virtually every continent, and its foreign relations were in a constant state of crisis and turmoil."[18]

Clearly, a unilateralist foreign policy did not mean being removed from the world. Rather, it was interpreted to mean that the United States would chart its own course and become engaged internationally at times and places that it chose, when it was perceived to be in the national interest to do so.

THE CIVIL WAR

By the time the American Civil War broke out in 1861, the United States was already on its way to becoming a major economic power. While the countries of Europe had been diverting economic resources toward their militaries, the United States had focused instead on domestic needs. The thriving trade between the United States and England (the United States exported raw materials, especially cotton, to England in exchange for British manufactured goods) tied the two countries closely together and further fueled U.S. economic growth. Pragmatically, one of America's former adversaries became one of its major trading partners.

The Civil War required the U.S. government to divert resources for military purposes necessary to fight that war. According to Paul Kennedy, the Civil War was "the first real industrialized 'total war' on proto-twentieth-century lines."[19] Although the conflict was a brutal and divisive one for the country, it further spurred U.S. industrial growth. As a result, by the end of the war in 1865, the industrial output of the United States had increased, and along with that came modernization of military technology. Coupled with the relative stability of the international system in the later part of the nineteenth century, the United States was then able to take its place in the "modern" world.

THE SPANISH-AMERICAN WAR

The Spanish-American War of 1898 represents one of the clearest cases where the United States broke from its unilateralist policy (as defined by political and military aloofness from other parts of the world) to become actively engaged internationally, both militarily and politically, while still remaining clear of "entangling alliances." The United States earlier had acted aggressively against Mexico to acquire contiguous territory seen as essential to the country's manifest destiny. The Spanish-American War represents a different case. The question to ask here is why the United States chose to declare war against Spain, a European country. How did this serve the national interest? Here we see the confluence of international and domestic politics, both of which must be considered in order to answer these questions.

The United States had had a troubled relationship with Spain for decades. Spain claimed some of the land that the United States wanted for its own. For example, the Florida cession in 1819 was the result of a long diplomatic campaign that was characterized by threats, bribes, and intimidation. At that time the United States also made it clear to Spain that any attempt by that country to reestablish its control over the colonies in the Western Hemisphere that had gained their independence (e.g., Argentina, Bolivia, and

Chile) would result in war between the United States and Spain. This history between the two countries helps frame the issues surrounding the Spanish-American War.

The U.S. decision to go to war against Spain in 1898 resulted from many factors, all of which reflected what was then understood as the "national interest." The result was a more aggressive foreign policy and an expansive, even imperialistic, interpretation of U.S. territory to include the Pacific Ocean. Spain's possession of the Philippines and Guam interfered with the U.S. desire to strengthen its role in the Pacific, especially after the opening of Japan in 1856, which was followed by a treaty with Korea in 1882.[20] And the United States saw Spain's control of the island of Cuba, ninety miles off the coast of the United States, as an infringement on its hemisphere. In addition, American businesses, which had invested millions of dollars in Cuban sugar, were pushing the government to do something about the political instability on the island.

McKinley was elected president in 1896 on the twin promises to protect American business and to free the Cuban people. Because of his experiences in the Civil War, he was reluctant to take the country to war again, but pressure on the president to do something grew. The press exacerbated U.S. claims on Cuba and pressure to go to war against Spain to "protect" the island. One newspaper, William Randolph Hearst's *New York Journal*, printed a letter written by the Spanish ambassador, Enrique Dupuy DeLome, that had been stolen by Cuban rebels. The DeLome letter described President McKinley as "weak and a bidder for the admiration of the crowd, besides being a would-be politician who tries to leave a door open behind himself while keeping on good terms with the jingoes of his party."[21] Although the ambassador subsequently resigned, the letter had the desired effect of further inciting "war fever" within the United States when it was published on February 9, 1898.

A few days later, on February 15, 1898, the U.S. battleship *Maine* blew up in Havana harbor, allegedly by an underwater mine, although a later investigation indicated that the explosion was caused internally.[22] Again, the press snapped into action and called for war against Spain, using the slogan "Remember the *Maine*" to rally public support. On April 11, McKinley went to Congress and asked for authority to "intervene" in Cuba, despite the fact that Spain had agreed to give Cuba its independence. Although this was not a formal declaration of war, Spain perceived it as such. In response, Spain declared war on the United States on April 23. By late July, the United States had overwhelmed Spain militarily in the Atlantic (Cuba and Puerto Rico) as well as in the Pacific (the Philippines), and peace negotiations started between the two countries. They signed the Treaty of Paris on December 10, 1898. As a result of the peace negotiations, Cuba was given its independence from Spain, Spain agreed to give Puerto Rico and Guam to the United States, and the United States purchased the Philippines for $20 million. The U.S. position in the Western Hemisphere, from the Atlantic into the Pacific, was secure.

Implications of the Spanish-American War

The United States justified the decision to go to war against Spain in part by the principles put forward in the Monroe Doctrine and the need to solidify its sphere of influence in the Western Hemisphere. Tied to this were humanitarian goals, as some U.S. political leaders believed Cuba needed to be "saved" from Spanish exploitation. An editorial in the *New York Times* of July 30, 1898, titled "Not for Cuba Only," notes that although this was a "war of humanity," to save the Cuban people from the barbarism of its Spanish colonial masters, it also notes that "it is not that alone. Our primary object, the real inspiring cause and chief end sought was the attainment of peace and tranquility at home."[23] Clearly, the decision to go to war was the result of a combination of commercial, political, and growing expansionist sentiments perpetrated in part by political leaders and members of the media.

To be understood fully, this decision must be put into a global context. For the countries of Europe, this was a time of imperialism, as each of the major powers scrambled to claim colonies in Asia and Africa. By confining itself to North America, the United States was being left out of this global power grab that threatened to undermine the place that the country was slowly securing for itself internationally. The Spanish-American War unambiguously made the United States an imperial power, rivaling the major powers of Europe. No longer seen as a new, young country, the United States now had its own colonies, which brought with them responsibilities. The United States could no longer be removed from the rest of the world, nor could it only look inward. Rather, its national interest now required that it protect its colonial interests as well as become more involved in world affairs. The foreign policy of the United States was changing.

It also is important to look at the role that domestic politics played in pushing the United States to war against Spain and toward expansionism. First, Americans were united against a common enemy, Spain, for the first time since the Civil War had divided the country. Northerners and Southerners fought side by side, thus helping to heal the bitter divisions, at least temporarily. Second, foreign policy, especially the role of the United States in the world, became an important issue in the presidential election of 1900. Theodore Roosevelt, leader of the Rough Riders, who had gained fame during the war, was on the ticket as McKinley's vice president, and he espoused an imperialist/expansionist agenda that he was able to enact once he became president upon McKinley's death in 1901. Finally, we see the power of the press, led by William Randolph Hearst, who used newspapers to foment public sentiment in favor of war. This fact alone marks an important transition in the role of the media in influencing policy.

The Spanish-American War and the defeat of Spain ended more than four hundred years of Spanish power and influence in the Western Hemisphere and Pacific and solidified the role of the United States as the major power in the region. This meant that the United States faced the new century in a different position internationally, and its foreign policy reflected that shift.

THE SCRAMBLE FOR CONCESSIONS

As a result of the Spanish-American War, the United States had a firm claim to the Pacific. But by 1899, the "scramble for concessions" in China threatened to leave the United States out of this market that was seen as important for American businesses. While the United States had been distracted by the Spanish-American War, between 1897 and 1899 the European countries had been acquiring territorial rights within parts of China. These "concessions" followed China's defeat in the Opium Wars and a subsequent weakening of the Qing Dynasty. This quickly led to an undermining of the Chinese empire as European countries and Japan began to carve up China for their own economic gain. To ensure America's place and to protect its own commercial interests in China, Secretary of State John Hay sent his Open Door note to the governments of Germany, Russia, and England; similar notes were subsequently sent to Japan, Italy, and France.[24] These documents called on the other imperialist countries to open their Chinese concessions (areas of interest) to trade and investment equally to all. Hay also requested that countries not interfere with any country's so-called "sphere of influence" within China. The Open Door notes were another assertion that the United States was a player in the international system and that it could not be taken for granted.

THE ROOSEVELT COROLLARY TO THE MONROE DOCTRINE

In 1902, Venezuela defaulted on debts to many of its European investors. In response, Britain, Germany, and Italy sent gunboats to blockade Venezuela's ports. In the United States these actions raised old fears that European powers would try to undermine U.S. dominance in the region. In 1904, President Theodore Roosevelt used an address to Congress to state clearly the U.S. position regarding the Western Hemisphere:

> It is not true that the United States feels any land hunger or entertains any projects as regards the other nations of the Western Hemisphere save such as are for their welfare. All that this country desires is to see neighboring countries stable, orderly, and prosperous. . . . Our interests and those of our southern neighbors are in reality identical. They have great natural riches, and if

within their borders the reign of law and justice obtains, prosperity is sure to come to them. While they thus obey the primary laws of civilized society they may rest assured that they will be treated by us in a spirit of cordial and helpful sympathy. We would interfere with them only in the last resort, and then only if it became evident that their inability or unwillingness to do justice at home and abroad had violated the rights of the United States or had invited foreign aggression to the detriment of the entire body of American nations. . . .

In asserting the Monroe Doctrine . . . we have acted in our own interest as well as in the interest of humanity at large. [25]

In this speech, Roosevelt established a policy that built on the principles espoused in the Monroe Doctrine. He gave notice that the Western Hemisphere was the responsibility of the United States and that the United States would use military force if necessary to protect its interests there. In effect, he laid out the conditions under which the United States would intervene in Latin America, and he also made it clear that the United States would take military action should any country engage in activities that could be seen as detrimental to U.S. interests. The United States was replacing European imperialist intentions in Latin America with its own, and its own foreign policy was being driven by a realist perspective backed up with its use of hard power.

Roosevelt's term in office was characterized by further U.S. expansion and involvement internationally. By the time Roosevelt became president in 1901, U.S. interests in Asia had been furthered by the Open Door policy that encouraged free and open trade rather than running the risk of having China divided into spheres of influence that might deprive the United States of its opportunity in this new market. In another assertion of U.S. interests in Asia, in 1905 Roosevelt helped negotiate the end to war between Russia and Japan, making sure that Russia would help balance the growing power of Japan. While Roosevelt won a Nobel Peace Prize for these efforts, they were driven in no small measure by Roosevelt's fear that if Japan got too strong, it could threaten U.S. markets and commercial interests in the Far East.

Consistent with Roosevelt's desire to dominate the Caribbean, which was seen as within the U.S. sphere of influence, he supported building a canal across the Isthmus of Panama that would connect the Caribbean with the Pacific Ocean. The canal would also allow the U.S. navy to move quickly from the Atlantic to the Pacific, making it possible to have one, rather than two, navies to protect U.S. interests. [26] Building the canal was made possible because of Roosevelt's intervention on behalf of Panama's rebellion against existing Colombian rulers. The success of that rebellion allowed the United States to acquire the land through which the canal would be built.

As noted above, the Roosevelt Corollary to the Monroe Doctrine and the building of the Panama Canal are but two examples of growing U.S. involvement internationally. When William Howard Taft, Roosevelt's successor, became president in 1909, he continued the policies started under Roosevelt. Taft pushed U.S. businesses to invest abroad as a way to further solidify U.S. interests. However, the expanding reach of the United States and its businesses meant that greater military involvement was necessary to protect them. Hence, Taft sent U.S. forces into Nicaragua and Honduras in 1910 and 1911, respectively, in order to protect U.S. lives and interests. In 1912, U.S. forces were deployed to Honduras, Panama, Cuba, and China, all in the name of "protecting U.S. interests." A detachment of marines was sent to Nicaragua in 1912 to "protect U.S. interests" and "to promote peace and stability," with a small group remaining until 1925. While some Americans opposed the United States' imperialist adventures, their voices largely went unnoticed. U.S. foreign policy and the place of the United States in the world had changed dramatically.

MARCH TO WORLD WAR I

By 1900 the international economic as well as geopolitical picture had changed. As one historian explains it when he speaks of "the great reversal," "By 1900, India accounts for barely 2 percent of world manufacturing output, China about 7 percent, while Europe alone claims 60 percent and the United States 20 percent, or 80 percent of the world's total" (see figure 2.2).[27] Thus, Europe and the United States replaced India and China as major centers of economic activity and, more important, industrial growth especially since the Civil War had allowed the United States to become a major power.

Within the United States, the era of industrialization brought both economic and social changes. The period from 1900 until the outbreak of World War I was a time of reform known as the Progressive Era. Not only did this change the face of labor and business, but it was also a time when the United States continued its international involvement, justified at least in part by the need to support U.S. business interests. The resulting changes in foreign policy were characterized broadly as "dollar diplomacy," in recognition of the importance of business and trade.

Woodrow Wilson, who was elected president in 1912, continued the policies set by his predecessors. The United States was actively engaged in those regions and parts of the world that had been defined as within its sphere of influence and critical to national interest, primarily Latin America and the Pacific. Wilson broadened the rationale for U.S. involvement so that U.S. assistance (and intervention if necessary) was extended to helping other peoples and countries become democratic. Wilson's idealism and commitment to democratic values would characterize his administration and become the basis for active U.S. engagement in the war that would rage in Europe.

Wilsonian Idealism and U.S. Foreign Policy

Wilson outlined the ideals that he valued in and for the United States in his first inaugural address, delivered March 4, 1913:

> Nowhere else in the world have noble men and women exhibited in more striking forms the beauty and energy of sympathy and helpfulness and counsel in their efforts to rectify wrong, alleviate suffering, and set the weak in the way of strength and hope. We have built up, moreover, a great system of government, which has stood through a long age as in many respects a model for those who seek to set liberty upon foundations that will endure against fortuitous change, against storm and accident. . . .
> . . . This is the high enterprise of the new day: To lift everything that concerns our life as a Nation to the light that shines from the hearthfire of every man's conscience and the vision of the right. It is inconceivable that we should do this as partisans; it is inconceivable we should do it in ignorance of the facts as they are or in blind haste. We shall restore, not destroy.[28]

Initially, U.S. interests in the first years of Wilson's administration centered on Asia, Latin America (primarily Mexico), and the Caribbean. Consistent

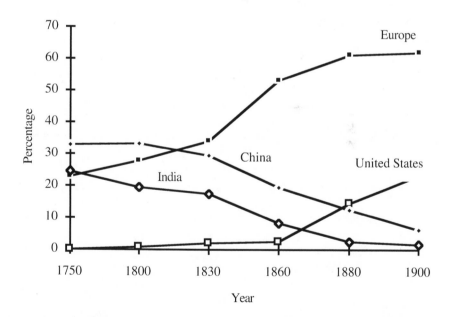

Figure 2.2.   World Industrial Output. Source: Originally published in Robert B. Marks, *The Origins of the Modern World: A Global and Ecological Narrative from the Fifteenth to the Twenty-First Century*, 3rd ed. (Lanham, Md.: Rowman & Littlefield, 2015). Data derived from Paul Kennedy, *The Rise and Fall of the Great Powers* (New York: Vintage, 1987), 149.

with his broadened interpretation of national interest, Wilson deployed U.S. military forces to those areas to help protect or maintain order (e.g., in Haiti, China, Dominican Republic) rather than just to protect U.S. interests.

Shortly after Wilson took office, Europe went to war. Wilson's goal was to keep the United States out of that conflict if possible. On August 4, 1914, he proclaimed the United States *neutral*. On May 7, 1915, the British passenger ship *Lusitania* was sunk by a German torpedo, resulting in the deaths of more than a thousand passengers and crew, including 124 Americans. In response, Wilson had the secretary of state deliver a note to the German ambassador in which the United States reiterated its neutrality but also gave warning that Germany should "not expect the Government of the United States to omit any word or any act necessary to the performance of its sacred duty of maintaining the rights of the United States and its citizens and of safeguarding their free exercise and enjoyment."[29]

In November 1916, Wilson was reelected president, in part because of his campaign slogan that he had kept the United States out of the European war. But ongoing trade with Britain, one of the belligerent nations, was drawing the United States into the conflict. The United States provided Britain and its allies with munitions, food, and raw materials, and it extended loans when the countries could not pay. During the first two years of the war (1914–1916), U.S. trade with Britain and its allies went from $800 million to $3 billion.[30]

Despite Wilson's intentions, he could not keep the United States out of the European war. In August 1915 German forces sank another British passenger ship, the *Arabic*, and then in March 1916, a French steamer, *Sussex*, and more American lives were lost. On January 22, 1917, as he was starting his second term in office, Wilson addressed the U.S. Senate and called for a "peace without victory." Specifically, he called for an end to the war on terms that "will create a peace that is worth guaranteeing and preserving, a peace that will win the approval of mankind, not merely a peace that will serve the national interests and immediate aims of the nations engaged." And he warned that "victory would mean peace forced upon the loser, a victor's terms imposed upon the vanquished. . . . Only a peace between equals can last."[31] In that prediction he was prescient, for the peace that was ultimately imposed on Germany contributed to the humiliation and economic devastation that fostered the rise of Hitler and Nazism and ultimately another war. Nonetheless, Wilson was not successful at either ending the war or keeping the United States out of it.

The resumption of German unrestricted submarine warfare in February 1917 and attacks on U.S.-flagged merchant ships made U.S. involvement inevitable. U.S. involvement was also spurred with the release to the Americans of a telegram intercepted by the British sent by German Foreign Minister Arthur Zimmermann to the German Ambassador in Mexico City in

January 1917. The so-called "Zimmermann Telegram" "promised the Mexican Government that Germany would help Mexico recover the territory it had ceded to the United States following the Mexican-American War. In return for this assistance, Germany asked for Mexican support in the war."[32] The Zimmermann Telegram was leaked to the press, and, as was the case with the Spanish-American War, helped convince the American public of the need to go to war. This implied threat coupled with the loss of American life by German torpedoes and the recognition that Germany had no interest in seeking a peaceful end to the conflict finally convinced Wilson of the need for the United States to take action. On April 2, 1917, Wilson went before a joint session of Congress and asked for a declaration of war against Germany, which was granted.

As the United States moved inexorably toward war, Wilson justified U.S. involvement in the most idealistic terms. "The world must be made safe for democracy. Its peace must be planted upon the tested foundations of political liberty."[33] In other words, the United States was going into this war for high-minded reasons and against an aggressive government that had violated international law.

Wilson's understanding of national interest and the ways in which he chose to implement American foreign policy represented a marked departure from the direction that the United States previously had taken. Whatever the actual reasons the United States had for going to war in Europe, Wilson put the decision into idealistic and moralistic terms. Further, his foreign policy in general was tied to a desire to actively extend democracy, thereby changing the U.S. policy posture from one that was unilateralist to one of active engagement internationally.

Wilson's Fourteen Points

On January 8, 1918, about ten months before World War I ended, Wilson again addressed Congress, giving what has become known as his Fourteen Points speech. Driven in part by his desire to avoid war in the future, the Fourteen Points outlined Wilson's vision to assure justice for all countries and peace in the future by creating an "association of nations . . . for the purpose of affording mutual guarantees of political independence and territorial integrity to great and small states alike."[34] The concept of uniting all states—large and small, powerful and those with less power—into one organization that would allow all of them to work together to thwart the imperialist or expansionist intentions of any one nation was a relatively new idea. Wilson's ideal notion of "collective security" was not to come to fruition, nor could the concept prevent another major war. Nonetheless, it provided the seeds that would eventually grow into the United Nations.

An armistice signed in Paris in November 1918 ended World War I. Wilson, Prime Minister Lloyd George of Britain, Premier Clemenceau of France, and Prime Minister Orlando of Italy negotiated the Treaty of Versailles. In a series of "secret" agreements, each of the allies was granted additional territory that was taken from the defeated countries. The German colonies were parceled out among the allies. New countries—Czechoslovakia, and Yugoslavia—were created as the existing European empires were disbanded, and Poland was again recognized as a sovereign state. The treaty imposed reparations on Germany, that is, payments that had to be made to the allies to compensate for the damage caused by the war. The treaty also included provisions for the creation of the League of Nations that would embody many of the principles espoused by Wilson.

Unfortunately, U.S. domestic politics intervened and thwarted Wilson's plans. With an election coming up in 1920, the issue of the League of Nations became highly politicized. The Republican majority in the U.S. Senate opposed the creation of the League, as did the Republican candidate for president, Warren G. Harding. This was one of the first times to date that Congress asserted its will on a foreign policy issue, thereby overriding the president's priorities. An indication of the growing power of the United States was that, without U.S. presence, the League of Nations could not succeed.

Although some of Wilson's goals for American foreign policy were defeated in the face of domestic opposition, many of his ideals and ideas influenced subsequent presidents and resurfaced periodically long after his death. [35]

U.S. INVOLVEMENT IN RUSSIA

In March 1917, while World War I was raging, a revolution in Russia toppled the government of Czar Nicholas II. Some months later, in November 1917, the Bolsheviks, a communist faction led by V. I. Lenin, overthrew the provisional government. Virtually all the European countries sent troops, allegedly to help Russia form a new stable government, although many of the Western leaders hoped to stop the nascent Bolshevik (communist) movement. In order to encourage the anti-Bolshevik forces, Wilson sent U.S. troops, which remained in Russia from 1918 through 1920, after World War I ended; nonetheless, the communist forces prevailed.

This involvement by the United States proved to have long-term implications. It planted seeds of mistrust, between the communist forces and the Western powers, that would continue to fester, finally emerging full blown in the Cold War that followed World War II. The leaders of the Soviet Union did not forget the way in which the Western countries, especially the United

States, did not hesitate to intervene in their civil war, including sending troops to their country. In turn, the leaders of the West were already defining the conflict as an ideological one that pitted the forces of democracy against those of communism. While the Soviet Union became an ally of the United States in its fight against Nazi Germany during World War II, the relationship was clouded.

DOMESTIC ISSUES:
THE EXECUTIVE AND LEGISLATIVE BRANCHES

As we review the foreign policy of the United States from its founding through World War I, one of the patterns that becomes most apparent is the dominance of the president in setting foreign policy priorities. Consistent with the beliefs of the early founders of the country, a strong executive was seen as the critical policy-maker and the one who set the priorities, with Congress playing largely a "balancing" role. As history shows, that generally was the case. Foreign policy was made by the president, working with other members of the executive branch (e.g., the secretary of state). While Congress played a role, it was largely secondary and compliant, with congressional attention more focused on enacting legislation for the growing and industrializing country.

One of the first, and perhaps most dramatic, examples of a departure from this pattern came in the Republican resistance to the League of Nations that was being pushed by Wilson. Article 10 was the heart of the League of Nations treaty; it stipulated that an attack on any member of the League was to be regarded as an attack on all members, and therefore that all should be prepared to go to war in response.[36] Republican opposition to the League was rooted in the concern that Article 10 would bind the United States too closely to other countries in opposition to the country's national interest and policy of unilateralism. The fear was that if the United States were to agree to the terms of the League, then the country could be plunged inevitably into foreign wars, whether or not it would be in its interest to do so.

Given congressional resistance, and knowing that entering into the League would require a two-thirds vote of the Senate, Wilson took his case to the American people, making it part of the presidential campaign of 1920. Harding, the Republican candidate, opposed the League, and his election meant that the United States would not join. Ultimately it was members of the Senate who asserted their feelings in opposition to the League, thereby assuring its defeat, regardless of Wilson's desires.

While an assertion of congressional opposition to presidential priorities was rare at the time, it would become more common later in the twentieth century, setting the stage for ongoing battles between the two branches about the making and implementation of U.S. foreign policy.

THE SHIFTING NATIONAL INTEREST

Although the dominant foreign policy pursued by the United States in the early years of the country was one of unilateralism, it did not take long for that concept to be reinterpreted in light of changing perceptions of national interest. While trade, commerce, and economic relationships were necessary to U.S. growth and prosperity, the founders of the country also saw political and military aloofness from other countries as essential to U.S. well-being. Gradually, however, U.S. prosperity was tied to the country's "manifest destiny" to expand across the continent. In many cases, this meant displacing those who were already on the land, whether European colonial powers or the Native Americans who had been there long before western exploration. Sometimes U.S. expansion was peaceful, as in the case of the Louisiana Purchase. At other times, the desire to grow brought the United States into direct conflict with other countries (e.g., Mexico and Spain) or with the native peoples. In each case, the United States justified that aggression because of national interest.

As the country grew and prospered, U.S. business and investment became more international or global in scope. This also changed the direction of U.S. foreign policy, as the country had to protect those interests, militarily if necessary, when they were threatened. By 1900, not only had the United States become a major industrial power, but it was emerging as a major political and military force to be reckoned with as well. By that time, U.S. territory had expanded beyond the Western Hemisphere into parts of the Pacific and Asia. Still under the same general foreign policy framework, the United States kept its involvement focused only on those parts of the world defined as being in its national interest. The Spanish-American War of 1898 represented a change in U.S. foreign policy, as the country aggressively declared war on Spain for dubious reasons. Nonetheless, the victory over Spain helped solidify the U.S. position in the world.

Until 1915, the United States remained largely within its own sphere of influence geographically, becoming more actively engaged militarily in the regions it defined as important. As president, Wilson added yet another dimension to the conduct of U.S. foreign policy by injecting ideals and morality as valid and legitimate reasons for intervention; U.S. involvement in World War I was justified in part by high-minded principles espoused by Wilson. These were further articulated in his Fourteen Points and in the creation of a League of Nations that was designed to make war less likely in the future.

By the end of World War I, the United States had established itself as a major power not only in the Western Hemisphere, but in Europe as well. However, if U.S. involvement in World War I is measured against Wilson's "lofty" goals, it proved to be a failure; the war neither ended war forever nor established a universal democratic system. But it did change the role of the United States in the international system, although in many ways the leaders of the country did not realize or acknowledge this for some time. In fact, it set the stage for active U.S. engagement during and following World War II.

Walter Russell Mead notes, "With fewer casualties than any other great power, and fewer forces on the ground in Europe, the United States had a disproportionately influential role in shaping the peace." But Mead also notes, "The United States was the only true winner of World War I. . . . World War I made the United States the world's greatest financial power, crushed Germany—economically, America's most dangerous rival—and reduced both Britain and France to a status where neither country could mount an effective opposition to American designs anywhere in the world."[37]

Following World War I, the highest priority of the Harding administration was a "return to normalcy," which meant changing priorities and focusing inward and away from international engagement. This also meant the creation of new laws restricting U.S. immigration and the passage of other laws that limited freedom for anyone thought to be associated with a communist organization. Under existing laws, American women who married foreigners lost their citizenship and could even be deported if they or their husbands were found to be suspect.[38]

By the 1930s, as fascism was growing in Europe, the dominant feeling in the United States was a desire for isolationism in the truest sense. After World War I, although the United States was a stronger and more powerful country internationally, the priorities—the national interest—were again focused inward. While the United States tried to remain outside the politics and problems of Europe and focus again on domestic priorities, it did not take long for the United States to engage internationally once again.

APPLYING FOREIGN POLICY CONCEPTS: THE SPANISH-AMERICAN WAR

Earlier in this chapter, we asked the following questions: Why did the United States choose to declare war against Spain, a European country? How did this serve the national interest? There are a number of factors that need to be considered in order to answer these questions.

Clearly, we now have a more complete understanding of the impact of the Spanish-American War on the United States. However, not all the information that we now have was available in 1896 when William McKinley was elected president. If you were an advisor to President McKinley and you knew then what we know now, what would you have advised him to do?

In order to determine this, you need to be able to identify the critical players at the time (e.g., role of Congress, the media, the public, business interests), what position or positions each of them took on this issue, and what you think was in the national interest at the time. This all must be put into the framework of U.S. foreign policy direction (unilateralist versus expansionist) as well as your own understanding of resources available to the United States, specifically, the use of hard versus soft power. Put another way, would you pursue a realist or an idealist or liberal policy?

With that background, what is your analysis of the Spanish-American War, and what would you have done?

The Case

William McKinley was elected president in 1896 on a pledge to protect American business. American businesses, which had already invested millions of dollars in Cuban sugar, were pushing the government to do something about the instability on the island of Cuba. Doing so would mean confronting Spain, which had been using repressive measures to battle an independence movement in Cuba. Within the Republican Party, Theodore Roosevelt and Senator Henry Cabot Lodge were already agitating for intervention, as this fit within their ideals for the United States, as were members of the press and some Democrats opposed to Spain's brutal methods. Lodge and Roosevelt were among a group of "expansionists" who met regularly to discuss national and international politics. (Roosevelt was an assistant secretary of the navy in the McKinley administration, before he became vice president in 1900.) These men believed strongly in "national greatness" and that the United States needed to assert its presence globally. Ultimately, they realized this would mean that the United States would have to expand across the Pacific. This desire was consistent with the goals of American business, which saw the Pacific as a potential market. "By the mid-1890s," according to Judis, this "merged into a single powerful case for an American imperialism."[39]

To appease his critics who were calling for action, McKinley sent the battleship *Maine* to Havana as a show of force. On February 15, 1898, the *Maine* blew up in Havana harbor, resulting in the deaths of 266 Americans. Although later investigations suggested that the explosion was most likely the result of a shipboard accident, the leading newspapers of the time used that incident to fuel what became known as "war fever." There were divisions within the government as to what the United States should do.

As president, McKinley was reticent to take the country into another war because of his own experiences during the Civil War. However, he also faced pressure from his own party (Lodge and Roosevelt, for example) as well as the American public, who had been churned up by the press into calling for war. McKinley was further concerned about the impact of the political uncertainty on the domestic economy. Finally, under mounting political pressure, McKinley went to Congress in April 1898 and asked permission to intervene in Cuba, which was granted.

The Spanish-American War lasted three months and was a clear victory for the United States. The Treaty of Paris that ended the war granted Cuba its independence from Spain and gave Guam and Puerto Rico to the United States. The United States also purchased the Philippines from Spain for $20 million. "The victory itself transformed American opinion and laid the groundwork for the McKinley administration's turn toward an imperial foreign policy."[40] The war showed that the United States could confront one of the major European powers and win.

The U.S. success in the war converted McKinley to a "new imperialist." Over the objections of the anti-imperialists, he decided to put a military governor in place in the Philippines. While the anti-imperialists warned of the danger of imposing American rule on the Philippines, the imperialists dismissed the concerns, reporting "that there was no 'nationalist sentiment'" and that the Americans "would be welcomed as liberators."[41] The anti-imperialists proved to be correct.

In the Philippines, a liberation army had been fighting against the Spanish for years before the Americans arrived in 1898 and was ready to fight the Americans. When the United States refused to grant independence to the Philippines, war broke out. Fighting continued in the Philippines; it lasted until 1916 and the passage of the Jones Act, "committing the United States to independence as soon as the Filipinos could establish a 'stable government.'"[42] The Philippines was given full independence in 1946 following World War II.

During the insurrection, the United States used brutal tactics against the Filipinos, which only fueled resentment and even hatred of the United States. Nonetheless, Roosevelt and the other imperialists never doubted the wisdom of the war against Spain, nor of taking the territory that it did for the United States. This was all part of the destiny of U.S. national greatness.

What Would You Do If . . .

The time is 1898. McKinley has been president for two years. His highest priority is economic well-being for the country, which means ensuring the success of big business. But the primary foreign policy orientation of the country since its founding has been unilateralist. To this time, that meant intervening internationally only in those cases where it would directly benefit business and commerce. It also meant staying removed from wars with Europe. A group within the Republican Party (McKinley's party) has been agitating for a more imperialist stance for the United States, while others have been clamoring for intervention in Cuba on humanitarian grounds.

What would you do if you were a close advisor to President McKinley and he looked to you for recommendations about whether or not to go to war with Spain? Given what you know now, including the consequences (both intended and unintended), would you recommend war, and why? Are there other options you would recommend exploring to satisfy the domestic pressures as well as to address prevailing foreign policy issues? What would be in U.S. national interest at that time?

Chapter Three

From Isolationism to Superpower

The Interwar Years through World War II, 1920–1945

The United States came out of World War I with a strong position internationally although also with a desire to turn inward once again. Therefore, the United States embraced a policy of *isolationism* during the period between the two world wars (roughly 1920 through 1941). If the foreign policy during the early years of the country was characterized by unilateralism and creeping engagement with other countries, the interwar period was a time when the United States preferred to remain removed from the international system as much—and as long—as possible.[1] While isolationism was the stated and overarching policy, the reality was that the United States continued to expand and solidify its role internationally.

Policies in the 1920s reflected the domestic political priorities of the time: a commitment to big business and economic growth, as well as the desire to shield the United States from the outside world. This was done by passing laws limiting who could enter the country and through policies that the leaders in Washington hoped would keep the United States out of another European war. As economic depression gripped the country in the 1930s, the highest priority was domestic recovery. Nonetheless, the United States found itself involved internationally, although initially this engagement was limited in scope. While the United States hoped to stay out of the conflict that later escalated into World War II, this proved to be impossible.

This chapter begins with a brief description of the interwar years and the relationship between domestic and foreign policies. The focus will then be on World War II, which brought the United States—and the rest of the world—into the new "atomic age" that changed the conduct of international relations and foreign policy. The chapter concludes with a discussion of one of the more controversial decisions made during this period, the decision to drop two atomic bombs. These two-fold decisions affected the country's foreign policy through the Cold War.

INTERWAR AMERICA

Although U.S. attention was focused inward in the 1920s and 1930s, the reality was that the country was fast becoming one of the most powerful nations in the world. Since the Monroe Doctrine, the United States had established a significant presence in Latin America. The United States also had a dominant place in Asia and the Pacific as early as the turn of the century, and subsequent policies ensured that it would retain that position. Where Europe was devastated by World War I, the industrial strength of the United States grew substantially, fueled in part by the material needs of its European allies who were at war. The combined military and industrial power of the United States meant that it had surpassed even the European countries, which looked to the United States not only for military help (which was limited in World War I), but also for economic support.[2]

In addition, building on the precedent set by Wilson, U.S. global dominance was not just military and economic but political and ideological as well. The ideals espoused earlier by Wilson continued to guide U.S. foreign policy. Even subsequent administrations, while more pragmatic than idealistic, pursued a foreign policy that was liberal—even idealist— in nature, tied to the desire to negotiate agreements and bring countries together to find ways of avoiding war to settle their differences rather than through armed conflict.

When he was elected president in 1920, Warren Harding inherited a country disillusioned by world war and whose attention was focused inward. Isolationism guided foreign policy, albeit with active involvement externally when it was perceived to be in the national interest. The main priority of the Harding administration was economic growth and commerce, priorities that continued under Calvin Coolidge, who took office on Harding's death in 1923. He was followed by Herbert Hoover who, before he was elected president in 1928, had served as secretary of commerce. In that role he had declared, "The dominant fact of this last century has been economic development. And it continues today as the force which dominates the whole spiritual, social and political life of our country and the world."[3] This was the attitude that predominated through the 1920s, during the administrations of Harding, Coolidge, and Hoover.

For the United States, the 1920s on the whole was a period of economic prosperity and consumerism; the average income rose by more than 25 percent between 1920 and 1929. The increase in income coupled with a drop in prices for many luxury items meant that Americans were buying products that they could not have afforded earlier. There were poor and unemployed in the country, but they were largely lost amid the prevailing sense of well-being.[4]

Consistent with the priority to look inward, and fearing an influx of foreigners who could disturb the domestic economic balance that existed, Congress passed a series of immigration acts that severely limited the number of people allowed to enter the United States from countries in eastern and southern Europe, especially Russia, Poland, and Italy. In 1921, national quotas for immigrants were imposed; the 1924 Immigration Act further restricted the number of people allowed to enter the country. Not only did the Immigration Act favor those countries with earlier emigration patterns (e.g., northern and western Europe), but it barred all Chinese, Japanese, and people from other Asian countries.[5] In many ways the act was a reaction to a growing nationalist/nativist sentiment within the United States that sought to "protect" the country from foreigners and to ensure that "undesirables," such as communists, could not enter the country. It was also consistent with isolationism and the desire to be removed from interaction with others.

Within the United States, this period also was marked by an increase in tensions between the races, with riots breaking out in many of the major cities. According to one historian, this was exacerbated by the 1924 Immigration Act, which was "deliberately designed to be both racist and discriminatory."[6] The Ku Klux Klan, which had been dormant, reemerged with its message of hate not limited to blacks but extended to include Jews, Catholics, and anyone else deemed a "foreigner."

This was also the era of prohibition and temperance, as the country looked for ways to control the increasing alcohol consumption, greed, gambling, organized crime, and political corruption that many believed were undermining the values of society. However, the imposition of prohibition only exacerbated these vices as trade in liquor became a new source of wealth and power for organized crime.

Women's suffrage was among the social advances during this period. The passage of the Nineteenth Amendment in 1920 gave American women who were U.S. citizens the right to vote. The international nature of World War I, coupled with recognition of the role that women played to help the war effort, ensured support of the amendment by Wilson and then passage by Congress in 1919. By 1920, it was ratified by the necessary thirty-six states.

During the 1920s, the primary emphasis of the Republican administrations was on helping and supporting big business, which had foreign policy implications. Congress imposed tariffs to protect American goods, raising duties on farm goods up to 28 percent. However, Europeans retaliated by raising their own tariffs on American goods, thereby making it harder to sell American products abroad. Congress reduced taxes on the wealthiest

Americans from 65 to 50 percent and passed the Budget and Accounting Act, thereby giving itself greater oversight over the budget process, consistent with its constitutional responsibilities.

Thus, for most of the 1920s the United States reveled in its prosperity and consumption while at the same time ignoring growing economic, social, and political problems, both domestic and international. But by the end of the decade, circumstances changed considerably.

U.S. Foreign Policy, 1920–1930

Although the United States was one of the major powers after World War I, its policy of limited international engagement evidenced in its foreign policy decisions did not reflect that status. Despite the movement toward isolationism and emphasis on domestic economic growth, the Harding administration did not completely abandon the internationalism or idealism of the previous Wilson administration. Rather, Harding's international focus was largely limited to participation in disarmament conferences in the belief that limiting the growth of weapons would help minimize the chances of war. Clearly, this would be in the best interest of the United States.

In fall 1921, Harding convened a conference in Washington, D.C., to find ways to control the size of countries' navies (especially Japan's) and to limit a possible military buildup that could potentially affect the United States by deflecting its economic growth. The Washington Conference resulted in a series of agreements that encouraged all countries involved to respect one another's possessions in the Pacific, and that also limited the size and number of naval vessels they could build.[7] One flaw in these agreements was that they could not be enforced (an important lesson in any arms control agreement). For example, Japan secretly built up to and ultimately exceeded the treaty limits while simultaneously building its air power as it moved toward militarism and aggression. However, the agreements provided at least some sense of stability for the next decade.

Harding died suddenly in 1923 and was replaced by Calvin Coolidge, who completed Harding's term and then won reelection as president. Like Harding, Coolidge's main priority was domestic economic stability, especially in areas like farming that had not yet recovered from the downturn following the war. And, like Harding, Coolidge was willing to engage internationally in a limited way in order to pursue the desired outcome of keeping the United States out of another war.

In August 1928, representatives of the United States and France coauthored the Kellogg-Briand Pact, idealistically designed to outlaw war. The leaders who signed the pact did so aware of "their solemn duty to promote the welfare of mankind." And they were "persuaded that the time has come when a frank renunciation of war as an instrument of national policy[8] should be made to the end that the peaceful and friendly relations now existing between their peoples should be perpetuated." Most important, the signers of the pact agreed that "the settlement or solution of all disputes or conflicts of whatever nature or of whatever origin they may be, which may arise among them, shall never be sought except by pacific means."[9]

In many ways, the Kellogg-Briand Pact reflected the idealism of the Wilson years and the goals of Wilson's Fourteen Points, which encouraged countries to find ways to avoid war. The pact was signed by sixty-five countries, virtually all that were then in existence, and was ratified by the U.S. Senate.[10] U.S. Secretary of State Frank Kellogg won a Nobel Peace Prize for this effort. Unfortunately it did not result in ending war as a means of settling disputes between and among nations.

In 1930 another naval conference was convened, this time in London, that brought together the United States, France, Great Britain, Italy, and Japan specifically to extend the limits that they had agreed on at the Washington Conference of 1921. However, the international situation had changed since the earlier conference. Both France and Italy, concerned that the agreement would limit their military power, refused to sign. The London Conference also included an "escalator clause," allowing a country to build more ships if it felt threatened by another country, thereby opening the door to an arms buildup. Despite the optimistic belief that international security could be assured with arms control and arms limitation agreements, war was brewing in Europe.

ESCALATION TO WORLD WAR II: 1930–1941

Even with international idealism and desire to avoid war, World War II was on the horizon. By the early 1930s, fascism was growing in Germany, Italy, and Japan, all of which harbored militaristic and expansionist goals. In 1931, in direct violation of the Nine Power Treaty to respect the integrity of China, Japan conquered the province of Manchuria and created the puppet state of Manchukuo. This was done by a group of Japanese military officials without the backing of the Japanese government. The United States sent a note of protest in response and invoked the Kellogg-Briand Pact in condemning Japan's aggression. In January 1932, Japan bombed the city of Shanghai, another direct violation of China's sovereignty. However, the United States did not intervene; this was outside what was perceived as its national interest at the time and was consistent with the desire to stay removed from international conflicts. Without unanimous action and U.S. participation, the League of Nations was powerless to do anything. In fact, facing censure for its invasion of Manchuria, Japan withdrew from the League, as did Italy following its takeover of Ethiopia in 1935–1936. This sent an important signal that collective security, as it was constructed at that time, would not succeed in preventing war.

Simultaneously, the world fell into deep economic depression. Although the warning signs were apparent earlier, they were largely ignored until the crash of the New York stock market in October 1929. Economic downturn in Europe and throughout Europe's colonies quickly followed. In 1931, Japan suffered poor harvests, and severe economic dislocations resulted. These economic conditions fueled the fascist movement already growing in Japan, and Germany followed a similar pattern.

The U.S. presidential election of 1932 reflected the disillusionment of the American people and the desire for change. Franklin D. Roosevelt headed the Democratic ticket and defeated incumbent Herbert Hoover by 472 electoral votes to 59. Roosevelt used his first inaugural address on March 4, 1933, to reassure the American people, stating that "the only thing we have to fear is fear itself—nameless, unreasoning, unjustified terror which paralyzes needed efforts to convert retreat into advance."[11] At that point, the American people had a lot to fear. As one historian points out, "In 1932, at the height of the Depression, 13 or 14 million Americans, a quarter of the workforce and mainly men, were out of work. Industrial output [which had fueled the U.S. economy] was down by 60 percent."[12] The price of livestock and agriculture (crops) had fallen, which had a devastating effect on the farmers in the country. Given the level of discontent, there was fear that the country might be heading for domestic unrest or even a revolution.[13]

Because of the deteriorating economic situation, Roosevelt's highest priority was domestic needs such as putting people back to work, creating and unifying existing "relief" (social welfare) agencies, and stricter supervision of the banking industry in order to guarantee that the crash of 1929 and the run on the banks that followed would not be duplicated. In his inaugural address, Roosevelt stated, "Through this program of action, we address ourselves to putting our own national house in order."[14] It was only after he outlined his domestic "program of action" (which was to become the New Deal) that Roosevelt addressed international issues. Even then his attention was not to the war brewing in Europe. Instead he expressed concern about the ways in which a change in "international trade relations" affected the United States.

Noting the interdependence that was already evident among nations, Roosevelt talked of the need to "spare no effort to restore world trade by international economic adjustment." He alluded to the situations in Europe and the Pacific, both of which were moving toward war, and to the need for the United States to face the crisis if national interests were threatened. To meet these joint crises, domestic and international, Roosevelt also informed the American public that he was "prepared under my constitutional duty to recommend the measures that a stricken nation in the midst of a stricken world might require." And while he asked for the help of Congress to take whatever actions were necessary (as specified in the Constitution), he also made it clear that he would invoke his executive power should that become necessary.[15]

In this inaugural address, Roosevelt foreshadowed a number of themes that became more prominent in his administration and as the United States headed toward war. First was the priority to focus inward and address the devastating economic situation facing the country. In his speech, when Roosevelt addressed the international situation, he did so in a way that made it clear that U.S. national interest was affected negatively because of the decline in international trade. By asking for the help of Congress, Roosevelt showed that he understood the relationship between the president and Congress. However, he also raised the possibility of acting outside the bounds of Congress should that become necessary. This was the statement of a strong executive, which made it possible for Roosevelt to do what he outlined as being in the best interest of the country.

Given domestic priorities, it is not surprising that during Roosevelt's early years the United States tried to continue a policy of isolationism not only with respect to Europe and the Pacific but toward Latin America as well. Many of the countries in that region were also suffering from economic disruption and inflation along with political instability as economic conditions worsened. Rather than get involved in Latin America, traditionally an area of U.S. interest, Roosevelt's approach was to assure the countries to the south that they would be treated as equals and with respect. Roosevelt pledged that the United States would be a "good neighbor," but he retreated from involvement in Cuba and Mexico, two countries that had been defined earlier as within the U.S. sphere of influence.[16]

Neutrality Acts

The outbreak of war between Italy and Ethiopia in May 1935 prompted Congress to pass a series of laws that prohibited the United States from providing arms or money to the belligerents or from sending U.S. ships into harm's way. Congress hoped that these "neutrality acts" would keep the United States out of the European war.

In 1937 war broke out between Japan and China, which threatened U.S. interests in China. The United States sent a note of condemnation, claiming that this was in violation of existing agreements, including the Open Door policy and the terms of the Washington Conference. Japan responded that because of changing circumstances, the Open Door was no longer applicable, in effect putting the United States on notice that Japan would not comply with any existing agreement.

In September 1938, in an attempt to stop German aggression without going to war, the leaders of Britain and France met with Hitler in Munich and agreed that Germany could annex part of Czechoslovakia in exchange for the promise of peace. One year later, despite his pledge, Hitler attacked Poland. Britain and France, both of which had promised to support Poland, declared war on Germany. War in Europe was inevitable; the lesson learned was that appeasement would not work.

During this period Roosevelt continued to appeal for peace internationally. He sent letters to Hitler and to Mussolini in Italy in September 1938 and in 1939, trying to persuade them to seek peace and affirming U.S. neutrality in the situation in Europe. In November 1939, Congress passed another neutrality act, but this time amended it to allow the belligerents to purchase war munitions and materials from the United States as long as they paid cash and carried the purchases in their own ships. "That was as far as American public opinion would go at that point; it was a step away from complete isolation, but a long way from intervention in Europe's quarrels."[17] Nonetheless, the United States was creeping toward involvement in the European war.

From Neutrality to Nonbelligerency

On June 10, 1940, Roosevelt spoke at the University of Virginia in Charlottesville and outlined a subtle shift in U.S. foreign policy from "neutrality" to "nonbelligerency." He said that the United States subsequently would pursue "two obvious and simultaneous courses: we will extend to the opponents of force the material resources of this nation; and, at the same time, we will harness and speed up the use of those resources in order that we ourselves in the Americas may have equipment and training equal to the task of any emergency and every defense." While he made it clear that "we still insist on the need for vast improvements in our own social and economic life," he also warned that the United States would gear up for a war footing should it become necessary.[18] One year later, it would.

The presidential election of 1940 was hard fought. Roosevelt's opponent, Wendell Wilkie, accused Roosevelt of trying to drag the country into the war. Nonetheless, the two candidates were not as far apart on foreign policy as it first appeared. Wilkie supported Roosevelt's policy to get the country on a war footing and to aid ally Great Britain. Both men favored instituting a draft, which Congress passed in September. But as the election got closer, Wilkie's campaign rhetoric appeared to become more extreme. He warned about the dangers of sending American men into a foreign war. He implied that the United States had no direct interest in the war and, therefore, that Americans should not fight and die in Europe. Ultimately, Roosevelt defeated Wilkie and won an unprecedented third term as president. According to one historian, Roosevelt believed that "in the interests of the United States,

Great Britain had to be supported both up to the limits his own public support and the law of neutrality would permit."[19] Roosevelt began to prepare the country for the possibility of war.

In his message to Congress on the "state of the union" in January 1941, Roosevelt spoke of the "four freedoms," which became a call to the American public to go to war if necessary. Roosevelt reminded the American public why the country went to war in the past—"for the maintenance of American rights and for the principles of peaceful commerce"—and that the war then raging on four continents was for the "armed defense of democratic existence." He reminded the country that "thinking of our children and their children, we oppose enforced isolation for ourselves or for any part of the Americas." And he presaged the U.S. reaction to the Japanese attack on Pearl Harbor when he warned, "As long as the aggressor nations maintain the offensive, they—not we—will choose the time and the place and the method of their attack."[20]

Roosevelt ended this speech with a call for personal sacrifice so that all Americans could respond to the call of "a world founded on four essential freedoms." These were freedom of speech and expression, freedom to worship God in one's own way, freedom from want, "which will secure to every nation a healthy peacetime life for its inhabitants," and freedom from fear— all to be guaranteed "everywhere in the world." Then, drawing on the idealism and appeal to moral virtue that had permeated much of American foreign policy since Wilson, Roosevelt called for a moral world order characterized by "cooperation of free countries, working together in a friendly, civilized society."[21] Hence, almost one year before the United States formally became involved in World War II, Roosevelt set the stage for U.S. involvement by asking the American public to sacrifice and by reminding them that the United States had a unique role to play in the world.

Two months later, in March 1941, Congress passed the Lend-Lease Act, allowing the United States to assist countries whose defense was seen as vital to the United States by lending or leasing them war supplies, equipment, or material. In August 1941, Roosevelt met with British Prime Minister Winston Churchill off the coast of Newfoundland, Canada, and issued the Atlantic Charter, affirming common principles "for a better future for the world." In this document, the two leaders reiterated many of the principles that Roosevelt had already laid out in his Four Freedoms speech, but they also echoed many of the ideas and ideals originally articulated by Wilson.[22] This statement moved the United States even closer to war.

WAR

U.S. entry into the war became inevitable when the Japanese attacked Pearl Harbor on December 7, 1941. On December 8, Roosevelt went to Congress and asked for a declaration of war against Japan. He began his message with the now famous words that December 7, 1941, would be "a date which will live in infamy" as "the United States of America was suddenly and deliberately attacked by the naval and air forces of the Empire of Japan."[23] Three days later, Germany and Italy declared war on the United States. The United States was at war in both Europe and the Pacific.

Although it took the bombing of Pearl Harbor for the United States to enter the war officially, it is clear that the country had been moving toward involvement for some time. Roosevelt's speeches for at least one year prior to the attack were preparing the country for what appeared to be inevitable. In addition, U.S. policies—gearing up industrially to help the war effort, assuring that the United States was prepared should it become necessary to go to war, moving from neutrality to nonbelligerency—were all designed to get the United States ready to enter the war. In many ways, the United States had no choice. It was one of the major powers in the world; by 1938, it had overtaken Britain and Germany as the greatest manufacturing producer.[24] The United States had been inching past isolationism, and Roosevelt was building public support for war, including warning the American people of the sacrifices they would have to endure for important reasons. The United States was once again going to fight the forces opposing democracy and freedom.

The Legacy of World War II

We are not going to describe the course of World War II, as that information is readily available elsewhere. However, what is important here is assessing the legacy and impact of the war on the United States and the evolution of the international system that followed. In many ways, World War II was a product of the twentieth century because of the role technology played; the surprise attack by Japanese aircraft on the naval base at Pearl Harbor was a reminder that all countries were suddenly vulnerable to such surprise attacks. Further, the war ended with the decision to use the newest technology, the atomic bomb. The emergence of these new technologies not only changed the way war was fought but also set the stage for the Cold War that would follow.

The United States became fully mobilized for the war effort, which led to some important changes domestically. Because men were drafted, women had to take on new roles domestically, including going to work to keep industry running. As women accepted these new roles, they were given more responsibility and proved themselves as professionals and corporate leaders, which had repercussions in the decades following the war. African Americans lobbied for greater integration, especially in light of a controversy that emerged during the election of 1940 about the segregation of the army. This push for integration also had important—and long-term—social implications for civil rights. [25]

This period was also characterized by one of the most inhumane policies seen in the United States since slavery. On February 19, 1942, President Roosevelt signed Executive Order 9066 authorizing the evacuation of more than 112,000 people of Japanese descent living on the West Coast to "relocation centers," where they spent the remainder of the war. [26] Many of these people were American citizens, and some had family members serving in the U.S. military. This policy was indicative of the fear that pervaded the country. The United States had been attacked by Japan, which was translated into a potential threat from the Japanese (and Japanese Americans) within the country.

The war also created strange, if fleeting, international alliances. It was not surprising that the United States joined with Britain and France, two traditional allies, to fight Nazi Germany. However, a new alliance was created when the Allied forces joined with the Soviet Union's communist leader, Joseph Stalin, to fight against Germany. Although the alliance with the Soviet Union was a necessary part of the war effort, Roosevelt and especially Churchill were suspicious of Stalin's motives as well as his ideology. This alliance lasted until the war ended and Germany was defeated.

By 1944, when it was clear that the Allied forces would win the war, one of Roosevelt's priorities was to start to prepare for peace. In January 1944, he again faced Congress and the American public to describe "the state of the union." This time, however, his speech dealt with both winning the war and the need "to maintain a fair and stable economy at home." To address both of these priorities, Roosevelt made a number of recommendations that he claimed would amount to a new bill of rights, appropriate for the time. These included the right to a good education, the right to a decent home, and the right to protection in case of illness and in old age. Roosevelt concluded his speech by noting:

> All of these rights spell security. And after this war is won we must be prepared to move forward, in the implementation of these rights, to new goals of human happiness and well-being.
>
> America's own rightful place in the world depends in large part upon how fully these and similar rights have been carried into practice for our citizens. For unless there is security at home there cannot be lasting peace in the world. [27]

In this speech, Roosevelt not only predicted the end of war, but also prepared the country for a return to postwar normalcy, with an emphasis on domestic issues once again.

Technology and World War II

Pearl Harbor was a wake-up call about the role of technology in redefining a country's security. At a time when oceans could only be breached by ship, surprise attack was difficult because of the time involved. Pearl Harbor made it clear what air power could do and mean. Suddenly, the United States and other countries were vulnerable, as this new technology could be used to attack in a way that had not been seen before. The role of air power changed the nature of warfare as well. Unlike World War I, where much of the war was fought on the ground and in the trenches, during World War II all countries depended on aerial bombing. This did not totally erase the need for ground or sea battles, as the history of World War II shows. Instead, it offered the belligerents more and different opportunities and ways to fight the enemy.

For example, the Battle of Britain in 1940 was an ongoing attack by German bombers sent to bring destruction on Britain. This part of Hitler's strategy of attrition against Britain was made possible by air power. British bombers attacked Germany as early as 1941, joined by U.S. air forces in 1942. The Germans responded with V-1 and V-2 flying bombs and rockets against Britain. While the Allies tried to confine their attacks to industry and "high-value" targets such as railroads, it was inevitable that civilians were killed and cities destroyed. Similarly, the German bombing of London did not differentiate between military and civilian targets. This showed both the strengths and weaknesses of the new technology: while it allowed countries to attack one another in the homeland, where they were most vulnerable, the risk to civilians increased and, with that, the number of noncombatant casualties. The allied bombing of Dresden, Germany, and the firebombing of Tokyo, Japan, are also examples of the destructive power of air attacks, which virtually leveled both cities and resulted in the deaths of hundreds of thousands of civilians.[28]

In June 1944, with the Germans apparently on the run, the Allies crossed the English Channel, landed on the beach at Normandy, France, and began the ground attack that would bring the war in Europe to a close. The fighting intensified in fall 1944, making the war the primary campaign issue in the U.S. presidential election in November. President Roosevelt and his running mate, Harry Truman, were elected overwhelmingly. In December, one month after the election, the final defeat of Germany began with the Battle of the Bulge. On May 8, 1945, not quite one month after the death of President Roosevelt, Germany signed the terms of unconditional surrender. However, fighting continued in the Pacific, leaving it up to President Truman to end that war.

The Decision to Bomb Hiroshima and Nagasaki

As president, Roosevelt was aware of the role of technology and the importance of dominating technologically. In May 1942, to make sure that the United States retained an edge, Roosevelt authorized the creation of the Manhattan Project, which brought together some of the greatest scientists of the time. The team's goal was to determine whether it was possible to split the atom and create a chain reaction that would result in the release of energy. If this energy could be harnessed and controlled, as some physicists thought, then the United States would be able to create a new and very powerful weapon.

On July 16, 1945, the new weapon was tested successfully in the desert near Alamogordo, New Mexico. The project was so secret that even Vice President Truman was unaware of its existence. Yet, when he became president, Truman was the one who had to make the decision to use the weapon. With the war in Europe over, U.S. forces were concentrated in the Pacific, and the Americans stepped up their bombing of Japanese cities, resulting in hundreds of thousands of civilian deaths.

On both military and moral grounds, scholars have thoroughly debated the decision to drop the atomic bombs, especially since Japanese defeat appeared inevitable.[29] Nonetheless, Truman ultimately made the decision to use the atomic bomb to force a quick end to the war, thereby minimizing further American casualties. On August 6, 1945, the *Enola Gay* dropped an atomic bomb, dubbed "Little Boy," on the city of Hiroshima, Japan, killing more than 70,000 people. Three days later, on August 9, a second bomb, called "Fat Man," was dropped on the city of Nagasaki. The atomic age had begun.

On August 6, the White House issued a press release: "With this bomb we have now added a new and revolutionary increase in destruction to supplement the growing power of our armed forces. In their present form these bombs are now in production and even more powerful forms are in development." The release continued: "It is an atomic bomb. It is a harnessing of the basic power of the universe. The force from which the sun draws its power has been loosed against those who brought war to the Far East."[30]

In this release, the White House noted the role of technology and how it had changed the face of warfare. "Before 1939, it was the accepted belief of scientists that it was theoretically possible to release atomic energy. But no one knew any practical method of doing it. By 1942, however, we knew that the Germans were working feverishly to add atomic energy to the other engines of war with which they hoped to enslave the world. But they failed."[31]

On September 2, 1945, Japan surrendered. In retrospect, it is clear that more than simply military reasons affected the decision to drop the atomic bombs. Influencing that decision was the desire to send a signal to the Soviet Union about U.S. military supremacy.[32] Once the war—and the need for the alliance—ended, the suspicion that characterized the relationship between the United States and the Soviet Union returned. The seeds of the Cold War that would follow World War II were already planted. (See the case study of the dropping of the atomic bombs at the end of this chapter.)

THE UNITED NATIONS: DEFINING THE POSTWAR WORLD

The horrors of World War II reinforced the importance of preventing such catastrophes in the future. Planning for the creation of an organization that could bring countries together with that goal had begun before World War II ended. President Roosevelt and Prime Minister Churchill worked together to bring this idea to fruition.

As a vice presidential candidate in 1920, Franklin Roosevelt supported the need to approve a "general plan" of the League of Nations. Over time, however, it was perceived that "the organization's inherent structure and its rules of procedure were grossly inadequate to the basic task of safeguarding peace and preventing war."[33] Roosevelt supported the basic liberal philosophy on which the League was structured, but he believed that an organization such as the League could not succeed if it required unanimous action by all member states. In other words, while he agreed with the values of cooperation and collective security in principle, he also understood the importance of power and the need to inject realist thinking if such an organization were to succeed.

The principles embodied in the short document called the Atlantic Charter, which Roosevelt and Churchill negotiated in August 1941, ultimately led to the creation of the United Nations.[34] Note that they worked on this document before the United States had even formally entered World War II, but clearly, Roosevelt was anticipating that step and the need to start planning for the postwar world. The two leaders sent the text of the charter to Stalin for his endorsement, but he saw it as an attempt at Anglo-American domination. Stalin told British foreign secretary Anthony Eden that the charter seemed directed against the Soviet Union.[35] The idealistic visions of a world that could avoid war were counterbalanced by the schism growing between East and West.

Creation of the United Nations

Despite Stalin's reservations, on January 1, 1942, representatives of the Soviet Union and China joined President Roosevelt and Prime Minister Churchill in signing the Declaration of the United Nations. The following day, twenty-two other countries signed as well, all of which were countries then at war with the Axis powers. They also agreed to remain united and not to sign any peace agreement individually with the Axis countries. Although the idea of a "united nations" then referred to the Allied countries, it quickly grew into the skeleton for an international peacekeeping and collective security organization.[36] Planning for the nascent organization continued with an eye toward learning the lessons of the League of Nations so that its weaknesses would not be repeated. The framers recognized the need for countries to work together in opposition to any aggressor nations (i.e., liberalism) balanced against the use of power and military might if and/or when necessary (i.e., realism).

One of the highest priorities was finding funding for the new organization. The planners (primarily the British and Americans) also had to address the problem of assuaging Soviet suspicions as well as the fears of smaller countries that they would be overwhelmed by the power of the larger ones. During these early years (1942 through 1943) in the midst of war, the mood within the United States was changing and becoming more international in outlook. This aided Roosevelt in his task to build domestic support for the new United Nations while also planning for the postwar order, although he still had to overcome the objections of isolationists, such as Senator Arthur Vandenberg of Michigan, if the treaty were to be ratified by the Senate.

Roosevelt and Churchill, met first with Chiang Kai-shek of China[37] in Cairo, Egypt, and then the two men met Stalin in Tehran, Iran, to discuss the war effort and what would follow the end of the war. In his Christmas Eve message to the American public on December 24, 1943, Roosevelt reflected on these meetings and noted that "those four powers must be united with and cooperate with all the freedom-loving peoples of Europe, and Asia, and Africa, and the Americas. The rights of every Nation, large or small, must be respected and guarded as jealously as are the rights of every individual within our own republic." He also noted, "The overwhelming majority of all the people in the world want peace. Most of them are fighting for the attainment of . . . peace that is as strongly enforced and as durable as mortal man can make it. If we are willing to fight for peace now, it is not good logic that we should use force if necessary, in the future, to keep the peace?"[38] In this message, he was reinforcing the idea that force might be necessary in order to continue to assure peace not only at the present, but in the future. And he reminded the American public that the end of the war was not yet in sight, although these world leaders were in the process of thinking about, and preparing for the peace to follow. The creation of a United Nations was part of that thinking.

By the summer of 1944, formal talks on the new organization were well under way. The organization would consist of a Security Council, a General Assembly, an International Court of Justice, and a Secretariat, with other agencies to address specific issues (especially economic and social) to be brought in as needed. The primary purposes of the organization were to maintain peace (using force if necessary) and to foster cooperation among all nations, leading to the common good. The leaders agreed that all countries should be bound by the decisions of the new organization, but they had questions about how best to achieve this. The structure of the Security Council would include permanent members, each of which would have a veto in recognition of the power that each held, both politically and militarily. This structure also acknowledged the reality that any action would require them to act in unanimity, and therefore ideally would foster cooperation among them. The General Assembly would be composed of all member nations and would be vested with broad authority, in contrast with the Security Council, which was primarily charged with peacekeeping.

Negotiations on the details continued through 1944. The four major powers issued a statement following a conference at Dumbarton Oaks in Washington, D.C., titled "Proposals for the Establishment of a General International Organization."[39] The proposals included expanding the Security Council to five permanent members (United States, United Kingdom, Soviet Union, China, and France) and six rotating members elected by the General Assembly. In addition to the International Court of Justice, the new structure would include an Economic and Social Council and a Military Staff Committee to direct the forces that would be employed in the event of a UN military action.

It is important to remember that Roosevelt had to present this idea at a time when the United States was in the midst of war that was costly in terms of lives and money. Yet it was also a period in which the United States was clearly solidifying its place as a world leader. The challenge facing Roosevelt was how to put forward, during the war, a framework for this international organization that would help to avoid such conflicts in the future, bearing in mind that this would not succeed without getting the support of Congress, including the isolationists who saw the world very differently than he did. On April 25, 1945, less than one month after Roosevelt's death, delegates from forty-six nations gathered in San Francisco for a conference on the United Nations. The basic structure of the organization agreed to at that time was the one negotiated at Dumbarton Oaks. Despite ongoing political issues, the goals of the organization were paramount, and the delegates approved the charter of the United Nations. President Truman submitted it to the Senate, which voted to ratify the charter on July 28, 1945. Then on December 4,

1945, the Senate voted 65 to 7 to approve full participation in the United Nations.

The United Nations was to embody the lessons of the League of Nations, and in many ways, it was successful. But, as history has shown, no organization could successfully ensure that war would be avoided. Although optimistically and idealistically the new organization would force the United States and the Soviet Union to work together, the tensions of the Cold War were already in place.

On the whole, the American public supported the notion of an organization that would help deter or avoid war. By the end of World War II, the American people had also come to the realization that the United States could no longer resort to isolationism or even unilateralism in its foreign policy. Rather, the United States would have to become actively engaged in the international system.

From Isolationism to Engagement

The period following World War I was a time when the United States turned inward once again, reverting to an isolationist foreign policy. Yet the decade following the war was one in which the United States was engaged diplomatically, for example, initiating the Kellogg-Briand Pact and convening the Washington Conference, in the idealistic belief that negotiations and agreements could avoid conflict and war in the future. It did not take long for this premise to be questioned. Once Japan invaded China and Hitler began his relentless drive for power, no international agreement would stop them. Furthermore, even the League of Nations, which had specifically been created as an instrument of collective security, proved to be powerless unless all countries agreed to work together to stop the aggression of any one.

Under a succession of presidents, the highest priority of the United States was to remain removed from the conflicts escalating in the Pacific and Europe. Yet, as Roosevelt saw, that would be impossible. The best he could do was to justify the reasons for U.S. involvement in these foreign wars and prepare the American public for the sacrifices they would have to make once the country went to war. The bombing of Pearl Harbor made U.S. involvement inevitable. The surprise attack also gave notice to all nations of the dangers inherent in new technology.

The way that World War II was conducted was important for a number of reasons. The advent and use of new technology made it clear that whatever country had the best and most advanced technology would be in a position of power internationally. This meant that even before World War II ended, the rush to technological dominance that characterized much of the Cold War had begun. During the war, the United States feared that Germany would be the first country to get new technology and then use it against the Allies. This drove the development of new weapons by the United States. The fact that the United States was able not only to build but also to use atomic weapons made an important point both during and after the war.

By the end of World War II, the international order had changed. The United States emerged from that war as the major power and was well positioned internationally. War had not been fought on its mainland, so unlike the European countries and Japan, it had an intact industrial base. The U.S. economy was thriving. The country was the dominant military power as well, with a close relationship that had developed between the economy and the military sector, or what Eisenhower would later call "the military-industrial complex." Further, the United States was instrumental in creating a structure that would define the postwar world, embodied internationally in the United Nations.

The Domestic Context

Domestically, the country faced a number of challenges. The return of men in uniform displaced women who had been in the workforce and who had taken on greater roles both in their homes and in society. Following the war there was a return to a more "traditional" family that was fostered by the growth of the new suburbs. Nonetheless, within twenty years, women were fighting for access to jobs, status, and pay equal to that of their male counterparts. African Americans, who had fought in the war, returned home only to face discrimination, and they, too, felt that a promise had been broken. This led directly to the civil rights movement that started in the 1950s and really took hold early in the 1960s.

The period following World War II was difficult as the United States adjusted to a changing international order as well as these domestic issues. It would be up to Harry Truman to lead the country through these many domestic and international issues.

APPLYING FOREIGN POLICY CONCEPTS: THE DROPPING OF THE ATOMIC BOMB(S)

As we have seen in this chapter, some of the foreign policy decisions that emerged during this period proved to be very controversial; the decisions to drop atomic bombs on Japan twice in a period of three days remain controversial to this day. In retrospect it is clear that the use of the atomic bombs was designed not only to end the war with Japan but also to send a signal to the Soviet Union and any other potential adversary about both U.S. capabilities and its credibility—that is, not only did the United States have these weapons of mass destruction, but it was willing to use them as well.

Whether the United States was justified in dropping the bombs then continues to haunt the U.S. Now, seventy-plus years later, whether the U.S. should formally apologize for that decision and the devastation it caused became a topic for discussion once again in May 2016, when President Obama became the first sitting president to visit Hiroshima. Interestingly, Obama had received a Nobel Peace Prize early in his presidency for his commitment to rid the world of nuclear weapons, an idealistic goal that has yet to be achieved.

With these factors in mind both about the situation then and also the longer-term implications of the decision, what is your understanding of the decision surrounding the dropping of the atomic bombs, first on Hiroshima and then on Nagasaki? And if you were in a position to make the decision or advise President Truman about it, what would you have done?

The Case

Historian and student of Japanese culture Bill Gordon wrote an essay in 2000, "Reflections on Hiroshima," in which he draws on a range of sources to support his conclusion that "no justification exists for the dropping of the atomic bomb on Hiroshima."[40] His argument reflects what other critics of the decision say: there was little military justification at that point as Japan was already on the verge of collapse and surrender, and even if Hiroshima had been warranted, there is little to support the decision to drop a second weapon on Nagasaki.[41] According to historian Brian McNulty, "President Harry S. Truman's decision to use the atomic bomb on two Japanese cities remains one of the most passionately debated historical events of the twentieth century. . . . Some respected historians say the bombing was avoidable at best, and analogous to Nazi war crimes at worst." McNulty also notes, "While . . . historians agree on the bomb's necessity [because of the conduct of the war to that point], some question the necessity of dropping the Nagasaki bomb only three days after Hiroshima."[42] Hence, not only is the decision to drop one bomb debated, but the question of whether the second one was needed is cause for additional discussion and debate. An essay published by the Pew Research Center in August 2015, seventy years after Hiroshima and Nagasaki, demonstrates the ways in which Americans' attitudes toward this decision have changed over time.[43]

While that controversial decision helped end the war, even before the United States got involved in the Second World War at all there was discussion about whether doing so would be in the national interest of the country. In fact, there was a group within the United States who wanted the country to remain isolationist and removed from the wars in Europe, as evidenced by the passage of the neutrality acts. Isolationist Senator Arthur Vandenberg, a Republican from Michigan and the "acknowledged but unofficial spokesman of Senate Republicans on foreign policy matters," prior to the bombing of Pearl Harbor "advocated strict neutrality and a rigid arms embargo to prevent American involvement in the war." He proved to be prescient when he wrote that "we have thrown ourselves squarely into the power politics and power wars of Europe, Asia, and Africa. We have taken the first step upon a course from which we can never hereafter retreat."[44]

Once the United States was involved in World War II, it played a unique role as a military leader, fighting both in the European and Pacific theaters. Clearly, this was also a period in which the United States was solidifying its place as a world power. Both Roosevelt and then Truman who followed as president were aware of the fact that whatever the United States did would set the stage for the period that would follow the end of the war and the reconfigured postwar political and military order. Therefore the decisions that they made during the war would have longer-term implications.

In 1939, before the United States was even involved in World War II, Albert Einstein wrote a letter to then-President Roosevelt specifically to inform him about recent research "on chain reactions utilizing uranium [that] made it probable that large amounts of power could be produced by a chain reaction and that, by harnessing this power, the construction of 'extremely powerful bombs . . .' was conceivable."[45] Einstein believed, and wrote in his letter, that research was already under way on this idea supported by the German government, and that the United States should be prepared to move ahead as well. Einstein was working with Leo Szilard, a physicist who had emigrated from Hungary to flee the Nazis, and was among the most vocal of those advocating for the creation of this type of weapons program. Along with a number of other scientists, such as Edward Teller, they saw it as their responsibility "to alert Americans to the possibility that German scientists might win the race to build an atomic bomb and to warn that Hitler would be more than willing to resort to such a weapon."[46] Roosevelt responded to Einstein that he had had set up a committee to study this possibility, and then formally approved this uranium research in October 1939.

It took a while for the research to come to fruition but on July 16, 1945, the first atomic weapon was tested in the desert in New Mexico. Ten days later, on July 26, 1945, then-President Truman, Churchill, and Chiang Kai-Shek, meeting in Potsdam, issued a proclamation defining terms for Japanese surrender. That declaration carried a clear warning to Japan:

> The result of the futile and senseless German resistance to the might of the aroused free peoples of the world stands forth in awful clarity as an example to the people of Japan. The might that now converges on Japan is immeasurably greater than that which, when applied to the resisting Nazis, necessarily laid waste to the lands, the industry and the method of life of the whole German people. The full application of our military power, backed by our resolve, will

mean the inevitable and complete destruction of the Japanese armed forces and just as inevitably the utter devastation of the Japanese homeland. [47]

And then they called upon the government of Japan to proclaim an unconditional surrender noting that "The alternative for Japan is prompt and utter destruction."[48]

It is important to note that even though Stalin was at the Potsdam conference, he did not sign this declaration since technically the Soviet Union was not then at war with Japan.

The press statement that the White House issued following the dropping of the bomb on Hiroshima on August 6, 1945, was very explicit: "Sixteen hours ago an American airplane dropped one bomb on Hiroshima, an important Japanese Army base. That bomb had more power than 20,000 tons of T.N.T. It had more than two thousand times the blast power of the British 'Grand Slam' which is the largest bomb ever yet used in the history of warfare." It then continued "The Japanese began the war from the air at Pearl Harbor. They have been repaid many fold. And the end is not yet. With this bomb we have now added a new and revolutionary increase in destruction to supplement the growing power of our armed forces. In their present form these bombs are now in production and even more powerful forms are in development."[49]

Perhaps even more telling, however, is the threat that followed:

> We are now prepared to obliterate more rapidly and completely every productive enterprise the Japanese have above ground in any city. We shall destroy their docks, their factories, and their communications. Let there be no mistake; we shall completely destroy Japan's power to make war.
>
> It was to spare the Japanese people from utter destruction that the ultimatum of July 26 was issued at Potsdam. Their leaders promptly rejected that ultimatum. If they do not now accept our terms they may expect a rain of ruin from the air, the like of which has never been seen on this earth. Behind this air attack will follow sea and land forces in such numbers and power as they have not yet seen and with the fighting skill of which they are already well aware. [50]

The justification in the complete statement was that Germany was already working on developing such a weapon and therefore it was incumbent on the United States to do so as well. But also that Japan had attacked first at Pearl Harbor and that now, since they had not yet surrendered, the United States would have no choice but to strike again.

Although Roosevelt was the one who made the initial decision to authorize the Manhattan Project and to put the resources into developing this new type of weapon, it came to Truman to authorize the dropping of the two atomic bombs.

What Would You Do If . . .

The time is August 1945. The war in Europe has ended in May 1945, and the war in the Pacific against Japan was clearly winding down. The major world leaders had issued an ultimatum at Potsdam warning Japan about the need for unconditional surrender and of the devastation that the country would face if they did not comply. When Japan did not surrender under the terms of the Potsdam Declaration, the United States and its allies faced a major decision: whether to go ahead and use the atomic bomb against Japan, not once, but twice in the period of three days.

What would you do if you were an advisor to President Truman and he was looking to you for recommendations about what to do next? There are clearly a number of options: do nothing and hope that Japan realizes that the end is in sight and surrenders; drop one bomb as a warning but target relatively unpopulated areas; drop a bomb on a major city to send a signal; drop one bomb and then be prepared to drop another if Japan does not surrender after the first; or perhaps there are other options that could be considered. You are aware of the fact that this new weapon has incredible power that will send a signal not just to Japan, but to the Soviet Union or any other potential adversary as well. Therefore, the implications of the decision are far greater than just for the immediate time period. What are the arguments that you could make for each option, and what decision would you finally advocate for and why?

Chapter Four

The Making of a Superpower

Cold War Foreign Policy, 1946–1980

Two countries emerged in positions of global power at the end of World War II: the United States, which came out of the war with its homeland intact, its economy strengthened by the war effort, and its military unsurpassed technologically, and the Soviet Union, which had joined with the United States and the Western allies against Germany, but which was also charting its own course. One of the unintended consequences of World War II was that it set the stage for the Cold War that followed by pitting these two "superpowers," as they came to be called, against each other. Neither of these two countries specifically wanted or sought this power; in fact, in the 1920s and 1930s, each had pursued an isolationist foreign policy, preferring to focus on domestic priorities rather than trying to secure a place of power internationally. Yet World War II thrust both countries into positions of international leadership that became even more important after the war ended. The Soviet Union emerged from the war as one of the most powerful countries in Europe, while the United States was the only country strong enough to "balance" that power, and it was in the United States' interest to do so.[1]

In contrast, the relative power of those countries that had been dominant before World War II (e.g., the countries of Western Europe—France, the United Kingdom, and Germany—and Japan) waned as they were forced to look inward, rather than outward, in order to recover from the devastation of the war. The result was a restructuring of the international system into a bipolar world in which the forces of democracy and free-market capitalism, embodied by the United States and its allies, faced the Soviet Union and its allies, the forces of communism.

Rather than the traditional "hot war," where countries fought one another directly on the battlefield, this was a "cold war," or a period of ongoing tensions played out in a number of arenas. First, the Cold War was a war of *ideology*, which assumed that the two divergent approaches (democracy and communism) could not coexist peacefully. Therefore, one side would have to emerge as dominant.

One of the misconceptions that guided U.S. foreign policy during the Cold War was the belief that communism was a single monolithic force. This suggested that *all* communist countries, whether China or Vietnam or even some of the left-leaning movements in Africa and South America, were loyal to and supported (and were, in turn, supported by) the Soviet Union. This belief gave rise to the domino theory that ultimately led to U.S. involvement in Southeast Asia. According to the domino theory, if one country in Southeast Asia became communist, then the other neighboring countries would fall like a row of dominoes and similarly become communist. Hence, any incursion of communism had to be stopped before it spread.

The Cold War was also a *political* war in which the two approaches were seen as antithetical to each other, leading inevitably to conflict. The belief in the expansive political nature of communism not only had foreign policy implications for the United States but important domestic ones as well. The growth of McCarthyism and the "Red Scare" created a domestic atmosphere that supported U.S. foreign policy priorities.

The Cold War involved *military* confrontation. While no war was fought directly between the United States and the Soviet Union, the two sides fought each other indirectly through "proxy wars." The battleground on which Cold War conflicts were fought expanded dramatically to include countries in Latin America and Africa as well as Asia. Often the Soviet Union and sometimes the People's Republic of China backed communist-led insurgencies and communist-leaning leaders, and the United States backed virtually any government or force that was not communist. These proxy wars made it possible for the two superpowers to avoid a direct military confrontation that could, potentially, lead to nuclear holocaust. The outcome was the same—victory for the forces of democracy or communism—but the danger to the rest of the world from nuclear weapons was diminished. What neither side seemed to consider (especially in the early years) was the desire of other countries, such as India and Pakistan, to acquire nuclear weapons so that they could better deter—or if necessary fight—their own enemies.

Finally, the Cold War was a war of *economics*. The United States and its allies were steeped in capitalist free-market economics. In contrast, the Soviet Union followed a communist economic system, where the state planned the economy and owned the means of production. Although the conflict between these two systems appeared to be secondary to political, military, and ideological competition, in reality, economics pervaded many of the foreign policy decisions that the United States made, especially in the early years of the Cold War. For example, the Marshall Plan to aid Europe had its roots in the U.S. desire to expand markets for its own goods and the need for stable trading partners that would not be tempted to turn to communism. This made economic tools important elements of the U.S. foreign policy of containment and set the precedent of using foreign aid (i.e., money) as an instrument of foreign policy.[2]

The Cold War period was an especially important time in the evolution of U.S. foreign policy. As we shall see in this chapter, domestic and international policies and priorities came together as the United States revised and strengthened not only its military but its decision-making apparatus to support the goals and needs of this new "cold" war. It was a time when domestic and international politics merged through movements like the "Red Scare," which helped build domestic support for policies that were seen as necessary for success in the Cold War. We see the role of a strong executive as a series of presidents—starting with Harry Truman—provided the guidance and direction for a new course of action. Then, in the belief that presidents had overstepped their powers, we see Congress asserting its constitutional authority and oversight role. And, most important, we see the creation of a framework for American foreign policy that is rooted in unapologetic internationalism and engagement. Not only did the United States move beyond unilateralism or isolationism, but it did so in a way that left no doubt about the country's belief in itself and its dominance in the new world order. The concept of national interest changed dramatically after World War II, and all aspects of U.S. policy during the Cold War were designed to promote the "new" national interest.

This chapter will illustrate the ways in which perceptions affect the making of foreign policy. Stalin's speech in February 1946 reinforced the perception that George Kennan, a U.S. diplomat stationed in Moscow, already had of the Soviet Union and its intentions, and Kennan's perceptions were quickly translated into policy recommendations. In turn, the U.S. policy of containment affirmed Soviet concerns of being encircled by hostile countries and the need for them to build their own military to deter and defend against any possible attack. In short, we see the making of a classic "security dilemma" or a situation where the actions of one state to ensure its security are seen as a direct threat to another state, which responds with its own military buildup. While each state was enacting policies perceived to be ensuring its own security, in effect it was creating a situation of insecurity, something that becomes especially apparent in retrospect.

THE EARLY YEARS OF THE COLD WAR

In many ways, the origins of the Cold War can be traced to 1917 and the Russian Revolution. As noted in chapter 2, U.S. troops remained in Russia from 1918 through 1920 to fight against the Bolsheviks (communists). This action was not forgotten by subsequent Soviet leaders and was part of the reason for their suspicion and mistrust of the United States. On the other hand, the United States and its allies (primarily Great Britain) harbored their own suspicions of Stalin and his intentions. Although it was in all sides' interest to fight together against the Germans during World War II, it was not long after the war ended that a chasm emerged between the former allies.

Germany surrendered in May 1945. In July, the leaders of the three major victorious wartime powers (Truman, Churchill, and Stalin) met in Potsdam, Germany, to address the postwar order in Europe. Germany was divided among the four powers (the three plus France), which together ultimately decided the future of that country. Berlin, the capital of Germany, was similarly divided among the four. Physically it was located in the heart of what was to become the Soviet sector of East Germany, so Berlin, more than any other place, became a barometer of the level of Cold War tensions.

Just as Roosevelt had prepared the American people for participating in World War II before the United States officially entered the war and then started preparing them for the peace before the war ended, so Truman began setting the stage for the Cold War before it started. In October 1945, he gave a major foreign policy address in New York City that became known as the "Fundamentals of American Foreign Policy." In this statement he outlined twelve points that he said would now guide U.S. foreign policy. Some of the points are reminiscent of Franklin Roosevelt's Four Freedoms speech, in which he pledged to support the basic freedoms to which all people are entitled.[3] For example, Truman stated his belief that all peoples "should be permitted to choose their own form of government by their freely expressed choice," and he spoke of the need for the establishment of "freedom from fear and freedom from want."[4]

Truman also used this statement to send a signal, especially to Stalin, about U.S. intentions in the emerging world order. For example, he made it clear that the United States had "no plans for aggression against any other state, large or small. We have no objectives which need clash with the peaceful aims of any other nation." And he warned Stalin and any other potential aggressor, "We shall approve no territorial changes in any friendly part of the world unless they accord with the freely expressed wishes of the people concerned." He also foreshadowed some of the major postwar programs: "By the combined and cooperative action of our war Allies, we shall help the defeated enemy states establish peaceful democratic governments of their own free choice."[5]

Suspicions about Soviet intentions were confirmed in February 1946 when Joseph Stalin gave a speech in which he noted that in the wake of the victory of World War II, "the Soviet social system is a fully viable and stable form of organization and society," despite Western assertions that "the Soviet social system was a 'dangerous experiment' that was doomed to failure." He also noted the strength of the Soviet armed forces, and that the Red Army is "a first-class modern army, equipped with the most up-to-date armaments, led by most experienced commanders." Achieving this required planning and economic development, as well as mobilization of the people behind the war effort. And, after outlining the path forward, Stalin concluded by reminding the people that "all are engaged in one common cause" that unites the Soviet people.[6] Although World War II was behind them, Stalin was telling the people of the Soviet Union that they won because of their planning, their military strength and their will, all of which they would need as they look to the future. Clearly, this speech sent an important message to the West as evidenced by the telegram that U.S. diplomat George Kennan sent back to Washington from his base in Moscow approximately two weeks later.

George Kennan and Early Cold War Policy

The foreign policy that the United States pursued during the Cold War had its origins in 1946 and 1947. Within a short time after the end of World War II, it was clear to the United States that the next battle would be between the United States and the Soviet Union. In order to understand the evolution of U.S. Cold War foreign policy, it is important to examine in some detail the critical events and ideas that framed the policy decisions that the United States made.

The assessment of George Kennan reinforced the beliefs about a fundamental clash between the two countries and ideologies. In February 1946, Kennan sent a document to Washington that became known as "the Long Telegram." This document and Kennan's subsequent article "The Sources of Soviet Conduct" (the X Article, discussed below), published in 1947, helped crystallize the thinking of U.S. policy-makers and changed the course of U.S. foreign policy.[7] Both documents warned about an aggressive Soviet Union and the need for the United States to be prepared to counter that aggression anywhere in the world. For the analyses he put forward and the impact that he had, Kennan has become known as one of the critical architects of U.S. Cold War foreign policy, especially the policy of containment.

The Long Telegram

Kennan sent the Long Telegram from Moscow on February 22, 1946, describing the Soviet threat as he saw it. The document, intended as information for the president and secretary of state, was in five parts and began with the statement that the "USSR still lives in antagonistic 'capitalist encircle-ment' with which in the long run there can be no permanent peaceful coexis-tence." Kennan saw the Soviet leadership as defining a world in conflict because "[i]nternal conflicts of capitalism inevitably generate wars" that are "insoluble by means of peaceful compromise." And based on the premises that he put forth, he concluded that "[r]elentless battle must be waged against socialist and social-democratic leaders abroad."[8] Hence, Kennan made clear that the United States would face an ongoing battle that would pit the United States against the Soviet Union.

In part 2 of the telegram, Kennan documented how he arrived at his conclusions and drew a distinction between the outlook of the Russian peo-ple, who are "friendly to outside world, . . . eager above all to live in peace and enjoy fruits of their own labor," and the attitudes of the Soviet leader-ship. In his analysis, the Communist Party line made peaceful coexistence between the two countries impossible.

Part 3 offered Kennan's assessment of what the Soviet outlook meant for future Soviet policy. In this section Kennan outlined his view of the Soviet Union's drive for power and for "increasing in every way strength and pres-tige of Soviet state." He also painted a grim picture of a country that will do whatever it takes to achieve that end, including taking advantage of the parts of Europe seen as being "of immediate strategic necessity," and where the Soviets sensed "strong possibilities of opposition to Western centers of pow-er."[9] Part 4 of the telegram identified the ways in which these policies might be played out via "unofficial" organs, such the Russian Orthodox Church.

In part 5, "Practical Deductions from Standpoint of U.S. Policy," Kennan prescribed what U.S. policy should be to counter the Soviet intentions, begin-ning with the need to recognize the nature of the enemy and to prepare the United States to fight against it. To that end, Kennan concluded that "much depends on health and vigor of our own society. World communism is like malignant parasite which feeds only on diseased tissue. *This is point at which domestic and foreign policies meet.* Every courageous and incisive measure to solve internal problems of our own society . . . is a diplomatic victory over Moscow" (emphasis added). According to Kennan, the United States "must formulate and put forward for other nations a much more positive and con-structive picture of sort of world we would like to see. . . . It is not enough to urge people to develop political processes similar to our own. Many foreign peoples, in Europe at least, are tired and frightened by experiences of past, and are less interested in abstract freedom than security." And he warned that the United States "should be better able than Russians to give them this. And unless we do, Russians certainly will." In other words, the Soviet Union will press for an advantage in Europe, and unless the United States intervenes, the Soviet Union will "win." It is instructive to note that about six months later, the Soviet ambassador to the United States, Nikolai Novikov, sent a cable from Washington to Moscow in which he painted a similar portrait of the United States.[10]

The X Article

One year later, in 1947, Kennan published an article titled "The Sources of Soviet Conduct" in the journal *Foreign Affairs* under the pseudonym "X."[11] This article went further than the Long Telegram in outlining ideas for the future U.S. foreign policy of containment. By publishing in *Foreign Affairs*, a respected journal read by policy-makers, among others, Kennan made his points publicly. In fact, one of the most important aspects of the article was that it was directed at the American public, or at least those members of the public who studied and cared about foreign policy (i.e., "the attentive public"). In doing so, Kennan built support for the policies he believed would be most important for the United States to win the emerging Cold War.

In the article, he reprised themes outlined in the Long Telegram, such as "the innate antagonism between capitalism and socialism." And he warned that out of the antagonism "flow many of the phenomena that we find disturbing in the Kremlin's conduct of foreign policy: the secretiveness, the lack of frankness, the duplicity, the wary suspiciousness, and the basic unfriendliness of purpose." From that he concluded, "This means that we are going to continue for a long time to find the Russians difficult to deal with." As he outlined the characteristics that influence Soviet behavior, he also noted that the "cumulative effect of these factors is to give to the whole subordinate apparatus of Soviet power an unshakable stubbornness and steadfastness in its orientation. This orientation can be changed at will by the Kremlin but by no other power."

Kennan then put forward his recommendations for the United States: "In these circumstances it is clear that the main element of any United States policy toward the Soviet Union must be that of a long-term, patient but firm and vigilant *containment* of Russian expansive tendencies" (emphasis added). With that, Kennan articulated the basic tenets that would guide U.S. foreign policy for the next fifty years, premised on an expansionist and aggressive Soviet Union and the need for the United States to contain those tendencies. He also described some of the ways that the United States could contain the USSR: "The Soviet pressure against the free institutions of the Western world is something that can be contained by the adroit and vigilant application of counter-force at a series of constantly shifting geographical and political points."

While Kennan made it clear in this article that he thought the Soviet Union was far weaker than the United States and the West, he also warned that the Russian leaders were dedicated to the success of their cause and that they had the patience to wait and continue their fight. He was prescient when he noted that "Russia, as opposed to the Western world in general, is still by far the weaker party, that Soviet policy is highly flexible, and that Soviet society may well contain deficiencies which will eventually weaken its own total potential." (This would not happen until approximately forty-four years later, when the Soviet Union imploded in August 1991.) But, for the short term, Kennan argued it was up to the United States to do whatever it had to do to contain the Soviet Union. [12]

The X article not only outlined the containment policy that was the framework of American foreign policy during the Cold War, but it also sowed the seeds for the U.S. alliance system that followed by encouraging the United States to align with countries surrounding the Soviet Union in support of the common goal of containing the USSR. While this strategy helped limit Soviet expansion by making it clear that if the USSR went into any of those countries it would have to deal with the United States, it also sent a signal to the Soviet Union, which perceived that it was being surrounded by hostile countries. The result was to exacerbate the cycle of mistrust and suspicion that characterized much of the Cold War.

1947: THE TRUMAN DOCTRINE AND THE MARSHALL PLAN

A series of communist takeovers in countries of Eastern Europe followed World War II. Bulgaria and Yugoslavia elected communist majority governments in 1945, and communist governments were created in Hungary, Poland, and Romania in 1946. In addition, the Soviet Union retained its control of the Baltic republics of Latvia, Lithuania, and Estonia after World War II. Not only did these lead to the creation of a "Soviet bloc" in Eastern Europe, but they validated Kennan's warnings of an expansionist Soviet Union (see figure 4.1).

The situation in Greece, engaged in civil war since 1945, grew very serious from the perspective of the United States. Britain had been sending money and troops to Greece in support of the forces defending the monarchy against communist insurgents. However, by 1947 it could no longer afford to do so. Instead, it would be up to the United States to pick up the slack. Similarly, unrest in Turkey and Soviet pressure on that country furthered U.S. concerns about Soviet intentions regarding Europe.

Thus, by 1947 the world was divided into two basic camps centered on the United States and the Soviet Union: West versus East. Drawing on the warnings put forward in the Long Telegram and the X article, Truman delivered a speech to the U.S. Congress in March 1947 outlining what became known as the "Truman Doctrine." In this speech, Truman formalized the policies that the United States would pursue, as well as the reasons behind them. It was a clear articulation of U.S. policies and intentions at the start of the Cold War.

In his speech, Truman specifically identified Greece and Turkey as two major areas of concern to the United States. Regarding Greece, Truman laid out the background of the ongoing war and the fact that the Greek government had asked the United States for assistance. Truman noted that "Greece must have assistance if it is to become a self-supporting and self-respecting democracy. The United States must supply this assistance. . . . There is no other country to which democratic Greece can turn. No other nation is willing and able to provide the necessary support for a democratic Greek government."[13]

Truman continued: "The British government, which has been helping Greece, can give no further financial or economic aid after March 1 [1947]. *Great Britain finds itself under the necessity of reducing or liquidating its commitments in several parts of the world, including Greece*" (emphasis added). The importance of this statement cannot be underestimated. Not only did Truman make the case for U.S. assistance to Greece, but he also made it clear that the United States would take on the global role that the British had played earlier and could no longer afford to continue. Thus, the power balance shifted from Europe in general and Britain in particular to the United States. It also set the United States on a particular course of action not only in Greece, but also in other parts of the world as both Britain and France

Figure 4.1.   Cold War Europe

withdrew from their colonial commitments and the United States replaced them as the major power. With that relative change in status, the United States became the major imperial power in the West.

Truman also noted that "Turkey now needs our support. Since the war Turkey has sought additional financial assistance from Great Britain and the United States for the purpose of effecting that modernization necessary for the maintenance of its national integrity. That integrity is essential to the preservation of order in the Middle East." And, once again, Truman argued that the United States had to step in because Britain could "no longer extend financial or economic aid to Turkey."

Leading to the call for Congress to act, Truman uttered the words that have often been quoted: "I believe that it must be the policy of the United States to support free peoples who are resisting attempted subjugation by armed minorities or by outside pressures. I believe that we must assist free peoples to work out their own destinies in their own way. I believe that our help should be primarily through economic and financial aid which is essential to economic stability and orderly political processes." To support these beliefs, Truman asked Congress to authorize $400 million in assistance to Greece and Turkey. Congress authorized the funds, and the role of the United States as the defender of countries fighting communist aggression was established. The United States was now firmly committed to using its hard power, economic and military, as well as its soft power (i.e., its influence) to support its allies and in opposition to communism.

The Truman Doctrine had a number of other important foreign policy implications. It established the precedent of using foreign aid and economic assistance as an instrument of foreign policy, something that continued through the duration of the Cold War and continues to the present (post–Cold War) period. It also made clear to the Soviet Union and to all other countries that the United States would use military force not only within its own hemisphere (Monroe Doctrine) or when democratic ideals were threatened (Wilsonian perspective), but also in support of any country fighting communism anywhere in the world.

The National Security Act of 1947

When Truman outlined a new and more muscular direction in U.S. foreign policy, he also needed to create a structure that would ensure its implementation. The bureaucratic structure for the conduct of U.S. foreign policy had been in place virtually since the creation of the country, when the foreign policy orientation was very different. That structure no longer was appropriate for a world in which the United States was going to be playing a dominant role. With the advent of the Cold War, the military became an important and overt instrument of U.S. foreign policy; the success of U.S. foreign policy was tied directly to military might. For the United States to play a major role globally, not only did it have to have a credible military force, but it also had to be perceived as willing to use that force in support of its foreign policy goals. Therefore, the country needed a structure that more firmly linked the military to the civilian sides of policy-making.

President Truman designed the National Security Act to create a structure that would accomplish these various goals, all of which were seen as necessary for success in the Cold War. Until the events of 9/11 precipitated rethinking the national security and intelligence sectors, the National Security Act of 1947 was the most sweeping change made to the military and foreign policy apparatus since the country was founded.[14]

The National Security Act of 1947[15] did a number of things. The War and Navy departments were merged into a single Department of Defense (DoD), which was more appropriate for the new direction in U.S. foreign policy. The DoD was to be headed by a civilian, and each military service would be headed by a civilian secretary who reported to the secretary of defense.[16] It authorized the establishment of a Central Intelligence Agency (CIA) headed by a director of central intelligence (DCI); the ability to keep track of the Soviet Union and other adversaries was seen as essential to preparing for and winning the Cold War. The act provided for the creation of a National Security Council (NSC) charged with coordinating domestic, military, and foreign policies relating to national security. The membership of the NSC would consist of the secretaries of state and defense with other officials (such as the director of the CIA and the chair of the Joint Chiefs of Staff) serving as advisors as needed. Starting in 1953, under President Eisenhower, the NSC staff was headed by an assistant for national security. Initially, this job involved little more than serving as secretary to the NSC; however, over time, and as U.S. foreign policy became more complex, the role of national security advisor grew so that now that position serves as one of the most important advisors to the president.

With the passage of the National Security Act, the United States was better equipped militarily as well as from a policy-process perspective to wage the Cold War.

The Marshall Plan

As Congress debated the Truman Doctrine, in June 1947 Secretary of State George C. Marshall delivered a commencement address at Harvard University outlining the basic principles for the postwar recovery of Europe. Marshall proposed a specific plan for European economic recovery to be implemented over the next several years in the belief that only if Europe were strong economically could it withstand any attempt at communist insurgency. But it also put the burden on the Europeans to determine their own needs:

Before the United States Government can proceed much further in its efforts to alleviate the situation and help start the European world on its way to recovery, there must be some agreement among the countries of Europe as to the requirements of the situation and the part those countries themselves will take in order to give proper effect to whatever action might be undertaken by this Government. It would be neither fitting nor efficacious for this government to undertake to draw up unilaterally a program designed to place Europe on its feet economically. This is the business of the Europeans.[17]

In response, Britain and France took the lead and invited twenty-two European countries, including the Soviet Union and its Eastern European allies, to a conference to draw up an outline for European reconstruction that could be presented to the United States. Although the USSR and members of the Eastern bloc refused to participate, virtually all the countries of Western Europe did, and on September 23, 1947, they submitted a report to the United States on general European needs.

On April 3, 1948, President Truman signed into law the European Recovery Act—widely known as the Marshall Plan. It provided for $5.3 billion specifically for European economic recovery for the following year. During the period from 1948 through 1950, the United States spent $12 billion in economic aid for Europe, more than half of which went to Britain, France, and West Germany. This infusion of money gave those countries the impetus they needed to begin to recover from the war. And, as planned, they became major trading partners of the United States (and, through the European Union, remain so today).

The Marshall Plan not only strengthened the economic systems of the partner countries, but by doing so, it helped stabilize their political systems as well. By forcing the countries of Europe to work together, it actually created the early framework for what would later grow into the European Union. It tied the United States more firmly to Western Europe, and it solidified the role of the United States as global leader. But it also exacerbated the divide between Western Europe and the countries of Eastern Europe, which were pulled more firmly into the Soviet orbit.

By 1947, just two years after World War II ended, the United States had secured its place as a "superpower" politically, militarily, and economically. Further, it had transformed its foreign policy into one that was actively engaged internationally, and its foreign policy–making process and national security apparatus were restructured to support that perspective. And Congress and the American public supported this direction for the country.

THE ESCALATION OF THE COLD WAR: BERLIN TO KOREA

A coup in Czechoslovakia in 1948 brought a communist government to power and furthered U.S. concerns about an expansionist Soviet Union. Those fears were made even more real in June 1948, when the Soviet Union closed all roads through East Germany into Berlin, blocking land access to the city. The United States saw this as an act of Soviet aggression against an ally and felt that it had to respond. To do so, the United States led a massive airlift that lasted one year. During that period, all necessary supplies, including food, clothing, and medicines, were brought into West Berlin by air (see figure 4.2). Stalin lifted the blockade in June 1949, but this would not be the last time that Cold War tensions were played out in this divided city.

The Creation of NATO

The Berlin blockade reinforced the importance of U.S. military involvement in Europe as well as the critical role of the United States in deterring the Soviet Union. The desire by the United States and Europe to formalize their relationship as well as to build on the need to contain communism contributed directly to the creation of the North Atlantic Treaty Organization (NATO) in April 1949. At the heart of the North Atlantic Treaty is Article 5, with its statement of collective security and mutual support that unequivocally links the United States and Europe.[18] In many ways, this statement of collective security/defense is similar to the one outlined in Article 10 of the League of Nations charter—that the collective power of nations working together would be sufficient to deter any aggressive nation.[19] In contrast to the earlier League of Nations, what made the NATO alliance credible was the link between the United States and its allies in Western Europe and, as evidenced by the Berlin blockade, the willingness of the United States to use its military power to support its allies when necessary.

The NATO treaty contains other components that were—and remain— important politically, if not necessarily militarily. For example, Article 2 specifically references the "further development of peaceful and friendly international relations by strengthening their free institutions. . . . They will seek to eliminate conflict in their international economic policies and will encourage economic collaboration between any or all of them."[20] While this made it clear that these like-minded countries (democratic and capitalist) would work together and cooperate, it further divided East and West.[21] In general, NATO represents one of the clearest, and also most enduring, examples of the U.S. postwar alliance system designed to contain communism.

Figure 4.2.   Germany after World War II Showing Allied Airlift to Berlin

The End of the Decade

Two other events occurred in 1949 that served as harsh reminders to the United States about the dangers of the Cold War. In September 1949 the Soviet Union tested an atomic bomb, making it the second country to acquire these new weapons of mass destruction. This happened years before the United States anticipated that the Soviets had the technology to do so. With that test, the world really was bipolar, and the United States could no longer count on technological domination to assure the defeat of the USSR.

Then, in October 1949, after years of civil war, Mao Tse-tung (Mao Zedong) proclaimed the creation of the People's Republic of China (PRC), a communist state. Despite the fact that Chinese and Soviet communism were different and that each country was pursuing separate goals,[22] to U.S. policymakers the creation of the PRC was another indication of the spread of communism, which they believed was monolithic and out for world domination. This perception colored many of the foreign policies that they made during the Cold War.

By 1950 the United States was established as a major power in European affairs. Further, it had started to play an active role in the Middle East when it supported the creation of the state of Israel in 1948 and was the first country to formally recognize Israel. In 1953 the United States cemented its place in that region when it supported the overthrow of Prime Minister Mohammed Mossadiq in Iran. Eisenhower wanted a pro-U.S. leader in Iran because of its strategic location bordering the Soviet Union as well as its supply of oil (which Mossadiq had nationalized). Thus, Eisenhower ordered the CIA to work with the Iranian military to overthrow Mossadiq. With the help of the United States, Shah Mohammed Reza Pahlevi was restored as leader of Iran following a coup in August 1953, regaining the role he had had before Mossadiq took power two years earlier. Iranian resentment toward the United States grew because, as one scholar noted, the shah was seen as "holding the American proxy in the Persian Gulf—as the protector of America's interests."[23] Those feelings would come to a head during the Iranian revolution of 1979 and the seizure of the U.S. embassy in Tehran.

NSC 68

In the 1950s, the United States was flexing its muscles globally. The National Security Act established the structure necessary for the United States to act as a global superpower. The Truman Doctrine and Marshall Plan outlined clearly the active role that the United States would take in Europe, and the creation of NATO reinforced the ties between the United States and its European allies. And the United States was willing to play an active role in parts of the world, such as the Middle East, in which it had not been involved before. However, all of these actions were guided by the strong belief in the need to contain communism led by the Soviet Union.

In April 1950, two months before the outbreak of war in Korea, the NSC issued a report to President Truman known as "NSC 68: United States Objectives and Programs for National Security." This document laid out the bipolar nature of the Cold War world and, like the Long Telegram, reinforced the belief that the goal of "those who control the Soviet Union and the international communist movement is to retain and solidify their absolute power, first in the Soviet Union and second in the areas not under their control." And because the United States is the "principal center of power in the non-Soviet world and the bulwark of opposition to Soviet expansion [it] is the principal enemy whose integrity and vitality must be subverted or destroyed . . . if the Kremlin is to achieve its fundamental design."[24]

The analysis put forth in NSC 68 (which was classified until 1975) led to the conclusion that the United States had to build up its military forces (conventional and nuclear) in order to meet its commitments and confront—and deter—the Soviet threat. Any questions about Soviet intentions were laid to rest in June, when war broke out on the Korean peninsula.

War in Korea

By the time that war in Korea started in June 1950, the United States had been involved in Asia for about a century. However, it was the U.S. occupation of Japan following the end of World War II that made the United States a major presence in that region. When civil war broke out on the Korean peninsula, precipitating invasion by the Soviet-backed North into the U.S.-backed South, Truman felt that the United States had to act on behalf of its ally, South Korea.

Truman asked Secretary of State Dean Acheson to bring the issue before the United Nations Security Council, which condemned the invasion as a breach of the peace agreed to at the end of World War II. Voting when the Soviet ambassador was absent (and therefore could not veto the action),[25] the Security Council agreed to call for an end to fighting and required the invading armies of the North to withdraw to the thirty-eighth parallel, an arbitrary dividing line that had been established earlier. When this did not happen, on June 27 the UN Security Council called on member states to aid South Korea, created a special military command, and invited the United States to lead it.

Truman never asked Congress for a formal declaration of war. Since this was not an act of war but merely a "police action" in support of the United Nations, he used his power as commander in chief and issued a statement consistent with the Security Council request: "I have ordered United States air and sea forces to give the Korean Government troops cover and support." He concluded the statement by asserting, "I know that all members of the United Nations will consider carefully the consequences of this latest act of aggression in Korea in defiance of the Charter of the United Nations. A return to the role of force in international affairs would have far-reaching effects. The United States will continue to uphold the rule of law."[26]

Initially under the leadership of U.S. General Douglas MacArthur,[27] the Korean War continued until an armistice was signed between North Korea and the United Nations on July 27, 1953. The armistice drew the dividing line between North and South Korea at the thirty-eighth parallel (where it had been before the war broke out) and established a demilitarized zone, patrolled by UN forces, to separate the two sides.

Approximately 35,000 Americans lost their lives in this Korean War, which was the first example of active U.S. military engagement under the new Cold War framework. The military was an important instrument of U.S. foreign policy and was used directly to support the foreign policy and ideological goals of confronting communism, a clear commitment to realist political thinking backed up by the use of hard power. The war was fought on the basis of President Truman's executive power to commit forces, and without a congressional declaration of war. It was a clear assertion of U.S. global superiority. But given the tenuous relationship between the United States and the Soviet Union, both of which had nuclear weapons, it was also a reminder of how fragile the peace could be, as well as the dangers of war between the superpowers.

The Cold War at Home

To be successful, foreign policy needs the support of the American public, which is often unsophisticated about the details. Hence, the U.S. political leaders simplified the policy into a depiction of democracy versus communism or "good" versus "evil." Truman helped draw the lines in some of his speeches, but actual events coupled with the coverage of those events reinforced the notion of a divided world. It was the rise of Senator Joseph McCarthy and the subsequent "Red Scare" that brought the Cold War home.

In February 1950, McCarthy gave a speech in which he charged that there were more than two hundred communists in the State Department. He followed this with speeches on the floor of the U.S. Senate, where he talked about "loyalty risks." Although many viewed him as an extremist and a demagogue, his attacks got the attention of the press and the public. McCarthy spoke in terms that the "average" American could understand, and his charges resonated. The Senate held investigations and hearings to look into McCarthy's allegations. Ultimately, the Senate censured him, and both McCarthy and the charges he made were discredited, but not before the damage was done and many innocent people suffered. Nonetheless, McCarthy and the "Red Scare" created the atmosphere at home that contributed directly to building support for U.S. military and foreign policy during the Cold War.

The Domino Theory

North Korea's invasion of South Korea exacerbated America's fears of communism and gave ammunition to those in Washington who felt that the United States was not doing enough to contain communism. Journalist Stewart Alsop wrote, "We are losing Asia fast" (referring not only to Korea but to China as well). He went further when he warned that after China, "the two pins in the second row are Burma and Indochina. If they go, the three pins in the next row, Siam, Malaya, and Indonesia, are pretty sure to topple in their turn. And if all of Asia goes . . . magnetism will almost certainly drag down the four pins of the fourth row, India, Pakistan, Japan and the Philippines."[28] This belief, that if one country were to fall to communism others would follow, became the rationale for increasing support to South Korea, and it was the basis for the domino theory that contributed directly to the U.S. decision to get involved in Vietnam.

EISENHOWER

The decade of the 1950s was characterized by brinkmanship and ongoing tensions between East and West. Both the United States and the Soviet Union arrived at policies that each felt would solidify its own power as well as send signals to the other country. This suggests that foreign policy and military decisions made by the United States during this period not only were designed to further those policies deemed to be in the national interest but also were based on a perception of the ways in which each country viewed the other. We will examine the policies and decisions made during this period from those multiple perspectives.

In 1952 the United States elected Dwight Eisenhower president based in part on his pledge to "bring the boys home from Korea." In June 1953, about six months after Eisenhower took office, the Korean War ended with the signing of an armistice. The United States deployed troops to help patrol the border between North and South Korea and reaffirmed its commitment to protect its allies against communism. With the war in Korea, the United States expanded its reach and demonstrated that it would use military force when necessary to contain communist aggression.

The United States made some of its foreign policy decisions during this period in reaction to external events over which it had no control. For example, Stalin's death in 1953 just before the Korean War ended had a direct impact on U.S. policies. So much of U.S. foreign policy was tied to *perceptions* about the Soviet Union that Stalin's death led to uncertainty about who would succeed him and what that would mean for Soviet decision-making. In 1956, after three years of unclear leadership, Nikita Khrushchev came to power. He used a "secret" speech at a session of the twentieth congress of the Communist Party of the Soviet Union to denounce Stalin and declare that "coexistence" would become the goal of Soviet foreign policy.[29] The speech was widely covered and, taken together with announcements of Soviet reductions in armaments, might have signaled a significant change in international relations. This was not to be; the Soviet army quickly quashed the Hungarian revolution of 1956, which served as a reminder not only of Soviet military power, but also of its willingness to use it.

Committed to containment, Eisenhower's foreign policy built on the recommendations of NSC 68 as well as the advice of "cold warriors" such as Secretary of State John Foster Dulles. Eisenhower shifted U.S. foreign policy to rely more heavily on weapons of mass destruction as the primary deterrent against Soviet aggression. With the advent of the hydrogen bomb and apparent technological superiority, the United States had a credible threat that if this country or its allies were attacked by the Soviet Union (or China), the response would be overwhelming. This was the doctrine of "massive retaliation." However, the success of this strategy was premised on U.S. military superiority.

That assumption was put to rest in October 1957 when the Soviet Union launched a satellite, known as *Sputnik*, using a rocket that had a range of five thousand miles (capable of hitting the United States). The fact that the Soviets had this capability came as a surprise to the United States, which had not yet tested its own long-range rocket (ICBM) successfully. As a result of *Sputnik*, there was a fundamental shift in the perceived balance of power between the United States and the Soviet Union; the Soviet Union had apparently surpassed the United States.[30] This came at a time when U.S. foreign policy was premised on the idea of military balance or even U.S. superiority, and it contributed to the acceleration of the arms race that had already started.

The Eisenhower years were characterized by international tension and a tenuous balance of power. The Suez Canal crisis of 1956 disrupted the delicate balance that existed in the Middle East. It also caused strains between the United States and France and Britain, its closest European allies. Precipitated by Egyptian president Nasser's nationalization of the Suez Canal, Britain and France conspired with Israel to overthrow the Egyptian leader. Israel invaded Egypt in October 1956, allegedly to destroy bases that had been used against Israeli settlers. As agreed, the British and French governments immediately claimed that the war would put passage through the Suez Canal in danger and called for a cease-fire. When Nasser rejected this, the two countries launched an attack against Egypt. Britain, France, and Israel all denied that they had colluded, and with U.S. pressure, the UN negotiated a cease-fire. All sides suffered as a result of this adventure. The British prime minister resigned, and the British government lost prestige within the British commonwealth. The attack by Israel fueled the hatred between Israel and the Arab peoples. The United States was angered that it had not been told of this plan by three of its allies. To many in the United States and Western Europe, Suez was an unnecessary distraction during a time of Cold War tension.

The U-2 Incident

In May 1960, Eisenhower was looking forward to a summit meeting with Khrushchev in Paris that was to be his final major diplomatic act before his term ended. However, just before that meeting, the Soviet Union shot down a U.S. U-2 spy plane that had been flying over the USSR.[31] Even more embarrassing to Eisenhower, the pilot, Francis Gary Powers, was captured alive by the Soviet Union.[32] A series of events followed, starting with Eisenhower's claims that a "weather plane" had been lost. When the Kremlin published a photograph of the plane along with the claims that the pilot was alive, Eisenhower faced a dilemma: admit that he lied about the plane, or say that he was unaware of its mission. Either way, the outcome would not be good for Eisenhower and perceptions of the United States, and it virtually guaranteed that the summit would fail. As reporter James Reston wrote in the *New York Times*, "This was a sad and perplexed capital tonight, caught in a swirl of charges of clumsy administration, bad judgment and bad faith."[33]

In many ways, this event set the tone for the election of 1960. The Cold War to date had been a delicate balancing act that included not only military might, as defined by actual numbers of weapons, but also perceptions. The U-2 incident and the subsequent failure of the Paris summit held in August 1960 were further indicators that the perception of balance had shifted in favor of the Soviet Union. It is little wonder that one of John F. Kennedy's major election themes was a "missile gap" and that the United States was losing the arms race to the USSR.

THE KENNEDY YEARS

John F. Kennedy defeated Eisenhower's vice president, Richard Nixon, in the election of 1960 and became president. While the American public saw Kennedy as youthful, handsome, and energetic, the Soviet Union perceived him as young and inexperienced. Here, too, perceptions became reality as that image of Kennedy played into the decisions that the Soviet Union made during Kennedy's brief tenure in office; the foreign policy decisions made by Kennedy defined the direction of U.S. foreign policy for the next decade.

In August 1961, after he had been in office about seven months, Kennedy faced a crisis over Berlin. The Soviets demanded that the Western powers evacuate West Berlin, and Khrushchev threatened to sign a peace treaty with East Germany, a move that would have further isolated the Western sector of the city. When Kennedy refused to comply with Khrushchev's demands, the Soviets sealed East Berlin from the West by erecting a wall. That wall became a symbol of the Cold War divisions between East and West; when the wall came down in November 1989, it was a tangible sign that the Cold War was over.

Berlin was an early crisis for the Kennedy administration. But Kennedy faced other areas of crisis and even conflict that further defined U.S. foreign policy under Kennedy and beyond. Two specific areas that had long-term implications for U.S. foreign policy were Cuba and Southeast Asia—specifically Vietnam.

Cuba

With the Monroe Doctrine, the Spanish-American War, and the Roosevelt Corollary, the United States had defined Cuba as being within its sphere of influence. Therefore, the United States initially welcomed Fidel Castro when he overthrew Cuban dictator Fulgencio Batista in 1959, believing that Castro would create a democracy on the island. However, in 1960, when Castro turned to the Kremlin for aid and support, the United States became concerned about the danger of creeping communism in its own hemisphere.

When Kennedy became president, he inherited and accepted a plan drawn up by the Eisenhower administration for a CIA-backed invasion of Cuba, executed with the help of Cuban exiles in the United States. The plan assumed that once the Cuban exiles landed in Cuba and the Cuban people learned about the invasion, they would rise up and overthrow Castro. But the Bay of Pigs invasion in April 1961 was a disaster. Not only did the people of Cuba not rise up, but virtually every member of the invading force was either killed or captured.

Kennedy gained respect domestically when he spoke to the American public and took responsibility for what happened. "There's an old saying that victory has a hundred fathers and defeat is an orphan. I am the responsible officer of the government," he said.[34] In contrast, the failed invasion undermined his credibility internationally by reinforcing the perception that he was inexperienced and not up to the task of managing U.S. foreign policy. At a time when perceptions mattered, this sent an important signal to the Soviet Union that, no doubt, helped prompt the other big crisis in Cuba during Kennedy's term.

The Cuban Missile Crisis of October 1962 was a critical turning point in the course of the Cold War. There are many reasons why the Soviet Union chose to put missiles in Cuba: the United States had invaded the island the year before, and the Soviet Union wanted to protect its client state; it was an assertion of Soviet superiority designed to send a signal to China;[35] Khrushchev wanted to demonstrate leadership domestically by taking a bold step internationally. But there is little doubt that the Soviet Union did so at least in part in the belief that, as a result of what happened at the Bay of Pigs, Kennedy simply was not strong enough to stop it.

The Cuban Missile Crisis undoubtedly was the most dangerous confrontation of the Cold War, a time when the two superpowers were indeed "eyeball to eyeball."[36] President Kennedy and his closest advisors reviewed a range of options and, as tensions grew, opted for a naval blockade of the island of Cuba coupled with "back-channel" diplomacy. In retrospect, it was the decision to pursue both courses of action simultaneously that made a peaceful resolution of the crisis possible.

Countless volumes have been written about the Cuban Missile Crisis.[37] Suffice it to say, the successful—and peaceful—resolution of the conflict led to an increase in stature internationally for both Kennedy and the United States and a concomitant diminishment of both Khrushchev's and the Soviet Union's prestige. At a time when perception of balance was relative (in that a relative increase in one side came at the expense of the other), this was an important shift. In part as a result of the failure of this gamble in Cuba, Khrushchev was removed from power shortly thereafter.

In 1992, thirty years after the missile crisis, former U.S., Soviet, and Cuban officials met in Havana to discuss and explore the circumstances of the event. Following that conference Robert McNamara, who had been Kennedy's secretary of defense, revealed that "the two nations were much closer to nuclear conflict than was previously realized."[38] McNamara also disclosed that he had learned at the conference that Soviet officials "had sent Havana short-range nuclear weapons and that Soviet commanders there were authorized to use them in the event of American invasion. . . . The short-range nuclear weapons were in addition to medium-range nuclear weapons that would have required authorization from Moscow to use." Given the new information, McNamara concluded, "The actions of all three parties were shaped by *misjudgments*, *miscalculations* and *misinformation*," and that "in a nuclear age, such mistakes could be disastrous" (emphasis added).[39]

Nonetheless, the outcome of the Cuban Missile Crisis changed the momentum of the Cold War by shifting the balance back in favor of the United States.[40]

Vietnam

The other area of tension growing at this time that affected U.S. foreign policy far beyond the Kennedy administration was Vietnam, in Southeast Asia. During the presidential transition, Eisenhower warned the newly elected president about the dangers in Southeast Asia from communist-backed insurgencies in Vietnam and Laos. The French colony of Vietnam, part of the area then known as Indochina, gained its independence after defeating France at Dien Bien Phu in 1954. This victory was followed by an agreement signed in Geneva to divide Vietnam at the seventeenth parallel until elections could be held two years later. The United States did not sign the agreement but promised to abide by its terms, pledging support to the government of Ngo Dinh Diem in the south. The northern part of the country was controlled by communists under Ho Chi Minh, who had led the fight for independence against the French. The elections were not held in 1956, and unrest continued to fester.

The seeds for protracted U.S. involvement in Southeast Asia were sown under Eisenhower when he sought congressional approval for limited U.S. involvement in the region. Congress then made clear its opposition to unilateral U.S. involvement to replace France, which had withdrawn after its defeat in 1954. Referring to the popularity of Ho Chi Minh, then-Senator John F. Kennedy, according to one historian, "warned that no amount of military aid could conquer 'an enemy which has the support and covert appeal of the people.'"[41]

At the time, Laos was in the midst of an uprising led by communist Pathet Lao forces allied with the Vietnamese communists (Vietminh). Eisenhower felt that Laos, rather than Vietnam, would be the trouble spot, and he warned Kennedy that the conflict in Laos was potentially destabilizing to the region. Eisenhower said of the communist insurgency that it was "the cork in the bottle . . . whose removal could threaten all of Southeast Asia." And in late 1960, as he was leaving office, Eisenhower warned, "We cannot let Laos fall to the Communists, even if we have to fight—with our allies or without them."[42]

Shortly after he took office, in March 1961, Kennedy made a statement on Laos echoing Eisenhower's concerns: "The security of all of Southeast Asia will be endangered if Laos loses its . . . independence. Its own safety runs with the safety of us all. . . . I want to make it clear to the American people, and to all the world, that all we want in Laos is peace, not war."[43]

However, it was Vietnam, not Laos, that proved to be the real dilemma. International negotiations settled the conflict in Laos in 1962 with an agreement that guaranteed neutrality for the country of Laos.[44] At the same time, the unrest in Vietnam grew, led by popular leader Ho Chi Minh, who continued to gain strength against the despised (and U.S.-backed) Diem. The Kennedy administration was very concerned about "losing" Vietnam to communism. Kennedy was also concerned about what such a loss (or even continued conflict) might mean for the rest of Southeast Asia, including Laos and Cambodia, both of which were neutral nations. To assuage this concern, in 1961 Kennedy authorized sending about four hundred U.S. special forces (Green Berets) to Vietnam and one hundred military advisors to aid Diem in the South. Nonetheless, Diem was overthrown and assassinated on November 2, 1963, and the civil war in Vietnam escalated. By the time of Kennedy's death three weeks later on November 22, 1963, there were 23,000 Americans in the country.[45] The United States clearly was committed to Vietnam, and the president had yet to seek authorization from Congress.

JOHNSON: VIETNAM AND THE GREAT SOCIETY

After Kennedy's assassination, Vice President Lyndon Johnson became president and inherited the problem of Vietnam. Johnson had had a long career in Congress, first in the House of Representatives and then in the Senate, where he served as majority leader from 1955 until he became vice president in 1961. That experience influenced the ways in which Johnson made decisions and especially his understanding of the need for congressional support for those policies that he thought were important.

Johnson came into office committed to making change domestically by enacting a series of laws to promote what became known as "the Great Society." However, Johnson also was aware that an unpopular and costly war in Vietnam could put his domestic policies at risk. A Congress that was pressured by constituents because of the war would be far less likely to compromise or support presidential initiatives in other (domestic) areas.[46] The policies of the Johnson administration illustrate clearly the confluence of domestic and international politics and how one can easily affect—and derail—the other.

The Tonkin Gulf Resolution

By 1964 domestic turmoil within the United States was increasing. The Civil Rights Movement was growing in strength, as was the women's movement. Leaders like Martin Luther King, Jr., energized the black community, and the Vietnam War became a rallying cry as minorities were disproportionately being asked to fight—and die—there. Johnson knew that there was a direct relationship between what would happen in Vietnam and domestic politics.

In 1970, after he was out of office, Johnson reflected on the dilemma that he had faced as president, trying to balance the escalating war effort and domestic reforms. At that time Johnson told historian Doris Kearns Goodwin, "If I left the woman I really loved—the Great Society—in order to get involved with that bitch of a war on the other side of the world, then I would lose everything at home. All my programs. All my hopes to feed the hungry and shelter the homeless. All my dreams to provide education and medical care to the browns and blacks and the lame and the poor. But if I left that war and let the Communists take over South Vietnam, then I would have been seen as a coward and my nation would be seen as an appeaser and we would find it impossible to accomplish anything for anybody anywhere on the entire globe."[47] Hence, Johnson believed that the United States would have to continue to fight in Vietnam, regardless of the costs.

The war in Vietnam escalated slowly, and still Johnson did not have official congressional authorization to send troops into combat. From his experience in Congress, Johnson knew that he needed to have congressional backing and domestic support for the war effort. His opportunity to get these came in August 1964 when two U.S. destroyers, the *Maddox* and the *Turner Joy*, were allegedly fired on in the Gulf of Tonkin in international waters approximately sixty miles off the coast of North Vietnam. The first attack against the *Maddox* came on August 2; however, a second one, two days later, was questionable. The commander of the *Maddox* later admitted that he did not think they were fired on at all. Rather, he indicated that "weather effects" and "overeager" sonar operators were probably to blame rather than an attack by the North Vietnamese.[48] Nonetheless, the incident gave Johnson the excuse to seek congressional support for the war.

On August 5, 1964, Johnson sent a message to Congress. The thrust of his public statement was the need for the United States to honor its commitments to meet communist aggression in Southeast Asia under the terms of the Southeast Asia Treaty Organization (SEATO) established initially by the Southeast Asia Collective Defense Treaty signed in 1954 and approved in 1955 as part of the Cold War alliance system.[49] Johnson asked Congress "to join in affirming the national determination that all such attacks will be met, and that the United States will continue in its basic policy of assisting the free nations of the area to defend their freedom."[50]

On August 7, 1964, Congress passed a joint resolution as Johnson requested. (The text of the resolution had been drawn up months earlier.) The resolution was sent with Johnson's message to Congress in which he outlined the events that precipitated the resolution. It is important to note that the message to Congress is far longer than the actual resolution. The heart of the resolution, and the power that Johnson sought, is found in Section 1: "The Congress approves and supports the determination of the President, as Commander in Chief, *to take all necessary measures* to repel any armed attack against the forces of the United States and to prevent further aggression" (emphasis added). Section 3 keeps the resolution active until "the President shall determine that the peace and security of the area is reasonably assured . . . *except that it may be terminated earlier by concurrent resolution of the Congress*" (emphasis added).[51]

Congress debated the resolution for two days before the House passed it on a 416 to 0 vote, and the Senate by a vote of 88 to 2. One of the two members of the Senate who voted against the resolution was Oregon Republican Wayne Morse, "who objected to the resolution on the basis of his belief that the resolution was indirectly a declaration of war and that it violated Article 1, Section 8, of the U.S. Constitution."[52] The other was Democratic Senator Ernest Gruening of Alaska, who called the resolution "a predated declaration of war."[53]

The Tonkin Gulf Resolution is significant for a number of reasons. First, it gave Johnson virtually open-ended permission to take whatever actions he deemed necessary in Vietnam. Second, it left the timing open ended so that the resolution (and the powers that went with it) would remain in force until either the president determined that the circumstances had changed or Congress terminated it, which it did in January 1971. And third, it clearly shifted the policy-making balance of power. Despite questions of constitutionality, when Congress passed the Tonkin Gulf Resolution, it gave the power to initiate military action to the president. (Congress would reassert itself and take some of that power back under President Nixon.) In remarks made when he signed the resolution into law on August 10, 1964, Johnson said that it stood "squarely on the corners of the Constitution," and "confirms and reinforces powers of the Presidency."[54]

After the resolution passed, Johnson escalated the war in Vietnam. By 1966, 450,000 American troops were in Vietnam, and General William Westmoreland, commander of U.S. forces in Vietnam from 1965 through 1968, requested an increase to 542,000 by the end of 1967.[55] By mid-1967, according to one historian, "Westmoreland conceded that if his request for an additional 200,000 men was granted, the war might go on for as long as two years. If not, he warned, it could last five years or even longer."[56] In other words, the United States was in the midst of what came to be known as a quagmire. Fighting intensified during this period, and so did battle deaths; the number of Americans killed in action rose to 13,500 by late 1967.[57] In order to keep the war effort going, draft calls increased as well. The increase in the number of men drafted coupled with growing American casualties and no end in sight to the conflict contributed to opposition to the war at home.

The Great Society

While Johnson was dealing with the Vietnam War, domestically he continued to push his Great Society policies. In 1964 in response to the Civil Rights Movement, Congress passed the Civil Rights Act, outlawing discrimination in public accommodations and in the use of federal funds, and giving more protection in voting rights. With pressure coming from the Civil Rights Movement, passage of this bill carried a powerful message that change is possible when the voice of the people is heard in Washington, a message that would be applied a few years later by war protesters. In 1965, under Johnson's direction, Congress also passed the Medicare Bill, a housing bill, the Voting Rights Act, an Economic Opportunity Act to fight the "war on poverty," a Clean Air Act, and measures to create a new Department of Housing and Urban Development and National Foundations for the Arts and Humanities. Between 1965 and 1968, Congress passed five hundred reform laws, made possible in part by Johnson's understanding of and ability to work with the legislative branch.

While these represented a great success for Johnson's domestic priorities, the war in Vietnam continued to escalate and was taking a toll economically.

In order to continue to pay for the war effort, ultimately Johnson had to cut back on spending for the domestic programs that he had fought so hard to enact. The size of the federal deficit rose, as did taxes. And public discontent over the course and conduct of the war was growing.

In January 1968, the situation in Vietnam worsened. During the cease-fire in place for the lunar new year—the Tet holiday—the forces of the North launched a major surprise offensive. The Tet offensive lasted about one month, and even though the South "won," defined by a greater number of North Vietnamese troops lost than South Vietnamese or U.S. forces, it was a propaganda victory for the North. The media played and replayed images of North Vietnamese and Viet Cong troops attacking the South, including the U.S. embassy in Saigon, which raised questions in the minds of the public about who really was winning the war. Walter Cronkite, the anchor of CBS nightly news and known as "the most trusted man in America," having recently returned from Vietnam, concluded his broadcast on February 27, 1968, with a commentary in which he said, "To say that we are closer to victory today is to believe, in the face of the evidence, the optimists who have been wrong in the past. To suggest we are on the edge of defeat is to yield to unreasonable pessimism. To say that we are mired in stalemate seems the only realistic, yet unsatisfactory, conclusion."[58] This commentary further fueled the antiwar movement at home.

In March 1968, at the time of the first Democratic primary contest for the presidency, Johnson's approval rating had dropped to 26 percent. When peace candidate Eugene McCarthy (Democratic senator from Minnesota) won 42 percent of the vote in the New Hampshire primary, it sent a strong signal to Johnson about how the public felt about his performance.[59] On March 31, Johnson announced "a unilateral halt of all United States air and naval bombardment of most of the populated areas of the north."[60] He called on the North Vietnamese government to join peace negotiations that would bring an end to the war. And then he announced: "I shall not seek, and I will not accept, the nomination of my party for another term as your President."[61] He later said that he had had enough.

> I felt that I was being chased on all sides by a giant stampede coming at me from all directions. On one side, the American people were stampeding me to do something about Vietnam. On another side, the inflationary economy was booming out of control. Up ahead were dozens of danger signs pointing to another summer of riots in the cities. I was being forced over the edge by rioting blacks, demonstrating students, marching welfare mothers, squawking professors, and hysterical reporters.[62]

Johnson learned an important lesson in American foreign policy: it doesn't matter how successful a president is domestically because an unpopular war will make a difference at the polls. While Americans generally vote economics and "pocketbook" issues, when the country is fighting a war that involves the deaths of Americans in a country far away and with a dubious relationship to national interest, foreign policy will become a more important issue.

NIXON

Richard Nixon defeated Johnson's vice president Hubert Humphrey in the 1968 election and became president in January 1969. He inherited the war in Vietnam as one of his foreign policy issues. The Vietnam War was fought against the backdrop of the Cold War; one of the most important foreign policy legacies of the Nixon administration was the way he handled two of the major communist adversaries of the United States, the Soviet Union and China, while also trying to extricate the country from Vietnam. Guided in part by Henry Kissinger, who served first as national security advisor and then as secretary of state, Nixon pursued a policy of détente, or reconciliation, with the Soviet Union and began the process that resulted in opening diplomatic relations with China. These two competing trends, fighting communism in Southeast Asia on the one hand and reconciliation with major communist powers on the other, are among the most interesting facets of the evolution of U.S. foreign policy in the period.

Escalation in Vietnam

The Vietnam War escalated during the Nixon years. As opposition to the war grew domestically, Nixon changed the strategy for fighting that war by reducing the number of troops on the ground and relying more heavily on air attacks. In 1969, in an assertion of congressional authority, Congress passed a nonbinding "Sense of the Senate" resolution that told the president he could not commit additional troops or encumber funds for the war without the express permission of that body. Although this did not have the force of law, it sent the important message that Congress was not pleased with the conduct of the war and that its members were "hearing" their constituents. It also made it clear that Congress would assert its constitutional powers, especially those aspects regarding declaring war, that it had given to the president, or that a series of presidents had taken. This was among the items that caused Nixon to rethink the strategy.

In July 1969, while on a major international trip that included his only visit to Vietnam, Nixon unveiled what became known as "the Nixon Doctrine." While the United States would still support countries struggling against communism by providing economic and military assistance, there would be a shift away from the deployment of combat units that would result in a large number of U.S. casualties. This announcement followed another one early in June after a meeting with Vietnamese President Nguyen Van Thieu that 25,000 U.S. forces would be withdrawn from Vietnam to be replaced by South Vietnamese forces. Reports at the time speculated that the new guidelines were prompted by the growing antiwar movement in the United States and by the belief that the withdrawal would help quiet the movement. The administration feared that the antiwar movement was helping to fuel North Vietnam's reluctance to negotiate by reinforcing the notion that public pressure at home would force Nixon into a weaker position. [63]

Nixon developed these ideas further for the American public in a speech that he gave on November 3, 1969, in which he returned to the "major shift in U.S. foreign policy" that he outlined in July. Specifically, that the United States would keep all its treaty commitments, will continue to provide a "shield" if "a nuclear power threatens the freedom of a nation allied with us" or threatens a nation that the United States considers "vital to our security," and that the United States will furnish military and economic assistance. But he also made clear that it will be up to the nation directly threatened "to assume the primary responsibility of providing manpower for its defense." In other words, the United States will no longer be expected to provide combat troops. And he concluded by appealing to "the great silent majority," the members of the American public who Nixon believed did not oppose the war, to support him and his plan to bring the war to an end. [64] In a poll taken shortly after that speech, Nixon hit a 67 percent approval rating, among the highest of his presidency. [65]

Implementing this new policy, in April 1970, Nixon informed the country that over the next year he had authorized the withdrawal of more than 150,000 ground troops from Vietnam. However, by the end of the month, the public was shocked to learn that U.S. forces had entered Cambodia, which was neutral in the conflict. This led to outrage and protests across the country. Public anger grew when on May 4, 1970, National Guard troops shot and killed four students who were protesting at Kent State University in Ohio. Many college and university campuses across the country suspended classes so that students and faculty could protest the war and the policies of the Nixon administration. Protestors went to Washington to demand that Congress take action to bring the war to an end.

Congress debated the wisdom of the Tonkin Gulf Resolution and the power it had given to the president, and opposition to the "blank check" given in the resolution grew. In response to the growing concerns about the conduct of the war, as well as the president's virtually unchecked ability to escalate it, on January 12, 1971, Congress repealed the Gulf of Tonkin Resolution.

By 1970, eager to find a way to end the war, Kissinger began "secret" peace negotiations. Meanwhile, Nixon continued to authorize bombing Vietnam and Cambodia. In 1972, even with the troop withdrawals, there were more than 40,000 Americans stationed in Vietnam.[66] On January 27, 1973, a cease-fire agreement was signed in Paris, and in 1975 Vietnam was unified as a communist country. Approximately 59,000 Americans had died in Vietnam.

War Powers

Congressional repeal of the Gulf of Tonkin Resolution in 1971 was the first step in the assertion of congressional authority to regain some control of the foreign policy process and to begin, once again, to enforce the checks and balances between the executive and legislative branches outlined in the Constitution. As the war went on with no end in sight, and as protests grew, Congress came under increasing pressure to limit what was seen as the abuse of presidential power regarding the ability to commit the United States to war. The impetus to do something was pushed further by the Watergate scandal and by questions about the integrity of the president. In response to these growing concerns, on November 7, 1973, Congress passed Public Law 93-148, known as the War Powers Resolution.[67]

The War Powers Resolution's stated purpose is "to fulfill the intent of the framers of the Constitution of the United States and insure that the collective judgment of *both* Congress and the President will apply to the introduction of United States Armed Forces into hostilities, or into situations where imminent involvement in hostilities is clearly indicated" (emphasis added).[68] The law clearly asserts that any time U.S. forces will be sent into hostile or even potentially hostile situations, the president must consult with and report to Congress. It also specifies the need for consultation between the president and Congress before introducing troops into hostility, and it contains the provisions under which the president must report to Congress "in the absence of a declaration of war." The resolution clearly was designed to limit the possibility of giving any subsequent presidents the blank check that Johnson and Nixon had had to commit the United States to conflict and to escalate that conflict without a formal declaration of war. It also was designed to make it very difficult for Congress to once again cede all its war-powers authority to the president.[69]

Nixon vetoed the bill and questioned its constitutionality, as have subsequent presidents (who have generally complied with it), but Congress overrode the veto. Specifically, presidents have questioned the provisions in Section 5, "Congressional Action," under which the president must end the use of force within sixty days unless Congress authorizes otherwise (Section b) and which require that forces be removed "if the Congress so directs by concurrent resolution" (Section c). Critics argue that these provisions usurp the president's constitutional power as commander in chief. And there are always questions of enforcement.[70] Nonetheless, the War Powers Resolution had the desired effect of putting the president on notice that he should report to Congress before deploying U.S. troops. That puts the burden on Congress to determine how to respond. In that sense, the law helped reaffirm the balance in roles and responsibility between the executive and legislative branches.

The Soviet Union, Détente, and Arms Control

As the war in Vietnam was growing, so were the number of nuclear weapons worldwide and expenditures for defense.[71] The vast number of nuclear weapons formed the basis of "mutually assured destruction"—or MAD—the deterrent allegedly keeping the United States and the Soviet Union from attacking each other or their allies. To help get spending and weapons proliferation under control, the Soviet Union and the United States entered into a process of discussion and negotiation designed to limit the spread of nuclear weapons.

The arms control process started in 1969 and was part of *détente*, defined by Henry Kissinger as "an environment in which competitors can regulate and restrain their differences and ultimately move from competition to cooperation."[72] One of the things that make this policy and the arms control process in general so intriguing from the perspective of American foreign policy is that it is a liberal/idealistic approach (the notion of cooperation) employed by a decision-maker (Kissinger) who, in many ways, was the ultimate realist. The process resulted in a successful agreement, the Strategic Arms Limitation Treaty (SALT I), signed in 1972, and set the stage for subsequent agreements. More important, it made relations between the United States and the Soviet Union more *predictable* by establishing an ongoing forum for discussion and conversation that continued through the duration of the Cold War. Regardless of the level of tension between the two countries, the discussion and negotiation process continued in the belief that it was in the national interest of both.

SALT I satisfied the immediate needs of both countries. "The Soviet Union gained recognition of its status as the United States' equal; the United States gained a commitment from the Soviet Union to moderate its quest for preeminent power in the world."[73] SALT I did not stop the arms race. Rather, it set limits for specific nuclear weapons, providing a ceiling up to which both sides could build, and then allowed both sides to channel additional resources into other weapon systems. At a time when both countries had enough nuclear delivery systems to obliterate each other, this was seen as an important step.

China and Normalization

As was the case with arms control and détente with the Soviet Union, in many ways only an administration known for its virulent anticommunist position could begin the process of normalizing relations with China.[74] The United States did not recognize the PRC, referring to the Nationalist government of Taiwan as "China." But in 1971, Nixon sent Kissinger to Beijing to begin the process of "normalization." The desire for rapprochement between the two countries was born of *pragmatism*, not idealism. For China, closer relations with the United States would serve as an important balance to its growing antagonism with the Soviet Union. For the United States and for Nixon in particular, stronger relations with China would allow him to play China against the USSR, appear to weaken China's ties to Hanoi at a time when the course of the Vietnam War was not going well, and help Nixon politically by allowing him to run for reelection in 1972 by stressing what he had done to help achieve a more peaceful world, rather than by having the Vietnam War as the main foreign policy focus.

In 1972, President Nixon visited mainland China, the first American president to do so. At the end of the trip, Nixon issued a statement known as the Shanghai Communiqué that has defined U.S. policy toward China and Taiwan since that time. Using language that had been negotiated earlier, the document states, "The United States acknowledges that all Chinese on either side of the Taiwan Strait maintain there is but one China and that Taiwan is part of China. The United States does not challenge that position. It reaffirms its interest in a peaceful settlement of the Taiwan question by the Chinese themselves." This phrase articulates the "one China" policy that remains in place today. In the document the United States also declared, "With this in mind, it [the United States] affirms the ultimate objective of the withdrawal of all U.S. forces and military installations from Taiwan. In the meantime, it will progressively reduce its forces and military installations on Taiwan *as the tension in the area diminishes*" (emphasis added).[75] Thus the United States will maintain forces and serve as a protector to Taiwan as long as it perceives there is danger of an armed attack by China and a forceful attempt to take over the island—that is, until the status quo changes. Because of this initiative, seven years later, in 1979 under President Carter, the United States established full diplomatic relations with China.

Nixon, the quintessential realist politician, had successfully orchestrated rapprochement with the Soviet Union and China, thereby easing Cold War tensions and shifting the balance of global international relations. By putting a process into place for ongoing negotiations between the United States and the Soviet Union, he ensured that the two sides would continue to talk, which would also help minimize tensions. And he negotiated an end to the war in Vietnam, although belatedly. Nonetheless, by the time of his resignation in

August 1974, his foreign policy successes were lost in the face of deep domestic divisions and political scandal.

When Nixon resigned, he was succeeded by Gerald Ford. Ford had been appointed vice president by Nixon when then-sitting Vice President Spiro Agnew resigned in October 1973. Prior to becoming vice president, Ford had been a popular member of Congress, serving as Minority Leader of the House during Johnson's tenure as president. As a member of Congress and critic of many of Johnson's policies, Ford understood Washington and the political process and felt the impact of the Watergate scandal as well as Nixon's resignation. When he took office, Ford's primary goal was to restore the faith of the American people in government in general and in the presidency in particular. One of his most controversial decisions was to grant Nixon an unconditional pardon, which he did on September 8, 1974, believing that this was an important step in healing the American people. In foreign policy, he had to face the unification of Vietnam as a communist country, which was seen as a major blow to the United States, but he also helped broker an interim peace agreement between Egypt and Israel, thereby paving the way for the Camp David Accord. Perhaps the most difficult part of his presidency, though, was inheriting an economy with rampant inflation (up to 12 percent in 1974) and a growing recession. In many ways, the situation that he faced as president was an impossible one. [76]

CARTER

Jimmy Carter defeated Gerald Ford in the election of 1976. Carter believed in the need to restore the perception of integrity to the government and he ran as an "outsider" who could bring a new tone to Washington. He also wanted to help the country recover from the "Vietnam hangover" that made the United States hesitant to get involved in any international conflict.

In his campaign and early in his presidency, Carter brought back to foreign policy the idealist perspective advocated by Woodrow Wilson, and he vowed to make the fight for human rights the centerpiece of his foreign policy agenda. In March 1977, Carter addressed the UN General Assembly and reiterated that commitment to global human rights. While the Carter administration pursued the foreign policy perceived as consistent with the basic tenets on which the United States was founded (freedom and liberty for all), it also angered many of the international leaders who saw this as a direct attack on their domestic policies. For example, Carter angered the Soviet Union by praising Soviet dissidents who had dared to speak up against the government.

The Carter years (1977–1981) were marked by a series of both dramatic successes and notable failures in foreign policy. The successes included the

Camp David accords signed in March 1979, the first major agreement between Israel and an Arab nation (Egypt), which resulted in Israel's withdrawal from the Sinai. (President Carter subsequently won a Nobel Peace Prize
for this accomplishment.) He also successfully negotiated the treaties returning the Panama Canal to the control of Panama and making the canal a
neutral waterway open to all shipping traffic after 1999. The United States
was given the permanent right to defend the waterway and its neutrality. The
Panama Canal treaties resulted in a fight between the president and Congress.
Given an increasingly assertive Congress that did not see why the treaties
were to the advantage of the United States, Carter had to fight for their
passage at great political cost.

He successfully negotiated the SALT II treaty with the Soviet Union,
thereby continuing the arms control process started by Nixon. But in the
wake of the Soviet invasion of Afghanistan in December 1979, and in the
face of a hostile Congress, Carter never submitted it for ratification, although
he did commit the United States to abide by its terms.

Perhaps the most spectacular foreign policy failure of the Carter years
was the Iranian revolution and the way in which Carter handled the taking of
American hostages at the embassy in Tehran.[77] Day after day nothing happened as network news anchors, such as Walter Cronkite, began each broadcast with an announcement about how many days the hostages had been held.
This contributed to an undermining of public confidence in Carter, and when
he finally did authorize a rescue attempt, it was over the objections of members of his cabinet such as Secretary of State Cyrus Vance, who resigned in
protest. The rescue attempt on April 24, 1980, was a dismal failure, and the
entire experience on top of four years of economic recession, high gas prices,
unparalleled inflation, and other domestic economic woes contributed directly to Carter's defeat at the polls in November 1980 by Ronald Reagan.

Carter's administration is instructive in the course of American foreign
policy. In part, Carter inherited the economic problems that were the result of
years of war as well as domestic ills and bad decisions. He chose to pursue a
foreign policy based on values and idealism at a time when pragmatism and
realism probably would have been more successful. He saw issues in black-
and-white terms and presented them to the American public and to the world
in that way. While this encouraged and empowered some, it also inflamed
and alienated others both at home and abroad. Implementing foreign policy
successfully requires domestic support as well as international cooperation,
and Carter was not able to get either. It was only after the Cold War ended,
and years after he stepped down as president and took on the role of "elder
statesman," that Carter came to play an important role internationally in
pursuit of peace and human rights and won a Nobel Prize for his efforts.

GROWING ENGAGEMENT

United States foreign policy evolved significantly between the end of World War II and the election of Ronald Reagan in 1980. The early Cold War years were defined by a foreign policy of realism and power politics, and every aspect of the policy-making apparatus was aligned to achieve its foreign policy and military goals. The United States was the unchallenged leader of the West, and its vision created and guided the international order for much of the Cold War.

U.S. engagement in Vietnam changed much of that. Involved initially as part of the global fight against communism, in Vietnam the United States learned that a superior military fighting force, created to deter or if necessary fight a war against another major power, is basically useless in the type of guerrilla war it fought in Vietnam. Further, U.S. decision-makers learned that a war cannot be fought (and won) without the ongoing support of the American public, and that support can come only from a clear articulation of why the war is necessary and its relationship to national interest.

By the end of the Carter administration, the United States was suffering from "Vietnam hangover" and national self-doubt. Ronald Reagan came into office determined to fight these negative forces. For Reagan, the United States was still a superpower, and it had to start acting like one again.

APPLYING FOREIGN POLICY CONCEPTS: THE TONKIN GULF RESOLUTION AND THE LESSONS OF VIETNAM

When Johnson went to Congress with the Tonkin Gulf Resolution in August 1964, the result was an escalation of the war in Vietnam. Johnson knew that he would need congressional approval to send in combat troops and to stage the military buildup that he thought would be necessary for the United States to win that war. What he did not know then and could not have anticipated was the fact that the United States would not win that war and that Vietnam would be unified as a communist country.

In May 1975, approximately one month after the fall of Vietnam, then–Secretary of State Henry Kissinger drafted a memo to President Gerald Ford outlining what he saw as the major lessons of the war. Although the memo was never sent nor signed, it is now available publicly and has some important insights. Among the lessons Kissinger notes are "the importance of absolute honesty and objectivity in all reporting, within and from the Government as well as from the press." Another lesson is "a dedication to consistency," in terms of the reasons given for going to war, and then for seeing that war through." And he speaks in this memo of the need to "ask ourselves whether it was all worth it, or at least what benefits we did gain."[78]

If they had been applied by Johnson in 1964, those lessons and others that Kissinger articulated in this memo might have changed the decisions that Johnson made and altered the course of the war.

The Case

By early 1964, President Lyndon Johnson realized that he needed to do something to address the growing conflict in Vietnam. President Kennedy had sent special forces units into that country, but he had not taken the issue to Congress. For the most part, the American public was largely ignorant about the war brewing in Southeast Asia.

Johnson was a product of Congress and understood the often difficult relationship that exists between the executive and legislative branches of government. Although he was not asking for a formal declaration of war, politically he knew that it would be in his best interest to seek congressional approval to escalate the war in Vietnam. Not doing so would mean running the risk that Congress would deny support for the domestic programs that he was working on, collectively known as "the Great Society."

Johnson faced a dilemma. Once he went to Congress to ask for congressional approval to escalate the war, it would be critical that the United States win the war. The United States had little experience fighting the type of guerrilla war such as the one growing in Vietnam, and the French, America's allies, had lost to the Vietnamese ten years earlier. And Johnson knew that he would have to make the case to the American people that fighting this war on the other side of the world was in the U.S. national interest.

Anticipating the need to go to Congress, Johnson drafted a resolution justifying the escalation of the war. In August 1964, he was given the opportunity to use that resolution. Two U.S. naval ships, the *Maddox* and the *Turner Joy*, were allegedly fired on in the Gulf of Tonkin. Although the circumstances surrounding the attacks were murky, Johnson wanted to take advantage of them to ask Congress for permission to meet such attacks with military force. Congress gave that permission along with support for the president to "take all necessary measures to repel any armed attack against the forces of the United States and to prevent further aggression."[79]

The Gulf of Tonkin Resolution allowed Johnson to do what he wanted to do and escalate the war. The United States ended its involvement in Vietnam in 1973, and North and South Vietnam were unified two years later as a communist country, but more than 59,000 Americans lost their lives in that war. Domestically, opposition to the war put enough pressure on Lyndon Johnson so that he decided not to run for reelection in 1968. A growing peace movement reached its climax in 1970, following the deaths of four students at Kent State University who were protesting the war and had been shot by members of the National Guard. In response, colleges and universities around the country closed as students and faculty protested the war and held "teach-ins" about it. In January 1971, Congress repealed the resolution, and two years later it passed the War Powers Resolution to rein in the power of the president to engage the United States in foreign conflicts or war without congressional approval.

It took many years for the United States to recover from the "Vietnam hangover." The perception of U.S. weakness as a result of its defeat clouded the ways in which other countries viewed the United States, which affected its foreign policy options. Veterans returning home from the war were shunned as domestic opposition to the war became confused with hostility toward those who fought it. The domino theory proved not to be true, as the creation of a communist government in Vietnam did not lead to communism sweeping the rest of the region. And the peace movement melded with the civil rights and women's movements, resulting in major social upheaval and later change within the United States.

What Would You Do If . . .

The time is 1964. President Johnson has been president for just over one year, and he inherited a war in Southeast Asia. His highest priority was his domestic agenda, but he knew that that could be held hostage to an unsuccessful war in Vietnam. Johnson knew that he needed to make some critical choices that would affect not only his administration, but his legacy and U.S. policies in general for years to come.

What would you do if you were a close advisor to President Johnson and he looked to you for recommendations on what to do about Vietnam? You have just received word that two U.S. ships may or may not have been fired on in the Gulf of Tonkin. But the details of the alleged attacks are sketchy at best. Given what you know now, including the consequences (both intended and unintended), what would you recommend that President Johnson do, and why? In your assessment, you will need to address what course would be in the U.S. national interest at that time and why.

Chapter Five

The Cold War and Beyond

Reagan through Clinton, 1981–2001

Thus far, we have identified a number of broad themes that help explain the direction of U.S. foreign policy from the nation's founding through the Cold War, as well as some of the decisions that were made and why. Under the leadership of a series of strong presidents, with domestic and congressional support, and as a result of changing international conditions, the United States became a major power militarily, politically, and economically. President Truman altered the foreign policy decision-making apparatus (i.e., the bureaucracy) to allow the government to implement more effectively the policies of a "superpower" during the Cold War, which lasted about forty-five years. However, the structure, framework, and approach that were then in place made it more difficult for the country to make the adjustments required for a post–Cold War world.

The 1980s started with the election of Ronald Reagan, who early in his administration referred to the Soviet Union as "the evil empire." He promoted building a weapons shield ("Star Wars") to protect the United States from incoming Soviet missiles, and he increased spending for defense and the military. In other words, he did everything that a Cold War president needed to do. And just as President Kennedy stood next to the Berlin Wall in 1963 to proclaim "Ich bin ein Berliner,"[1] in 1987 President Reagan told Mikhail Gorbachev, the leader of the Soviet Union, to "tear down this wall."[2] Two years later, in 1989, that would happen. If Cold War tensions could be measured by policies regarding Berlin, then the fall of the Berlin Wall was the best indicator that the old order literally was crumbling. It would take two more years for the Soviet Union to fall. After years of waiting for this to happen, was the United States ready for it when it did?

117

When Reagan's vice president, George H. W. Bush, was elected president in 1988, the Cold War international order was disintegrating. Democratic revolutions were sweeping Eastern Europe. One after another the communist governments fell and were replaced by democratically elected leaders who believed in capitalist market economies. President Bush proclaimed the creation of a "new world order," as distinguished from the "old" Cold War order.

After decades of proclaiming that the West would inevitably win the Cold War, it did. Yet it happened so suddenly that all the United States could do was react to international events: wars in the Middle East, ethnic strife and genocide in Yugoslavia and Africa, and an apparent increase in terrorism. Divisions arose between the United States and its closest allies about what policies to follow in each of these cases. While hints of these issues were present during the Cold War, they were either ignored or dealt with as "side-shows" to the more important issue of U.S.-Soviet relations. The Cold War goal of containing communism (broadly defined) provided the focus for all aspects of U.S. policy since 1945. After 1989,[3] the United States had new and different challenges to face. And without the Cold War framework as its guide, U.S. foreign policy often appeared rudderless.

Brent Scowcroft, National Security Advisor to President George H. W. Bush, describes the changes this way: "The cold war was an intense concentration on a single problem. . . . And suddenly, historically in the blink of an eye, that world came to an end, and it was replaced by a world without the existential threat of the Cold War. If we made a mistake, we might blow up the planet—that was gone. Instead there were one hundred pinprick problems."[4]

This chapter focuses on the period from 1981 and the start of the Reagan administration through the administration of Bill Clinton (elected in 2000) with an emphasis on what the changing international order meant for U.S. foreign policy without the Cold War. We begin with the prelude to the end of the Cold War, including the fall of the Berlin Wall, the implosion of the Soviet Union, and the democratic revolutions that swept the countries of the former Eastern Bloc. We will conclude with the Clinton administration, which articulated what the increasingly globalized world meant for the United States while also puzzling about how to address the plethora of ethnic and nationalist conflicts that emerged and the challenges that they posed to American foreign policy.

FROM COLD WAR TO DEMOCRATIC REVOLUTIONS

"On the day of Mr. Reagan's inauguration as president in 1981," writes one historian, "the Iranians released their American hostages. That closed a humiliating and frustrating episode."[5] One can speculate as to why Iran chose to release them on that day; suffice it to say, it provided a powerful start to the Reagan administration. Whereas Jimmy Carter's administration ended in apparent failure, Ronald Reagan came into office the image of American strength. No longer would U.S. foreign policy be based on "soft" ideas, such as human rights, but it would once again be tied to strength and power.[6] While the American public might have yearned for such a change, it came at a price.

Reagan's election signaled a return to a strong executive whose administration defined the policies and the priorities of the nation at that time. And, for the most part, despite its earlier assertions of oversight, Congress complied with and approved Reagan's domestic policies and priorities, even though they resulted in budget deficits. In what became known as "the Reagan Revolution," Reagan focused his attention on domestic issues, especially the economy. He cut taxes across the board and, concomitantly, slashed social programs, many of which had been in place since the New Deal. He focused on "supply-side economics" that promised prosperity by putting more money into the hands of people who would spend it, thereby stimulating the economy. He blamed the recession that hit the country in 1981 and 1982 on residual effects of Carter's policies (as opposed to the impact of Vietnam), and when the economy started to recover before the congressional elections of 1984, he took the credit. And Reagan authorized an increase in spending for defense in order to counter what he had called "America's weakened defense" during the election campaign.

Reagan successfully energized the American public and instilled a sense of pride in the country once again. The United States returned to the policies of "us versus them," good versus evil, democracy versus communism, that were tempered under Carter. However, Reagan's hardline rhetoric, such as his "evil empire" speeches in June 1982 and March 1983,[7] reawakened Cold War fears in the Soviet Union as well as within many in the United States.

The hostile rhetoric put the Soviet Union on warning that the Cold War was not over. In response, the Soviet leadership once again denounced the United States. In the words of one historian, "Matters were not helped when, within a few months of Mr. Reagan's inauguration, America's nuclear force was twice in one week activated following erroneous computer warnings that Soviet missile attacks were on the way."[8] Hence, U.S. foreign policy during at least the first years of Reagan's eight years in office was characterized by increasingly hostile rhetoric, an arms buildup, and a sense that the United States was reliving the policies of decades earlier, before détente and arms control.[9]

When the Berlin Wall fell in 1989, then-President George H. W. Bush as well as Reagan took the credit. Yet the end of the Cold War was the result of the confluence of many factors; Reagan just happened to be president when a series of critical events started to unfold. Shortly before he left office, when asked about the role he had played in facilitating the end of the Cold War, Reagan referred to himself as "a supporting actor." When asked at a press conference who deserved the credit for the changes in the Soviet Union that ultimately led to the end of the Cold War, Reagan replied that "Mr. Gorbachev deserves most of the credit, as the leader of this country."[10]

There is little doubt that Reagan's policies of increasing spending for defense and ratcheting up the hostile rhetoric pushed an already significantly diminished Soviet Union to the brink. The priority of Mikhail Gorbachev, who became general secretary of the Communist Party of the Soviet Union in 1985 just as Reagan was beginning his second term in office, was to demilitarize the Soviet Union so that much-needed resources could be diverted to the depleted economy. Further, since he came of age in the post-Stalin era, Gorbachev had a different perspective on the West than previous leaders, and he saw Europe and Russia as sharing a "common home."[11]

Reagan also was receptive to Gorbachev's ideas and was willing to work with him on implementing new policies. Reagan believed that a change in the direction of the Soviet Union would be in the best interests of the United States and therefore modified his own approach over time, becoming less "cold warrior" and more the diplomat whose primary goal was to encourage Gorbachev to continue down the new path that he had chosen. Doing this required personal contact, and the two leaders met periodically to outline areas of common interest. By the time that the Reagan administration ended, the Cold War was on a course to its inevitable end.[12]

Reagan and Gorbachev actively pursued arms control talks as part of their mutually beneficial policy agenda. The meeting between the two men in Reykjavik, Iceland, in 1986 initially appeared to be a failure, yet it led directly to the treaty, signed in December 1987, limiting intermediate-range nuclear weapons. This treaty specified the destruction of all land-based missiles with a range of between 500 and 5,500 kilometers (which could strike from Europe into Soviet territory and vice versa), with specific provisions for on-site inspection. Not only was this treaty seen as important because it eliminated a certain type of weapon system, but it laid the groundwork for further arms control agreements leading to the destruction of other types of weapons. As was the case with Richard Nixon, whose anticommunist stance made it possible for him to negotiate with both the Soviet Union and China without charges that he was "selling out" the country, Ronald Reagan, another "cold warrior," was able to negotiate successfully with Gorbachev.

IRAN-CONTRA

In the West, Reagan was celebrated for helping to bring about the fall of communism. But the Iran-Contra affair was a different type of foreign policy situation that also defined this administration. "Iran-Contra" refers to a complex set of policies and actions that led to congressional hearings and a federal commission to explore what really happened. One outcome of Iran-Contra was a clear statement of presidential responsibility. It is also another example of the assertion of congressional oversight regarding the executive branch. And it raised—and then clarified—some important points about who holds ultimate responsibility for making and implementing U.S. foreign policy, something that had become fuzzy over time.

A revolution in Nicaragua in 1980 resulted in the overthrow of the Somoza regime, which had been supported by the United States. It was replaced by the left-leaning Sandinista government, which the Reagan administration saw not only as communist but also as a potential threat to U.S. influence in Latin America. Hence, overthrowing the new Sandinista government by supporting a group of rebels, known as the Contras, became a U.S. policy priority. However, within the United States, public opinion polls indicated that the American people did not support military involvement in Nicaragua, which led the government to try to conceal any possible involvement in the conflict. In 1984, in response to CIA actions to mine the harbors of Nicaragua, Congress passed the Boland Amendment, making it illegal to support "directly or indirectly, military or paramilitary operations in Nicaragua." This was one of three amendments limiting U.S. action in Nicaragua. Ignoring this prohibition, members of the National Security Council (NSC) staff devised an undercover operation to aid the Contras secretly, through third-party support.[13]

In 1986, stories surfaced that the United States had secretly sold weapons to Iran, an enemy of this country since the revolution of 1979, with the profits from the sale funneled to the Contras. Further, in exchange for getting the weapons, Iran promised to ensure the release of hostages being held in Lebanon. When asked about the reports of this linkage, Reagan denied the basic facts. But critical questions remained unanswered, and the president convened a special commission to investigate. As a result of the commission's investigations and findings, most of the blame fell on Robert (Bud) McFarlane, Reagan's former national security advisor, and NSC staff member Colonel Oliver North, who was found guilty of lying to Congress in hearings about the incident. It was clear that the whole scheme was set up in a way that sheltered the president and vice president by keeping the details from them. (During the Watergate hearings, this approach was known as "plausible deniability.")

Although neither President Reagan nor Vice President Bush was charged with or indicted on any specific crime related to Iran-Contra, the uncertainty about whether they were—or were not—involved raised important questions about who is responsible for making and implementing U.S. foreign policy, and what responsibility the president does or should have when illegal actions are committed by members of the administration in the name of foreign policy or "national interest."

THE TOWER COMMISSION AND REPORT

The special review board convened to look into Iran-Contra was headed by Republican former-Senator John Tower. The other two members were Democratic former-Senator and Secretary of State Edmund Muskie and Brent Scowcroft, a retired air force general who had been national security advisor to President Ford (and who would become George H. W. Bush's national security advisor). The goal of the Tower Commission was to look into the allegations and then issue a report on what happened. It was this report, published in 1987, that provided the clearest picture of Iran-Contra. But the report did something else; it clarified, once again, the relationships among the various actors who make foreign/national security policy (for in this case they were interchangeable) for the country, and it made it clear that ultimate responsibility rests with the president.

> Ours is a government of checks and balances, of shared power and responsibility. The Constitution places the President and Congress in dynamic tension. They both cooperate and compete in the making of national policy. . . .
>   The Constitution gives both the President and Congress an important role. The Congress is critical in formulating national policies and in marshalling the resources to carry them out. But those resources . . . are lodged in the Executive Branch. As Chief Executive and Commander-in-Chief, and with broad authority in the area of foreign affairs, it is the President who is empowered to act for the nation and protect its interests. [14]

The report is even blunter in its recommendations: "The primary responsibility for the formulation and implementation of national security policy falls on the President." The authors, all of whom had experience with the executive and legislative branches, warned, "The departments and agencies—the Defense Department, State Department, and CIA bureaucracies—tend to resist policy change." This makes it even more incumbent upon the president to "bring his perspectives to bear on these bureaucracies for they are his instruments for executing national security policy. . . . His task is to provide them leadership and direction."[15]

After years in which it appeared that a strong president was leading the country, the Tower Commission report served as a reminder about the difficulties and complexities of making foreign policy. It also provided a warning of how easily the system can go awry when the president is not really in control of nor taking responsibility for those who work under him.

GEORGE H. W. BUSH AND THE "NEW WORLD ORDER"

Despite Iran-Contra, Reagan left office a popular president. He was succeeded by his vice president, George H. W. Bush. But the world in which Bush took office in January 1989 was changing quickly. The country of Yugoslavia was disintegrating and on the path to ethnic conflict. The government of Somalia was collapsing, leaving the country in a state of chaos and clan warfare. In May, 1989, Hungary began the process of opening its border with Austria, one of the first signs of the cracks between the East (Hungary) and West (Austria) and on November 9, 1989, the Berlin Wall came down. The Solidarity Party, led by Lech Walesa, gained power in Poland, and by Christmas the (communist) Polish People's Republic was replaced by the democratic Republic of Poland. Other countries in the Soviet Eastern European bloc started the process of removing their communist leaders and replacing them with democratically elected governments. And the Soviet economy was declining steadily, leading to the assumption that change in that country was inevitable.

In contrast to the optimistic changes taking place in Eastern Europe, in June 1989 the government of China brutally and violently cracked down on students calling for reform who were protesting in Tiananmen Square in Beijing. As many as two thousand were believed killed in that incident. At a time when democracy appeared to be sweeping most of the communist countries of Eastern Europe, government hold was tightened in China.

Amid uncertainty about the direction of the Soviet Union or Eastern Europe, and unwilling to push too much, Bush pursued a tentative and status quo foreign policy, preferring to limit U.S. involvement internationally. Nonetheless, Bush also recognized the significance of the changes taking place. As international events were unfolding rapidly, President Bush spoke of the creation of "a new world order" that would emerge in the wake of communism. He coined the phrase in a speech on September 11, 1990, in which he used Iraq's invasion of Kuwait the month before to outline his vision for the future. At that time, he said, "At this very moment, they [American soldiers] serve together with Arabs, Europeans, Asians, and Africans in defense of principle and the dream of a *new world order*" (emphasis added).[16] In other words, in a rapidly changing world, old adversaries, such as the United States and the Soviet Union, could work together and share responsibilities that would make for a better future.

Unfortunately, while the Cold War was ending, other "hot wars" were emerging that would require the attention of the United States. The most immediate of these was Iraq's invasion of Kuwait.

The Persian Gulf War

On August 2, 1990, Iraq invaded Kuwait, which provided the impetus for the Bush administration to get involved internationally. Shortly after the invasion, the Security Council passed Resolution 660 condemning the action, demanding immediate withdrawal of Iraqi troops from Kuwait, calling upon Iraq and Kuwait to enter into negotiations to settle their differences, and reserving the right to meet again as necessary.[17] Over the next few months, President Bush and members of the administration used the United Nations to build support for a military response to this act of aggression. When Iraq did not comply with Resolution 660 on November 29, 1990, the Security Council passed Resolution 678 authorizing "member states . . . to use all necessary means to uphold and implement Resolution 660 . . . and to restore international peace and security to the area." The Security Council also set a deadline of six weeks for Iraq to withdraw from Kuwait. Otherwise, the UN would authorize military force.[18]

As early as September 1990, shortly after the invasion, when it became apparent that the United States might get involved in an armed conflict, Bush knew that he would need approval from Congress under the terms of the War Powers Resolution. According to his memoirs, Bush used the Gulf of Tonkin Resolution as a model so that he, too, could get the same kind of open-ended support from Congress that President Johnson had been given in 1964.[19] In addition, Bush met with congressional leaders from both parties to build support for his position. In the meantime, UN Secretary General Javier Perez de Cuellar tried to resolve the situation peacefully to avoid armed conflict. On January 9, 1991, Secretary of State James Baker met with the Iraqi deputy prime minister, Tariq Aziz, in Geneva and warned him that the only way to avert war was for Iraq to comply with Resolution 678 and withdraw completely from Kuwait.

On January 10, Aziz made it clear that Iraq would not comply with the terms stated. At that time, joint resolutions were introduced into both houses of Congress authorizing the deployment of U.S. forces to Iraq under the terms of the UN resolution. On January 12, both houses of Congress voted to support the joint resolution; the House vote was 250 to 183, and the Senate vote was 52 to 47, "the smallest margin ever to vote for war."[20] The attack started early in the morning (Iraq time) on January 17, 1991.

The war lasted forty-three days and resulted in the defeat of Iraq and its withdrawal from Kuwait. Most notable about this effort is that "the coalition," as it was known, of military forces working with the United States was not tied to traditional alliances but rather was made up of forces drawn from a range of countries that came together in pursuit of a common outcome. For the first time since World War II, the United States and the Soviet Union cooperated and worked together on the same side—a remarkable event.

In addition, the Persian Gulf War was a true product of new technology both within the military and the media. While coverage of the Vietnam War earned it the moniker of "the first television war" for the nightly news coverage of battles and body bags, the Persian Gulf War was the first CNN war, leading to what has become known as "the CNN effect."[21] For the first time, the American people as well as the rest of the world got "live" coverage of what was happening in Baghdad and throughout Iraq and Kuwait. This changed expectations of what war coverage should be, something that would be taken even further during the presidency of George W. Bush, when reporters were "embedded" with troops to cover the 2003 war against Iraq.

Since the first Persian Gulf War, and given the subsequent decision to invade Iraq by then-President George W. Bush, much has been written and analysis done about the decision made by the first President Bush *not* to invade Iraq at that time and go after Saddam Hussein. Brent Scowcroft, then National Security Advisor to George H. W. Bush, when asked about that decision said "[T]hat was not unfinished business. We early on decided it was not up to us to drive him from power. And, as you know, in much of foreign policy you never have a complete success." When pushed further about this decision, Scowcroft offered the administration's rationale, which is telling given the events that subsequently transpired. Scowcroft said that they could have gone on to Baghdad, but "it would've changed the whole character of the conflict into one where we were occupiers in a hostile land. Our troops would've been subjected to guerilla activity. And we had no strategy for getting out. And that was a situation which I thought would be a disaster to get into."[22] As you will see in the next chapter, that assessment describes the situation following the decision to send U.S. troops into Iraq in 2003.

The End of the Soviet Union

In August 1991, shortly after the Persian Gulf War ended, there was an attempted coup in the Soviet Union. With Mikhail Gorbachev under house arrest at his vacation home in the Crimea by hard-liners who had initiated the coup, it was Boris Yeltsin, then-leader of the Soviet republic of Russia, who faced the rebels. Standing on a tank in front of the "Russian White House," Yeltsin declared that he would be in charge of all security forces on Russian territory until order was restored. With that statement, as well as the forceful image of him facing down the troops, Yeltsin emerged as the de facto leader of the country. The end of the Soviet Union was near. On December 8, 1991, the leaders of the Soviet republics of Russia, Ukraine, and Belarus announced the end of the Soviet Union, leading to the creation of a new Commonwealth of Independent States (CIS). This was confirmed on December 21 at a meeting of representatives of eleven of the former Soviet republics.

The end of the old Soviet Union was finalized on December 25, 1991, when Mikhail Gorbachev resigned as president of the USSR.

The dissolution of the Soviet Union, and with it the end of the Cold War, came as a surprise to the United States. While leaders of the United States and other Western countries had long called for this as well as for the victory of democracy over communism, the reality is that few actually thought it would happen. Since 1991, one of the questions that political scientists, historians, and policy-makers have asked is whether the United States was responsible for the end of the Soviet Union. But the death of the Soviet Union was the result of the confluence of a number of factors. These ranged from the perceived need to continue an arms buildup, which had a detrimental effect on the Soviet economy; to the democratic revolutions sweeping Eastern Europe, which clearly undermined the power of the Soviet government; to the liberalizing policies of Mikhail Gorbachev, which suggested that change was possible. As one historian noted, "Collapse, when it finally came, had come from within."[23]

The Balkans and Ethnic Conflict

Even with the euphoria surrounding the end of the Cold War, U.S. foreign policy remained unsettled. The existence of ethnic warfare and genocide in countries around the world became more prominent when not overshadowed by the Cold War. According to noted foreign policy analyst Leslie Gelb, the Bush administration "did not understand that these nasty civil wars could become breeding grounds for terrorists. . . . Bush's team performed better in putting the old world's problems to bed than in getting ahead of the new ones."[24] Somalia and especially the wars in the former Yugoslavia illustrate that point, which went beyond the Bush administration to bedevil the Clinton administration that followed.

The country of Yugoslavia had been artificially created after World War I, and its diverse groups (Serb, Croat, and Bosnian Muslim primarily) had been held together in part by the strength of the country's leader, Josip Tito. After his death in 1980, and with no designated successor, nationalist leaders emerged and called for independent states for each of the ethnic groups (e.g., "Serbia for the Serbs"). This meant that it was simply a question of time until the country dissolved into civil and ethnic warfare as each group vied for territory and power.[25]

On June 25, 1991, Croatia and Slovenia, two of the six republics that made up Yugoslavia, declared their independence.[26] Two days later, on June 27, the first of the wars that would wrack the Balkans for the next eight years began. The Yugoslav-Slovene War lasted ten days, until the UN negotiated a settlement. This falsely conveyed the idea that these "little" ethnic wars in the Balkans could be resolved quickly by negotiation. As the crisis grew and the conflict spread, the United States had to decide whether or how to deal with this situation. The dilemma facing the Bush administration was defining what was in the national interest. On the one hand, this was a war being fought in Europe, close to U.S. allies. This raised concerns that if the United States did not take action, the situation would escalate and the United States would no longer have a choice as to whether or not to get involved. On the other hand, the war was outside the formal NATO guidelines area, it was in a country with which the United States had little involvement, and therefore it would be a stretch to see it as directly relevant to U.S. national interest.

President Bush chose to deal with the situation using a combination of diplomacy (soft power) and threats (hard power). He sent Secretary of State James Baker to meet with Serbian leader Slobodan Milosevic to warn him not to take military action that would make the situation worse. On the whole, though, it fell to the Europeans to address the deteriorating situation in what remained of Yugoslavia, and the Bush administration was content to leave this "European problem" to the Europeans. But the problem would not go away; rather, it would be left to the Clinton administration to decide how to deal with it.

The administration of George H. W. Bush was a period of transition in U.S. foreign policy. Initially the victory in the Gulf War suggested that the post–Cold War period would be a time of shifting alliances created as necessary to meet specific threats. This suggested a flexibility in U.S. foreign policy that the Cold War had not allowed. Further, it indicated that Congress would be willing to grant to a president "permission" to use force against a specific enemy even when the United States was not directly threatened, as long as the case could be made that "national interest" was at stake. It also showed that the American public could and would support such a war, even in a distant country.

This new era in U.S. foreign policy also carried dangers that were not yet fully formed or understood. Ethnic conflict and genocide in other countries were threats to human rights but were difficult to articulate to the American public in a way that tied them to U.S. national interest. It was far more difficult to justify military involvement in a distant country on humanitarian grounds than on economic ones. In short, the concepts of "threat" and "national interest" were starting to have different meanings outside the context of the Cold War. Going into the presidential election of 1992, war was under way in the Yugoslav republic of Bosnia; the Bush administration was debating what to do about the conflict in Somalia; and unrest was building in Haiti, a country within the traditional U.S. sphere of influence. But overshadowing these foreign policy issues was a faltering economy. President Bush's popularity had gone from a high of 89 percent in February 1991, at the start of the ground war in Kuwait, to a low of 29 percent in July 1992, about four months before the election.[27] With the foreign policy victory in the Persian

Gulf behind them, the American public wanted to know what President Bush would do to address the domestic economic situation. It was Bush's challenger Bill Clinton who seemed to have the answers.

THE CLINTON YEARS

To meet domestic concerns raised during the campaign, candidate Clinton focused on the economy and the recession that was sweeping the country. The budget deficits that had started under President Reagan were taking their toll domestically and Clinton, accusing President Bush of being out of touch with America, promised to "focus like a laser beam on the economy." Clinton's priority was going to be domestic politics, but like other presidents before him, once in office Clinton discovered that international events have a way of interfering. Thus Clinton had to balance domestic priorities with responses to foreign policy crises.

Clinton suffered two foreign policy disasters early in his administration, in Haiti and Somalia, both of which affected his views on foreign policy and the role of the president. Those situations directly influenced his subsequent decisions about Bosnia and later Kosovo. And, in a clear example of the interaction between domestic and international politics, a Republican-controlled Congress and questions about the president's personal conduct further limited his foreign policy options.

With the end of the Cold War, the United States was the last remaining superpower. This gave the United States a unique and important role in the international arena. Without the Cold War, foreign policy priorities shifted once again; no longer would the focus be on using the military to deter a single (communist) threat. Instead, Clinton's acknowledgment of a globalized world meant recognition of the interdependence of countries and a return to trade and economic relations as a central component of U.S. foreign policy. This was a marked departure from previous policies, especially for a Democratic president, but it set the stage for the changes of the twenty-first century. While the military would still have to be prepared to fight two wars simultaneously (which was the established military posture), ideally it could also be used as a force for good in support of human rights and humanitarian missions. But many of these idealistic (i.e., Wilsonian) goals were derailed by domestic politics, specifically the conflict between President Clinton and Congress, as well as by international political realities.

President George H. W. Bush understood that the old international order was changing, but his administration really did not articulate a clearly defined direction for U.S. foreign policy in the wake of the Cold War. In contrast, Clinton saw that the future of foreign policy and international relations would be defined by interdependence, trade, and the use of technology.

But he also was bedeviled by ethnic and civil conflicts in various parts of the world, and by questions of what role, if any, the United States should play in them. Looking at a number of issues that Clinton had to address, and how he chose to do so, is instructive for understanding the problems associated with American foreign policy after the Cold War and in a globalized world. The Clinton administration holds important lessons about the impact of domestic politics and the ways in which domestic and foreign policy are intertwined. It also serves as a reminder that international events cannot be controlled by a president who is often forced to react and how, without the Cold War framework, international relations became unpredictable.

Somalia

U.S. involvement in Somalia predated President Clinton; it originated in a decision made by President George H. W. Bush in December 1992 (after he was defeated by Clinton in November) to send troops into Somalia on a humanitarian mission. This case serves as an example of how ill-prepared the United States was to meet the challenges that it would face after the Cold War. It also shows the ways in which foreign policy decisions often are made in reaction to events.

The ouster of dictator Mohammed Siad Barre in 1991 resulted in instability and clan warfare in Somalia that, coupled with years of drought, led to widespread famine and internal chaos. Although in August 1992 Bush had ordered an airlift of food as a short-term solution, it became clear that more help was needed. The NSC held a series of meetings throughout November, after the U.S. presidential election, to determine what to do to address the situation, which was seen as a humanitarian crisis. In one meeting on November 25, Bush was given three possible options: "increased support for existing UN efforts, a U.S.-organized coalition effort without the participation of American ground troops, or a major U.S. effort to lead a multinational force in which U.S. ground troops took the leading role." Then-chair of the Joint Chiefs of Staff, Colin Powell, "expressed concern about the use of ground troops." After "a broad discussion," President Bush decided that if other countries would join the effort, "U.S. combat troops would lead an international force to Somalia."[28]

The United States deployed troops to Somalia in December 1992 on a humanitarian mission to ensure that food was distributed to those who needed it. The deployment was authorized with the promise that U.S. forces would be out by Inauguration Day in January 1993. U.S. diplomat Robert Oakley was sent to Somalia to try to negotiate among the various clan leaders in order to restore some stability to the country. Despite earlier promises, when Clinton came into office, U.S. ground troops were in Somalia with no end to their deployment in sight.

By the end of summer 1993, about six months after Clinton took office, the administration faced a series of issues regarding Somalia. First, there did not seem to be an easy diplomatic solution to the problem. Second, in what was becoming a pattern, Congress was asking questions and raising issues about the role of the U.S. forces in Somalia. Finally, Clinton was facing the possibility of U.S. intervention in the growing war in Bosnia, and he saw the two as related. Clinton told his advisors, "unless we can get the Somalia mission under control . . . it's going to be very hard to convince Congress to provide the forces to implement an agreement on Bosnia."[29] Nevertheless, U.S. troops had already been deployed to Somalia by the previous administration.

On October 3, 1993, U.S. forces staged a raid in the city of Mogadishu to capture the warlord Mohammed Farah Aidid and his top lieutenants, but the United States paid a high price for that military action. The battle fought on the streets of Mogadishu resulted in hundreds (perhaps thousands) of Somali casualties and the death of eighteen Americans. U.S. public opinion was directly affected by pictures of a dead American soldier being dragged through the streets of Mogadishu.[30] This battle, "the largest firefight Americans had been involved in since Vietnam,"[31] evoked strong reactions from Congress as well as the public. Clinton addressed the American public to remind them of why U.S. troops were in Somalia, but he faced a dilemma. To leave would send a message about U.S. impotence in the face of nonstate actors, such as the warlords in Somalia. But staying would only put more U.S. soldiers in harm's way with an unclear objective. Clinton set a deadline of March 31, 1994, for a political settlement to be finalized so that U.S. troops could be withdrawn. The reaction to this solution among Republican members of Congress was especially hostile. For example, Senator Nancy Kassebaum stated, "I can think of no further compounding of the tragedy that has occurred there for our forces than to have them withdraw and see what started out to be a very successful, noble mission end in chaos."[32] Clinton also was criticized for sending troops into a mission that they were not prepared for and then for wanting them to withdraw in order to save more lives.

Clinton learned a lesson from this about sending U.S. troops to distant lands that were seen as removed from American national interests. As a result of Somalia, the Clinton administration chose not to interfere in the genocide that took place in Rwanda in 1994.[33] But perhaps more important, it helped frame the Clinton administration's perceptions regarding whether—and when—to intervene for humanitarian reasons.

Haiti

As Clinton was dealing with the situation in Somalia, another potential crisis was growing in Haiti. Half of the Caribbean island of Hispaniola, Haiti was well within the U.S. sphere of influence going back to the days of the Roosevelt Corollary. Consequently, instability in Haiti put Clinton into a position where he felt that he had to act. This military action also proved to be disastrous and further reinforced the administration's as well as congressional and public perceptions about the limits to U.S. military involvement.

President Clinton came into office a strong supporter of Jean-Bertrand Aristide. Aristide was Haiti's first democratically elected president, but he was overthrown in a military coup in 1991, eight months after his election. The United States brokered an accord between Aristide and Haiti's military rulers stipulating that Aristide would return to power on October 30, 1993. U.S. forces were then to be sent to Haiti as part of a UN contingent to train Haitians in engineering (such as building roads and other infrastructure) and to help serve as an internal police force.

In September 1993, the CIA reported that the Haitian leaders did not intend to keep the agreement. Nonetheless, some in the Clinton administration felt that the United States had to live up to its side of the agreement. Clinton authorized the deployment of a naval ship to Haiti carrying engineers and other forces to fulfill the U.S. commitment. When the ship arrived on October 11, 1993, it was met by a mob, many armed with guns and other weapons, while the police simply stood by. The Haitian leaders refused to guarantee the safety of the U.S. forces, and the ship anchored in the harbor, awaiting orders. On October 12, Washington ordered the ship to leave without allowing the forces to set foot in the country, and this became another foreign policy embarrassment for Clinton.

Clinton felt pressed to intervene in Haiti at least in part for domestic political reasons—to avert the possibility of an influx of Haitian refugees into the United States. Further, a significant African American constituency wanted to see the United States do something to help end the military dictatorship in Haiti. Despite his desire to respond to domestic concerns, Clinton learned quickly the limits of U.S. force in the face of civil unrest and without the support of the people and government that it was allegedly trying to help.

In addition, Clinton provoked Congress by not seeking congressional approval to send troops to Haiti, arguing that he possessed "executive authority" to do so. In response, Congress passed a resolution stating that "the President should have sought and welcomed congressional approval before deploying U.S. forces to Haiti."[34]

In 1994, with the situation in Haiti still unresolved, Clinton ordered a larger invasion force to the island. However, prior to their landing, former president Carter was able to negotiate a deal with rebel Haitian leader Cedras, allowing him to leave the island and authorizing American troops to come in to restore order.

Clinton learned harsh lessons from Haiti, another foreign policy debacle that undermined his credibility. To the members of Congress, it was an abuse of the power of the president, which further exacerbated the strains that already existed between the two branches.

The Balkans

When candidate Clinton was campaigning for the presidency against George H. W. Bush, he condemned the then-president for not acting more forcefully to address the situation in the Balkans. By the time Clinton took office as president in January 1993, the siege of Sarajevo, which became the longest siege in modern history to that time, was well under way, and stories of the genocide taking place throughout Bosnia were already hitting the American media. The issues were far from clear-cut, and explaining to the American public why involvement in this area would be in U.S. national interest would be difficult. As a result, Clinton called this "the most frustrating and complex foreign policy issue in the world today."[35]

Under Clinton, the United States pursued a bifurcated policy toward the Balkans. Policy was characterized either by an overwhelming desire not to get involved, which was the attitude of the administration toward the war in Bosnia in 1993 and into early 1994, or by the impulse to jump in and take a leadership role, which the United States did later in 1994. The former was the result of a number of factors: the harsh lessons of Somalia and Haiti of the difficulties of a humanitarian mission; the desire to let the Europeans take the lead under UN auspices (through the United Nations Protection Forces, or UNPROFOR); and concern about getting support of Congress and the public at a time when Clinton's popularity was low.[36] The decision to take a leadership role in the Balkans was the result of a change in the political landscape so that once the administration decided it was time to act, it did so decisively, resulting in a negotiated end to the war.

One of the events that prompted the Clinton administration to act was the "Sarajevo Market Massacre" on August 28, 1995, which resulted in the deaths of thirty-seven civilians, with eighty-eight wounded. It prompted a public outcry that provided the political support Clinton needed. Pushed by the United States, NATO accelerated its air strikes against Serb targets. This helped provide the military cover necessary for the Bosnian and Croat forces to launch a major ground offensive in preparation for the start of negotiations that would bring an end to the war. Negotiations were held at Wright-Patterson Air Force Base outside Dayton, Ohio, under the leadership of Assistant Secretary of State Richard Holbrooke. The major political leaders of Serbia (Milosevic), Croatia (Tudjman), and Bosnia (Izetbegovic) participated in the discussion, and in November 1995, President Clinton announced that an agreement had been reached. The peace agreement was signed in Paris on December 14, 1995, and the war in Bosnia ended.[37] Unfortunately, that was neither the end of war in the Balkans nor of U.S. military involvement there.

Kosovo and the Clinton Doctrine

The 1997 report "National Security Strategy for a New Century" suggests that U.S. military intervention may be appropriate "to respond to, relieve, and/or restrict the consequences of human catastrophe."[38] The willingness to use military force in this way defines what has been called the "new interventionism," one of the foundations of the Clinton Doctrine that was central to justifying the operation in Kosovo in 1999. This doctrine has at its core many of the ideals that Jimmy Carter espoused when he spoke of the need to make human rights central to U.S. foreign policy, and it echoes the earlier ideas of Woodrow Wilson.

Kosovo was another foreign policy issue that Clinton faced. The Dayton Peace Accords that ended the war in Bosnia did nothing to address the ethnic violence growing in the Serb province of Kosovo. Kosovo had been declared an "autonomous province" in 1963. But it had few rights until the Yugoslav constitution of 1974 allowed the province to write its own constitution, thereby giving it the same status as the six republics of then-Yugoslavia. After Serbian leader Milosevic came to power in 1987, the Serb minority in Kosovo increasingly repressed the Albanian majority, imposing more and more restrictions on what they could and could not do. In 1997, violence erupted when a group calling itself the Kosovo Liberation Army (KLA) began a series of terrorist-type attacks against the Serbs. Under the auspices of the European Union, a negotiation was called to take place at Rambouillet, outside Paris, in the hope of averting armed conflict. The negotiators gave Milosevic an ultimatum: withdraw from Kosovo or risk NATO military action. When the talks failed, the United States and Europe had little choice but to follow through, and in March 1999, NATO began bombing Serbia.

Kosovo was a difficult situation for the United States in many ways. While there was little doubt that human rights abuses were taking place, there were also divisions among the NATO allies as to what form an intervention should take. Clinton made it clear that he would not authorize sending U.S. ground forces into Kosovo, which put him at odds with the allies, especially Britain, and it publicly sent a signal as to military limits; one official in the Clinton administration later claimed that to state this so publicly had been a mistake.[39] Clinton did agree to support air strikes.

Clinton understandably was cautious about the deployment of U.S. military forces at this time. He had easily won reelection in 1996 because of domestic reasons. The economy was doing well, and despite a hostile Republican Congress, Clinton's public approval rating hit a high of 73 percent in December 1998.[40] In 1999, at the same time that he was facing decisions about Kosovo, he was under investigation for his affair with White House intern Monica Lewinsky. He was under additional scrutiny by Congress because he did not seek congressional approval for the earlier U.S. involvement in Bosnia and Kosovo, which he claimed had not been needed because these were NATO (as opposed to U.S.) missions. However, to the Republican-controlled Congress, this was part of a pattern of presidential disregard for congressional oversight.

With U.S. support, NATO made a decision to begin bombing Serbia; the attacks started in March 1999 and continued as a NATO operation tied to the need to assure international intervention when human rights abuses call for it or when it is in support of humanitarian goals. However, Clinton came under scrutiny regarding the U.S. policy on Kosovo. On the one hand, there were those who felt that the United States should have become involved sooner because of the clear human rights abuses. On the other hand, there were questions about whether Clinton had overstepped his responsibilities by agreeing to deploy U.S. troops and aircraft without broad support by Congress.

Domestically, a thriving economy took precedence over foreign policy situations, even those perceived as failures. As outgoing president in January 2001, Clinton had an approval rating of 67 percent, "the highest of any outgoing president since modern polling began—even surpassing Dwight Eisenhower and Ronald Reagan."[41]

Economics: Trade and Globalization

In approaching foreign policy from a broad perspective, Clinton understood that the world was changing and becoming more interconnected economically, a phenomenon referred to as "globalization." The economic failure of one country could have repercussions for other countries, and therefore it was in the United States' national interest to be sure that the global economy was strong. Clinton also understood that technology altered the way international business was conducted. Just as détente with the communist countries was best achieved by conservative Republicans, so was free trade pursued more successfully by a president from the Democratic Party, which was traditionally aligned with labor and was seen as protectionist.

With bipartisan support and despite objections from the largely Democratic unions, which claimed that it would result in the loss of jobs, Clinton successfully enacted the North American Free Trade Agreement (NAFTA) in 1994, uniting the United States, Canada, and Mexico. NAFTA strengthened both economic and political ties among the three countries, and now, years after the agreement went into effect, there is little evidence that it resulted in a loss of jobs in the United States. In 1995, when Mexico was in financial crisis, the Clinton administration provided that country with a $12.5 billion loan. While this was seen as a significant risk at the time, it not only stabilized the country, but Mexico repaid the loan within two years. This further strengthened the ties between the two countries.[42]

It is now clear that Clinton had an understanding of some of the changes taking place in the international system and was able to use them to strengthen the United States economically. While he had his foreign policy failures, notably Haiti and Somalia, his understanding of economics, both domestic and international, can be seen as one area of success.

Terrorism

One of the hallmarks of the post–Cold War world was the emergence of nonstate actors playing a major role in the international system. At a time when politicians are debating how to ensure the safety and security of the United States, a brief look at the pattern of terrorism during the Clinton years leading to the attacks of September 11 is instructive.[43] Perhaps the most important point is that "state-sponsored terrorism"—such as the acts perpetrated or supported by Libya, Syria, and Lebanon—has declined overall and is being replaced by a growth of independent organizations, many of which are seen as extremist and radical.[44] This pattern created a foreign policy dilemma for Presidents Clinton and then George W. Bush of how to respond to attacks that are not tied to a nation-state (country). Since international relations and international law are based on and assume a nation-state as the primary actor, there are few guidelines about how a country should interact with, or respond to, a nonstate actor.

According to Gelb, "when terrorists tried to blow up the World Trade Center in 1993, and later struck U.S. embassies in Africa, he [Clinton] did nothing at all for five years, until 1998 when he ordered small cruise missile attacks against Afghanistan and Sudan. These erratic, fragmentary, and feeble acts showed that Clinton [and his administration] had no comprehension of the nature and magnitude of the growing global terrorist threat, let alone what to do about it."[45] In a world in which perceptions become reality, the administration's inability to respond sent a signal that one could argue contributed to the attacks of 9/11.

In September 1998, Clinton addressed the UN General Assembly, and global terrorism was one of the central points of his talk. At that time, he admonished the international community that "all nations must put the fight against terrorism at the top of our agenda." He warned that terrorism is not only an American problem, but "a clear and present danger to tolerant and open societies and innocent people everywhere." And he also said, "If terrorism is at the top of the American agenda—[it] should be at the top of the world's agenda." He then offered common solutions to the problem, especially the need for countries to work together to counter this threat. He concluded that "together we can meet it and overcome its threats, its injuries, and its fears with confidence."[46] Despite this optimistic call for international unity against a common threat, terrorist acts against Americans (and also U.S. allies) increased.

In the aftermath of September 11, 2001, significant questions have been raised about what was then known about the terrorist cells acting in or against the United States, and whether the Clinton administration should have done more to stop Al Qaeda. Those questions might never be answered.

RETHINKING FOREIGN POLICY PRIOR TO 9/11

By the end of the Clinton administration it was clear that U.S. foreign policy had no overarching framework as it did during the Cold War. Rather, each of the two immediate post–Cold War presidents, George H. W. Bush and Bill Clinton, was unsure how to address the emergence of ethnic conflicts and civil wars and the humanitarian and human rights crises that accompany them. The result was the emergence of policies that were inconsistent and often opaque. While the Bush administration showed little doubt about the need to send U.S. troops to the Persian Gulf in the wake of Saddam Hussein's invasion of Kuwait or to deploy troops to Somalia to aid the humanitarian crisis unfolding there, he was unwilling to send troops to the former Yugoslavia, preferring instead to leave that to the Europeans to deal with. Similarly, Clinton appeared to be aggressive in his deployment of U.S. troops to Haiti for a mission that became a foreign policy fiasco and that raised questions about both his and the United States' intentions regarding the use of force.

From the start of the Cold War, American presidents based U.S. foreign policy on fighting that war with the hope of "winning." But the end of the Cold War was anything but easy from the perspective of U.S. foreign policy. The Cold War provided a framework and clear guidelines for foreign and military policy. In the post–Cold War period, U.S. foreign policy has been guided largely by the need to respond to the most pressing crisis or conflict. President George H. W. Bush spoke of a "new world order," but that lofty ideal was not translated into a foreign policy direction for the United States. The war in the Persian Gulf in 1991, fought by a coalition of countries brought together against one enemy, suggested one approach. However, the inability to address the ethnic conflict in the Balkans and the genocide in Rwanda, for example, suggest that such an approach would not be all-encompassing.

President Clinton came into office wanting to focus on the economy but found quickly that he, too, had to respond to more immediate foreign policy issues and that they could easily deflect time, attention, and political capital from domestic priorities. Clinton authorized a number of military actions (e.g., in Somalia, Haiti, and Bosnia) that were justified on humanitarian and human rights grounds. Clinton presented these to the American public by defining "national interest" rather broadly. But these cases also indicated a significant change in the use of military force in the post–Cold War environment to support more idealistic goals, specifically the U.S. military as a "force for good."[47] This hinted at the start of a new pattern in the direction of U.S. foreign policy, or a return to a policy advocated by Jimmy Carter, unsuccessfully, and by Woodrow Wilson decades earlier. In retrospect, one of the things that Clinton understood clearly was the fact that globalization was becoming the major force that would dominate the international system. Much as Truman saw the role that the military would have to play to support U.S. foreign policy in the Cold War period, Clinton understood the growing importance of economics and what that would mean for the United States as countries became more interdependent. Thus he embarked on policies that would position the United States as a global leader in that area. This did not mean ignoring the role of the military as an instrument of U.S. foreign policy. Rather, it elevated the role of economics and trade so that they, too, would become important tools for the United States to use.

When George W. Bush came into office in January 2001, his primary foreign policy goal was for the United States to return to a more unilateralist policy guided by pragmatic priorities, rather than the more idealistic goals of humanitarian aid, nation building, or preventing genocide. Once again, events beyond a president's control intervened, and with that the course of U.S. foreign policy changed. George H. W. Bush, Bill Clinton, and George W. Bush each started to frame a new direction for U.S. foreign policy in the post–Cold War world, only to be confronted with events demanding a different response. The events of September 11 severely disrupted the foreign policy course that George W. Bush had laid out. More important, September 11 carried a warning that the future of U.S. foreign policy will require anticipating the actions of and threats from nonstate actors as well as traditional nation-states. Since all aspects of foreign policy are premised on the nation-state, this creates another set of challenges for America. Just as the Cold War required new thinking about foreign policy, the notion of the threat, the military force structure and types of weapons needed to meet the threat, and the domestic governmental structure, so the post–September 11 world means rethinking all of these factors once again.

APPLYING FOREIGN POLICY CONCEPTS: THE USE OF U.S.
TROOPS FOR HUMANITARIAN PURPOSES

One of the dilemmas that any president faces comes in trying to decide when to deploy U.S. troops and how that deployment is in the national interest of the United States. This has been especially true since Vietnam, when members of Congress and the American public felt that the president had abused his power to send troops to fight and die in a war that was not in the national interest. Since Woodrow Wilson reframed U.S. foreign policy to inject the role of values, presidents have had to balance when, and whether, to take this country to war in support of ideals such as democracy and freedom. Especially since the end of the Cold War and the apparent rise of ethnic and civil conflicts, the United States has tried to determine whether it would be appropriate to intervene in the affairs of another country. In making this determination, the dilemma facing presidents has been balancing issues of the sovereignty of the state, which would preclude external interference, with the moral right to intervene in cases of human rights abuses. If, in fact, one of the roles of the military is to be used as a "force for good" to support basic values and human rights, then is it not part of the national interest of the United States to intervene when those rights are abridged?

Both Presidents George H. W. Bush and Clinton faced this issue during their presidencies. Clinton, even more than Bush, chose to intervene early in his administration and then paid a heavy political price later on. In retrospect, however, did he make the right decision and draw the wrong lesson in choosing *not* to intervene in Yugoslavia?

The Case

When Bill Clinton became president in January 1993, U.S. troops were already deployed in Somalia. They had been sent by his predecessor specifically to address what was seen as a humanitarian crisis, resulting from civil war in that country. Among the conditions for that deployment were supposed to be that the troops would be there for a limited amount of time and would be out by the time Clinton took office, which proved not to be the case. Clinton made the decision to authorize the military to try to capture the warlord Mohammed Farah Aidid, which resulted in a major battle on the streets of Mogadishu. Ultimately, the United States withdrew, leading to congressional and public criticism about the wisdom of the decisions made both to intervene and then to withdraw. As Clinton was dealing with the situation in Somalia, he also had to deal with a crisis unfolding in Haiti and, once again, Clinton made the decision to send in U.S. troops. This resulted in another foreign policy and military fiasco for Clinton.

One result of these two early lessons on the dangers of deploying troops in support of humanitarian missions was Clinton's decision to restrict "U.S. involvement in future peacekeeping missions and by refusing to intervene in other failed states."[48] A consequence of this decision was that "[w]hen a much bloodier conflict broke out in nearby Rwanda and Burundi, leaving 1 million dead, the United States, fearing a repeat of the Somalia disaster, let the carnage run its course. With no other major powers willing to step in, the UN, too, stood by as the genocide unfolded."[49]

Not only did the United States choose not to intervene in Rwanda, but it also stood by as Bosnia erupted into civil war, ultimately resulting in the deaths of at least 200,000 Bosnian Muslims in an act of "ethnic cleansing," with more than two million refugees who were displaced during the war. Despite his campaign rhetoric that "the United States should take the lead in seeking United Nations Security Council authorization for air strikes against those who are attacking the relief effort," and that "the United States should be prepared to lend appropriate military support to that operations,"[50] when he became president, Clinton proved to be unwilling to use force. Rather, not only did Clinton refer to the war in Bosnia as a "frustrating and complex foreign policy issue," but he also was unsure as to what to do. While he saw his main priority as the domestic economic situation, he also realized that he had inherited this situation, as he had the case of Somalia, and he stated that "if the United States does not act in situations like this nothing will happen." He also said that "a failure to do so [to act] would be to give up American leadership."[51] As one policy analyst notes, "Presidents inherit the leftover problems that their predecessors fail to resolve, or the tasks that simply require more time or resources to be completed."[52] This was the situation that Clinton faced.

Thus, Clinton had a dilemma. On the one hand, he knew that unless the United States took action, the fighting and genocide in Bosnia would continue. On the other hand, he had already suffered a number of military defeats in Somalia and Haiti, Congress was skeptical because he had initiated these attacks without congressional approval,[53] and he was not sure how to tie any U.S. involvement in Bosnia to U.S. national interest.

What Would You Do If . . .

The time is 1994. This is an election year, something that President Clinton is acutely aware of. He and his advisors are also aware that they had inherited a situation in Somalia, but that it was his administration that was blamed for the failure. It was Clinton's decision to move forces into Haiti, but that proved to be disastrous for the United States, both politically and in terms of public perceptions. The war in Bosnia is escalating, and the Europeans have proven themselves unable to contain the situation. Only the force of the United States would possibly make a difference.

What would you do if you were an advisor to President Clinton? You see a human rights catastrophe unfolding in Bosnia, but the United States has suffered when it chose to intervene in other cases. On the other hand, to do nothing would fly in the face of many of the values that the United States holds dear. Given what you know now, what policies would you recommend the president engage in, and why? In formulating a policy decision, you need to take into account how this will be presented to the American public, Congress, and the U.S. allies and how any decision ties directly to U.S. national interest.

Chapter Six

George W. Bush

A New Direction for U.S. Foreign Policy? 2001–2009

The administration of George W. Bush started in controversy when the contested presidential election of 2000 was decided by the Supreme Court, and it ended in controversy as well because of the results of decisions that were made in the wake of 9/11. While few would dispute the trauma of September 11, 2001, many have debated and continue to debate the wisdom of the administration's decisions to go into Afghanistan and especially Iraq for the disruption that those attacks caused in each of the two countries, the resulting regional instability that contributed to the growth of terrorist groups such as ISIS,[1] and the economic impact these wars had on the United States. The decision to attack Iraq in 2003 was especially suspect in light of the uncertain evidence provided about alleged weapons of mass destruction. A 2016 biography of President Bush is extremely critical in its assessment when the author writes in the first sentence that "Rarely in the history of the United States has the nation been so ill-served as during the presidency of George W. Bush."[2] And he concludes the book by stating, "Whether George W. Bush was the worst president in American history will be long debated, but his decision to invade Iraq is easily the worst foreign policy decision ever made by an American President."[3]

While the Bush administration initially came into office with a call for a neo-unilateralist, almost isolationist foreign policy, it took the attacks of 9/11 to forge a new direction for U.S. foreign policy. Suddenly, the United States was actively involved internationally, following an "either you are with us or against us" brand of foreign policy. Relatively quickly the United States went from trying to remain disengaged to an almost Wilsonian brand of interventionism tied to the imposition of democracy around the world. When Bush pursued policies that he felt were in the best interest of the United States, including the decision to go into Iraq and after Saddam Hussein in March 2003 without UN approval, it created rifts with NATO allies and also shifted world opinion against the United States. While few argued the wisdom of, or justification for, the war with Afghanistan, alleged to be harboring Al Qaeda and those who were behind the 9/11 attacks, many saw the war with Iraq as an unnecessary diversion. Others, however, saw it as evidence of a more muscular and militarized United States once again. That decision remains controversial more than ten years later. [4]

The foreign policy of George W. Bush can be divided into two parts: before and after September 11, 2001. The implications of the shift in foreign policy were far-reaching, as the United States, in seeking to establish itself as a global leader following 9/11, ended up pursuing policies that alienated many of its traditional allies. The post 9/11 period was also characterized by the growing threat from terrorism, which, as we will see, was a difficult one for the United States to counter as it was not tied to any nation-state but to a group that was harder to define—and to fight. Some argue that the decisions made in the wake of 9/11 contributed to the growth of terrorist groups, such as ISIS, that bedeviled the Obama administration. Further, how to deal with this elusive nonstate actor played into the rhetoric of the 2016 presidential election.

FOREIGN POLICY BEFORE SEPTEMBER 11

During the presidential campaign of 2000, then-candidate George W. Bush made it clear that the United States would chart its own course in foreign policy. Bush indicated that under his administration, the United States would return to a more unilateralist policy characterized by actions consistent with what the president perceived to be in the national interest. He stressed his desire to strengthen ties south of the border (especially to Mexico), rather than look primarily to the traditional allies in Europe. And he made it clear that the United States should not be in the business of "nation building," stating his intention to pull U.S. troops out of places like the Balkans. In short, candidate Bush outlined a marked shift in the direction of U.S. foreign policy, especially compared with that of his predecessor, Bill Clinton, and even his father, George H. W. Bush.

In the January/February 2000 volume of *Foreign Affairs*, Condoleezza Rice, then a Stanford University professor who had become part of the Bush inner circle and who would become Bush's national security advisor and then secretary of state, laid out what she saw as the priorities of the United States in a Republican (George W. Bush) administration. She began by stating that "the United States has found it exceedingly difficult to define its 'national interest' in the absence of Soviet power." But she also noted that such times "of transition" are important because "one can affect the shape of the world to come."[5] While many of the subsequent Bush administration policies were affected by the events of September 11, the article is instructive for the priorities and policies it outlined.

Rice foreshadowed Bush administration policy when she stated, "The president must remember that the military is a special instrument. It is lethal, and it is meant to be. . . . [I]t is certainly not designed to build a civilian society." Rather, in her estimation, "[m]ilitary force is best used *to support clear political goals*, whether limited, such as expelling Saddam from Kuwait, or comprehensive, such as demanding the unconditional surrender of Japan and Germany during World War II" (emphasis added).[6] At the time of the publication of this article, Rice, and presumably the entire Bush defense and foreign policy team, appeared to be focused on defining U.S. national interest in the absence of the Soviet threat.[7]

The events of 9/11 significantly altered the priorities of the Bush administration, creating the "global war on terror" and making this the highest foreign policy priority. From that time forward, all aspects of Bush administration foreign and security policy stemmed from, and were justified by, the need to support the war on terror. It is therefore instructive to go back to the Rice article and note the attention that she paid to U.S. national interest, which she defined "by a desire to foster the spread of freedom, prosperity and peace."[8] It was the desire to spread freedom and democracy that ultimately was used to justify the United States decision for war in Iraq, eclipsing the initial rationale for the attack, which was "regime change" and the desire to eliminate the spread of weapons of mass destruction allegedly found in Iraq. And despite his willingness to use military force, a realist characteristic, Bush's emphasis on spreading freedom and democracy is inherently idealist in perspective.[9]

Contested Election and Implications for U.S. Foreign Policy

In order to put the Bush administration's decisions into broader perspective, it is necessary to go back to the election of 2000, which was fraught with controversy. Marked by questions about election fraud in Ohio, a critical swing state, and the "hanging chads" and "butterfly ballots" in Florida, the election was characterized by accusations of irregularities in voting procedures as well as the ways in which ballots were counted. The Florida issue was especially contentious, and ultimately the issue of a recount went to the U.S. Supreme Court for a decision. On December 12, 2000, by a vote of 5 to 4, the members of the Court ordered a halt to a recount, thereby overruling the verdict of the Florida Supreme Court and effectively ensuring the election of George W. Bush as president.

Despite—or because of—his disputed victory in the presidential election, Bush moved quickly to fulfill the campaign promises he made, many of which involved a reversal in the patterns of foreign policy set by the Clinton administration. In June 2001, over the objections of the European allies as well as many environmentalists in the United States, Bush declared that the 1997 Kyoto Protocol to the UN Framework Convention on Climate Change "was fatally flawed in fundamental ways," and that the United States would not participate in that agreement but would offer an alternative. The United States, Bush said, was committed to "work within the United Nations framework and elsewhere to develop with our friends and allies and nations throughout the world an effective and science-based response to the issue of global warming."[10] These statements left other countries wondering how the United States was going to live up to this commitment or to others that had been made by previous administrations, as the Bush reaction seemed to be especially negative toward anything done by the Clinton administration.

Bush also withdrew the United States from the 1972 Anti-Ballistic Missile Treaty so that the United States would not be constrained by its terms in developing new weapon systems, especially a ballistic missile defense system. He said that the United States would limit continued engagement in the Middle East peace process, which had been a hallmark of U.S. foreign policy since the Carter years. In effect, Bush halted the Oslo process that had been pursued by Clinton. In another repudiation of his predecessor's policies, Bush also suspended talks with North Korea and criticized the agreement signed in 1994 by the United States and North Korea under the Clinton administration.[11] He said that the United States would not send additional troops to the Balkans as part of the peacekeeping force deployed there in 1995 following the end of the war, and implied that he would withdraw those which were there. And he made it clear that the United States should not be in the business of "nation building," a direct slap at previous administrations' foreign policy decisions, including his father's.

These early policy decisions led to criticism domestically and internationally about the direction of U.S. foreign policy. The European allies charged that this policy of unilateralism was undermining the basis of U.S. (and European) national security. They also raised concerns not only about the apparent destruction of the existing foreign policy framework, but about what (if anything) Bush was putting in its place. To many opponents both within and outside the United States, the perception was that the Bush administration's policies were tied to the desire to please special interests and were made for domestic political reasons rather than in the greater national interest. These criticisms stopped abruptly on September 11, 2001.

SEPTEMBER 11 AND THE RESPONSES

Using the military actively as an instrument of foreign policy was the hallmark of Bush administration foreign policy after September 11. On that day hijackers captured four aircraft, crashing two into the World Trade Center in New York and one into the Pentagon in Washington. The fourth, which by all accounts was also headed to Washington, crashed in Pennsylvania after passengers wrestled control of the aircraft from the hijackers and diverted it from its target. The responses to these events are instructive as they pertain to U.S. foreign policy.

One of the most immediate effects of September 11 was that NATO invoked Article 5 for the first time in its history. The North Atlantic Council issued a press release on September 12, 2001, affirming that Article 5 "stipulates that in the event of attacks falling within its purview, each Ally will assist the Party that has been attacked by taking such action as it deems necessary. Accordingly, the United States' NATO Allies stand ready to provide the assistance that may be required as a consequence of these acts of barbarism."[12] By early October, under the framework of Article 5, NATO had started to deploy Airborne Early Warning Aircraft (AWACS) to the United States. However, it should be noted that this was the *only* act that NATO took in support of the United States at that time, not because NATO did not want to do more—in its role as a collective security alliance, NATO was prepared to work with the United States to formulate a response to the attack—but because the United States, under the Bush administration, preferred to work outside the NATO framework, or any other formal alliance, in determining next steps.

Acting unilaterally, the Bush administration thereby determined how to respond to the attacks.[13] The administration quickly began exploring military options, including "a strike against al Qaeda forces in Afghanistan, where Osama bin Laden had been given sanctuary by the country's Taliban government, led by Muslim fundamentalists who had imposed a rigid Islamic regime."[14] The decision to attack Afghanistan was to be part of a larger "global war on terror" that would not end "until every terrorist group that had attacked Americans in the past, up to and including the 9/11 assaults, or might launch attacks in the future, had been destroyed."[15] As political scientist Peter Irons described it, perhaps the more important point about the decisions that Bush made was that "the 9/11 attacks created abrupt, far-reaching changes in the nation's political and military situation—changes that would, in turn, *raise significant constitutional issues*" (emphasis added).[16] These issues pertained to the decision to prosecute the war not only with Afghanistan but also with Iraq, and especially in the expansion of the role of the executive branch to make decisions not only about military and foreign policy, but also about domestic issues—all justified under the broad umbrella of the war on terror.

War with Afghanistan

After gathering intelligence information that linked the hijackers to the terrorist group Al Qaeda, based in Afghanistan, the Bush administration made the decision to send military forces to attack that country and oust the Taliban government, which supported and harbored terrorists. Consistent with the terms of the War Powers Act,[17] the president consulted with Congress and got its support for this venture. According to the president, this was a clear-cut case of an attack on the United States and a military response to that attack. The draft joint resolution was sent to the leaders of the House and Senate on September 12, 2001. It was passed by the Senate on September 14 by a vote of 98 to 0, and in the House later that same day by a vote of 420 to 1.[18]

According to a Congressional Research Service report, the floor debates surrounding the resolution "make clear that the focus of the military force legislation was on the *extent* of the authorization that Congress would provide to the President for use of U.S. military force against the international terrorists who attacked the U.S. on September 11, 2001 and those who directly and materially assisted them in carrying out their actions" (emphasis in original).[19] The resolution that was passed includes five "whereas clauses," "expressing opinions regarding why the joint resolution is necessary."[20] But the critical part is Section 2, "Authorization for Use of United States Armed Forces," which states that "the President is authorized to use all necessary and appropriate force against those nations, organizations, or persons he determines planned, authorized, committed, or aided the terrorist attacks that occurred on September 11, 2001, or harbored such organizations or persons, in order to prevent any future acts of international terrorism against the United States by such nations, organizations or persons." The document also makes it clear that "[n]othing in this resolution supersedes any requirement of the War Powers resolution."[21] (See chapter 4 for a description of the War Powers Resolution.)

In the signing statement that accompanied his signature, Bush asserted that S.J. Res. 23 "recognized the authority of the *President* under the Constitution to take action to deter and prevent acts of terrorism against the United States." He also stated that "in signing this resolution, *I maintain the longstanding position of the executive branch regarding the President's constitutional authority to use force*, including the Armed Forces of the United States" (emphasis added).[22] Although the president made it clear that he was complying with the terms of the War Powers Resolution and that the military action requested was necessary to protect the American people and homeland, he clearly was also asserting what he saw as the authority of the president to make these decisions. This is an example of the way in which Bush used "signing statements" to insert his opinion and interpretation of bills passed by Congress and is also another example of the way in which the Bush administration expanded the power of the executive branch in general, and the president in particular.

However, some in Congress were already concerned about the broad scope of the war on terror envisioned by Bush. In fact, both Democratic Senate majority leader Tom Daschle (D-SD) and Senator Robert Byrd (D-WV), the senior member of the Senate, urged the president to "choose his words carefully" in a proposed speech to Congress and the nation. "Disturbed by the sweeping language [of the resolution initially proposed], congressional negotiators finally persuaded the president to accept a resolution that limited him to retaliating only against those nations, organizations, or persons responsible for the 9/11 attacks."[23] After some compromise, Bush signed the resolution into law on September 18, 2001, and less than three weeks later, on October 7, 2001, the United States launched ground and air strikes against Afghanistan.[24]

Despite the reservations expressed by some in Congress, few argued with the president's decision to respond to the attacks of September 11 by attacking Afghanistan. In fact, Bush's public approval rating hit a high of 90 percent following September 11, the highest popularity rating ever recorded.[25] The swift military victory over the Taliban in Afghanistan proved that the Bush administration was willing to take a decisive stand militarily when it mattered, reinforcing the confidence of both the allies and the American public in the president and his policies. What Bush did not take into account at that time was the fact that removing the Taliban from office was not going to end the war in Afghanistan.

The initial decision to attack Afghanistan, one of the known homes for Al Qaeda bases, was seen as justified and, on the whole, was received positively both at home and abroad. British Prime Minister Tony Blair stated that "even if no British citizens had died [in the attacks of September 11], it would be right to act. This atrocity was an attack on us all."[26] Within a few months the war expanded and ultimately became a NATO mission. The International Security Assistance Force (ISAF) was created as a UN-mandated, NATO-led international force in December 2001 after the United States had ousted the Taliban regime. It was created initially to assist the Afghan Transitional Authority to reconstruct the country. Although other countries joined in this NATO mission, the United States had the largest number of troops deployed.

Despite the lofty goals of ousting the Taliban, confronting Al Qaeda, mounting a serious NATO mission, and rebuilding the country, the war in Afghanistan did not go as planned. In fact, between 2001, when the war with Afghanistan started, and January 2009, when the Obama administration came into office, attention given to Afghanistan by the United States became secondary to what became the major foreign policy issue of the Bush years: the war with Iraq.[27]

The Bush Doctrine and the War with Iraq

By early 2002, Bush made it clear that the United States would not stop with the attack on Afghanistan but would expand the war on terror. In his State of the Union speech in January 2002, Bush identified Iraq, Iran, and North Korea as an "axis of evil," and he stated that "some governments will be timid in the face of terror. . . . If they do not act, America will."[28] He followed that up with a speech on March 11, 2002, the six-month anniversary of September 11. At that time, he said, "Our coalition must act deliberately, but *inaction is not an option*" (emphasis added).[29] In other words, President Bush was sending notice to the American public and the world that the war on terror was going to expand beyond Afghanistan.

The Bush Doctrine, as it was popularly known, became the basis for the decision to go to war against Iraq in March 2003 and to do so without the formal backing of the international community. Formally titled the "National Security Strategy of the United States," this document, which was issued in September 2002, puts forward a new direction for American foreign policy: "While the United States will constantly strive to enlist the support of the international community, *we will not hesitate to act alone, if necessary, to exercise our right of self-defense by acting preemptively*" (emphasis added).[30]

This doctrine states clearly and unequivocally that the United States is justified in going to war preemptively against any group that potentially threatens the country or its allies, and that it will do so alone if necessary. This is a departure from the policies that the United States followed since the end of World War II, when much of its foreign policy was tied to formal alliances and the belief that security is best achieved if countries work together against a common enemy, rather than trying to defeat the enemy alone. Furthermore, it is a marked departure from the stated idealistic goals for the Bush administration that now made clear it would be relying on U.S. hard power to do whatever it thought was necessary. For the first time since the Cold War, the United States was again relying on its military might to pursue its foreign policy goals. And, once again, foreign and security policy became inextricably linked.

The Rise of the "Neocons"

One of the other important points to note about the Bush Doctrine and the decision to go to war against Iraq that followed is that, to a large extent, it was the product of the thinking of a group of foreign policy analysts collective known as the "Neoconservatives," or Neocons. Exemplified most notably by high-level decision-makers such as Vice President Dick Cheney, Secretary of Defense Donald Rumsfeld, and Deputy Secretary of Defense Paul Wolfowitz, as well as a number of pundits and supporters, this group started with the assumption of the United States as a great power that needs to be more assertive in promoting its ideals, including using its military might. Inherent in the Neocons' ideology are: concern with democracy, although that might be equated with the imposition of American values; the belief that U.S., power "can be used for moral purposes"; and skepticism of international law and organizations.[31] The Neocons who had been around during the administration of George H. W. Bush, including Cheney, Rumsfeld, and Wolfowitz, were adamantly opposed to the decision made at the end of the first Persian Gulf War to end hostilities and allow Saddam Hussein to remain in place. According to one political scientist, from the time of the election of George W. Bush the Neocons were determined to revisit Iraq. The fact that Dick Cheney became vice president and had a significant role in the appointment of other Neocons to high-level positions helped ensure that not only was Iraq a high priority but so were other policies that they deemed important. And the approaches that they advocated were consistent with President Bush's worldview. Thus, September 11 provided an opportunity for the Bush administration to enact policies that were long in the making.[32]

The Path to War with Iraq

The path to war in Iraq can clearly be traced back to the first Persian Gulf War and the unsatisfactory outcome according to a number of members of the George W. Bush administration. Further, it became "the first test case in the Bush administration's new foreign-policy doctrine of America's right not only to preeminence in world affairs, but to preemption, by military might if necessary, of whatever threats it perceives to its security at home and abroad."[33] The decision to go into Iraq was not without dissenters even within the administration. Then–Secretary of State Colin Powell, who had been the military director of the first Persian Gulf War, warned of the possible dangers of such a mission and at a meeting with the president in August 2002 was quoted as saying "'We'd own a country,' he told the president." And he also made the case that building international support would be essential "not only to legitimize any war in the eyes of the world, but also to lay the groundwork for the postwar reconstruction of Iraq."[34]

Despite the suspicion that Bush and the Neocons had of international organizations like the UN, Bush was persuaded of the necessity of going to that organization. In a speech before the General Assembly in September 2002, Bush made it clear that unless Iraq complied with the UN Security

Council Resolutions to allow weapons inspectors back into the country, actions would be taken, and he also left no doubt that the United States would go it alone if necessary. But Germany was already voicing opposition to any war in Iraq, as was France, which was pushing for the need to focus on the inspectors and only later on the threatened consequences. In other words, it is clear that six months before the war with Iraq there were already disagreements brewing between the United States and some of its closest European allies as to next steps. Only Great Britain was showing complete support.

While Bush was pressing the international community through the UN, he was already building support in Congress for a military action. On September 19, he sent a draft of a resolution to Congress asking for authority "'to use all means he determines to be appropriate, including force' to disarm and dislodge Saddam Hussein."[35] Aware of the 2002 Congressional election campaign and the need to build support for its position both domestically and internationally, the administration continued to use this same story line about weapons of mass destruction through the fall. On October 2, 2002, Bush submitted to Congress a resolution authorizing the use of force against Iraq. The resolution itself includes a litany of all of Saddam Hussein's wrongdoings for more than a decade, going back to the first Persian Gulf War and even earlier. It describes an Iraq that was building weapons of mass destruction and demonstrated willingness to use such weapons in the past; the clear implication is that it will do so again, this time against the United States. And it *suggests* that Iraq was somehow involved in the attacks of 9/11—"Whereas the attacks on the United States of September 11, 2001, underscored the gravity of the threat posed by the acquisition of weapons of mass destruction by international terrorist organizations"—although it does not mention Iraq by name in that particular clause.[36]

The resolution then concludes with these important clauses: "Whereas the President and Congress are determined to continue to take all appropriate actions against terrorists and terrorist organizations, including those nations, organizations, or persons who planned, authorized, committed, or aided the terrorist attacks that occurred on September 11, 2001, or harbored such persons or organizations"; and then, "Whereas the President has authority under the Constitution to take action in order to deter and prevent acts of international terrorism against the United States" the "President *is authorized to use the Armed Forces of the United States as he determines to be necessary and appropriate*" (emphasis added).[37] It is also interesting to note that this resolution refers explicitly to Public Law 107-40, which authorized the use of force "against those responsible for the recent attacks launched against the United States"[38] and was used to authorize the war with Afghanistan.

On October 11, 2002, the resolution was passed by both houses—in the Senate by a vote of 77 to 23 and in the House by a vote of 296 to 133—and it was signed into law by President Bush on October 16, 2002. All the dissenters were Democrats with the exception of Republican Senator Lincoln Chaffee of Rhode Island, who subsequently was voted out of office. The U.S. attack against Iraq began on March 19, 2003.

The administration also started a concerted public campaign to make the case for military action against Iraq. Directed at both the American public and U.S. allies, the administration put forward two interrelated arguments: "One was that Iraq had ominous, if still largely unspecified and unproven ties, to Al Qaeda. The other was that Saddam remained determined to build a nuclear weapon that could directly threaten the United States and the world."[39] It should be noted that both of these allegations had been debated within the government.

The political pressure by the United States and some of its allies was enough for Iraq to authorize the return of the weapons inspectors, but under pressure from the United States in November, the Security Council also passed Resolution 1441, which gave Iraq "a final opportunity to comply with its disarmament obligations under relevant resolutions of the Council" or "it will face serious consequences as a result of its continued violations of its obligations."[40] Although Iraq allowed inspectors back into the country and released thousands of pages of files on its weapons program, the Bush administration was quick to announce that Iraq was not fully in compliance. Early in 2003, the governments of France and Germany noted that Iraq was complying and should be given additional time. What seemed to be happening was that the United States was pushing for war while many of the allies were willing to wait.

Bush took the opportunity of the State of the Union message in January 2003 to make the implicit case for war:

> Twelve years ago, Saddam Hussein faced the prospect of being the last casualty in a war he had started and lost. To spare himself, he agreed to disarm of all weapons of mass destruction.
>
> For the next 12 years, he systematically violated that agreement. He pursued chemical, biological and nuclear weapons even while inspectors were in his country.
>
> Nothing to date has restrained him from his pursuit of these weapons: not economic sanctions, not isolation from the civilized world, not even cruise missile strikes on his military facilities.[41]

Then in February, Powell went to the United Nations to make the case against Saddam Hussein and to persuade other countries of the need to go to war. France, Russia, and China all defied the United States, arguing that the inspectors needed more time, while Bush ordered troops and combat helicopters to the Persian Gulf in anticipation of a conflict. As the various sides tried to reach a diplomatic solution to this impasse, the United States continued to deploy troops to the region. A UN Resolution that had been pending was withdrawn in the face of mounting opposition, and UN Secretary General Kofi Annan warned that without the support of the Security Council, the legitimacy of any military action would be questioned. Nonetheless, the decision was made and on March 19, 2003, President Bush announced to the American public that "at this hour American and coalition forces are in the early stages of military operations to disarm Iraq, to free its people, and to defend the world from grave danger."[42]

In authorizing that attack without United Nations approval, Bush charted another new course for U.S. foreign policy. The war against Iraq became the defining moment for the Bush administration. Unlike his father, who was able to build a strong international coalition before mounting the 1991 Persian Gulf War, George W. Bush had the support of only a few major nations and, perhaps more important, that action was directly opposed by many of the United States' traditionally strongest allies, such as France and Germany.[43] This resulted in a significant schism between the United States and its allies, which proved to be especially damaging at a time when the United States was building support for, and needed to sustain allied commitment to, the ongoing war in Afghanistan.

The War with Iraq and Its Aftermath

Where the first Persian Gulf War in 1991 was covered widely in the media (the "CNN effect"), the 2003 invasion was characterized by reporters "embedded" with troops, thereby enabling the U.S. public to watch the progress of the war in virtually real time and with first-person commentary. The course of the first phase of the war—"shock and awe"—was swift and apparently successful. The initial military attack was sufficient to bring about the end of the regime of Saddam Hussein. In a show of victory aboard the USS *Abraham Lincoln* on May 2, 2003, Bush spoke under a banner that declared, "Mission Accomplished." However, that declaration of victory proved to be premature. What Bush did not count on was the difficulty of both ending the war and building the peace.[44]

Much has been written about the issues and problems associated with the war in Iraq,[45] and we are not going to review or critique the decision here. Suffice it to say, the decision to invade Iraq without UN or allied support had a devastating impact on perceptions of the United States internationally. It also divided the country domestically.[46] Further, the longer the war continued, the more skeptical the American public and especially the allies became. But this did not stop George W. Bush from winning a second term in the election of 2004. When it comes right down to it, the American public does not like to change leaders during a war. And, as Bush kept reminding the American public, he was a wartime president. It was not until later in Bush's second term and then after Obama took office as president in January 2009 that the full impact of many of Bush's decisions started to be felt.

The Iraq War and the Economy

In his State of the Union speech on January 29, 2002, Bush made it clear that "it costs a lot to fight this war [in Afghanistan]. We have spent more than a billion dollars a month—over $30 million a day—and we must be prepared for future operations." And, he continued, "My budget includes the largest increase in defense spending in two decades—because while the price of freedom and security is high, it is never too high. Whatever it costs to defend our country, we will pay."[47] What was not, and could not, have been anticipated at the time of that speech was the additional costs of fighting two wars simultaneously, one in Afghanistan and the other in Iraq, or the longer-term costs to deal with the veterans of the two wars. According to a nonpartisan Congressional Budget Office (CBO) report released in 2011, the estimated costs for Iraq from fiscal year 2003, when the war started, through fiscal year 2011, when the report was compiled, was $805.5 *billion*.[48] According to an analysis in *Bloomberg News*, "Direct federal spending on the war through 2012 will reach $823 billion" and that does not include the resulting payment on the debt accumulated for the war or ongoing costs for veterans of that war.[49] The actual costs of the war are far greater than economic forecasts made by the Bush administration; a projection made by Lawrence Lindsey, Bush's Director of the National Economic Council, that the war could cost between $100 and $200 billion was dismissed by Secretary of Defense Rumsfeld as "baloney." Lindsey was subsequently forced from the position.[50] When the costs for Afghanistan are included, the economic costs of the wars on terror go up considerably.

While it is also true that the U.S. economy has grown, the economic drain has been significant, especially the decision to pay for the war by borrowing and budget deficits rather than by raising taxes. This had a longer-term impact on the economy that succeeded the Bush administration. The major point here is that the decision to expand the war on terror, while popular with many Americans, also had longer-term economic consequences as the country had to pay the price for the "guns versus butter" decisions that had been made.

Freedom and Democracy for All

As George W. Bush started his second term in office in January 2005, public opinion polls showed an increasing number of Americans were skeptical about the mission in Iraq and whether the goal of establishing a truly democratic Iraq would succeed. At that time, polls found an overall approval rating for Bush of 50 percent, versus a disapproval rating of 43 percent. A poll taken in May 2004, about six months prior to the election and just about a year after the war in Iraq started, indicated that overall, 50 percent thought that the war was going well, while 46 percent thought it was not. What this suggests is a country that was deeply divided.[51]

Despite candidate Bush's claim that the United States should not engage in nation building, a direct criticism of the Democrats, as President Bush began his second term, not only was the United States engaged in doing so in Iraq, but Bush's inaugural address suggested that the United States would continue its involvement globally, pursuing the Wilsonian ideals of freedom and democracy for all. The war on terror in general and the war in Iraq in particular were part of President Bush's broader policy agenda to spread freedom and democracy. He articulated this concept in his second inaugural address when he said, "There is only one force of history that can break the reign of hatred and resentment, and expose the pretensions of tyrants, and reward the hopes of the decent and tolerant, and that is the force of human freedom." And in language reminiscent of an earlier era, he continued, "So it is the policy of the United States to seek and support the growth of democratic movements and institutions in every nation and culture, with the ultimate goal of ending tyranny in our world."[52]

In his foreign policy decisions following September 11, and especially going into his second term, Bush appeared to be drawing on Wilsonian idealism using America's military might to accomplish his goal.[53] The term coined by the administration to describe this foreign policy direction was "practical idealism," which refers to "the policy's underlying premise that in a post-Sept. 11 world, America's national security is tied directly to the spread of free and open societies everywhere, including the Middle East."[54]

In his book *Winning the Right War*, foreign policy analyst Philip Gordon notes that the Bush administration, early in its second term, started to recognize the reality that an America "that is popular, respected, reliable, and admired has a far better chance of winning needed cooperation than an America that is not." He also contends that the administration was aware of the high price it paid "for gratuitously alienating allies and that diplomatic efforts to repair relations were worthwhile."[55] This awareness resulted in an effort by then–Secretary of State Rice to attempt to mend relations with the allies by traveling to Europe. President Bush made similar trips, including one to European capitals in June 2008, dubbed his "farewell tour." According to one account of that visit, "[t]he question of his legacy hangs over his eight-day visit to Europe." But this account also notes the fact that the war in Iraq "did more to strain relations with Europe—not to mention with the Muslim world—than any issue since Ronald Reagan deployed intermediate missiles in Europe in 1984 at the height of the cold war. As a result, he [Bush] remains deeply unpopular in Europe, as he does at home."[56]

What is clear is that during most of its tenure, the Bush administration was trying to define a new direction for U.S. foreign policy in the post–Cold War world and that despite the administration's protestations to the contrary, this policy was formulated in response to external events. In many ways, these events and the Bush administration's reactions to them defined the direction of U.S. foreign policy for the early part of the twenty-first century. They are also further proof that regardless of how much a president might try to initiate a particular course of action, ultimately he or she will be forced to react to the most immediate and pressing issues that arise.

Shortly before he left office, December 2008 polls show that Bush's approval rating had dropped to 24 percent and his disapproval rating had gone up to 68 percent. The only group that overwhelmingly remained supportive was conservative Republicans.[57]

It is important to note that it was not just his decisions about Iraq that undermined Bush's popularity at home. Domestic events, such as his handling of Hurricane Katrina and the failure to enact some of his signature policies such as Social Security and immigration reform, combined with skepticism about what was going on in the prison at Guantanamo in the wake of Abu Ghraib and the deteriorating situation in Iraq and Afghanistan contributed to rising doubts among the American people about Bush's leadership. The lack of consultation and the perception of abuse of prisoners as well as apparent abuses of the rights of citizens through legislation such as the Patriot Act also undermined U.S. moral leadership both at home and abroad.

President Bush and Wilsonian Idealism

Even though the Bush administration initially justified the war with Iraq based on the need to find weapons of mass destruction, it quickly morphed into the need for "regime change" to get rid of a nasty dictator who used such weapons against his own people and who posed a threat to the United States and its allies. There was talk of the ways in which the United States would be greeted as "liberators" who freed the Iraqi people from their dictator, and the assumption was that tribal differences within the country would be swept aside as the people of Iraq worked together to rebuild their country as a democracy. Using religious terms, Bush often spoke of America's mission to "'rid the world of evil' and to promote 'God-given values' around the world. The ability of the United States to 'shape events' added to that mission a license to depose 'evil' leaders such as Saddam Hussein."[58]

In writing about Bush and the influence of the Neocons, one political scientist writes that "the problem with the Bush reaction to 9/11 was not merely in its unilateral and comprehensive nature. It was also in the administration's insistence on discussing the challenges in *moralistic, religious, and even missionary terms* (rather than in political ones)" (emphasis in original). In so doing, Bush defined the terrorist challenge as a "biblical struggle of good versus evil" that resulted in the loss of support both at home and abroad, despite the overwhelming sympathy that the United States got immediately following the attacks.[59]

In that regard, Bush is often equated with Wilson in the zeal with which he pursued the ideals of promoting democracy and pursuing a foreign policy based on values. However, Bush did not learn all the lessons of history, specifically, that values such as "democracy" and "freedom" cannot be imposed; nor will the rest of the world see the distinction and the fight in quite the same way. For example, after becoming president in 1913, Wilson boasted "that he could transform Latin America, if not the rest of the world, into constitutional democracies in America's image." He was vocal in his opposition to Mexican dictator Victoriano Huerta, but, as he discovered, "attempts to instill American-style constitutional democracy and capitalism through force were destined to fail. . . . In Mexico, Wilson came to understand in practice what he had written in his theories of government—that 'self-government is not a thing that can be "*given*" to any people'" (emphasis added).[60]

In the Bush administration, the forces of the neoconservatives, who had been pushing for war with Iraq and the overthrow of Saddam Hussein since the end of the first Persian Gulf War, adopted Wilson's values but "insisted upon employing McKinley's and Theodore Roosevelt's means to achieve it. They believed in transforming the world in America's image, but sought to do so through the unimpeded use of American power rather than through international cooperation and organization."[61] As author John Judis notes, "If the administration's experience in Iraq increasingly resembles past American imperial ventures, Bush's experience was remarkably similar to McKinley's in the Philippines more than a century before."[62]

Wilson had changed the underlying framework of American foreign policy to inject values, such as democracy, which he saw as a universal given. However, Bush tempered that set of values with his own beliefs of the United States as an imperial power with a preordained role to play in the world. These values guided his decisions to go to war with Iraq. But as one political scientist notes, "As the Iraq war turned into a protracted and costly struggle, both the rationale for the American presence in Iraq and the aim of the war shifted substantially. The Iraq war was less about relinquishing Iraq of its weapons of mass destruction than about bringing freedom and democracy to the Middle East."[63]

Clearly, Bush's foreign policy embodies some of the idealism of Wilson with the imperialism of McKinley and Theodore Roosevelt. In understanding the impact of this blend of foreign policy orientations, Judis summarizes it well when he states that "America's true power has always rested not only in its economic and military strength, but in its determination to use that strength *in cooperation with others* on behalf of the equality of individuals and nations" (emphasis added).[64]

The Iraq War: A Postscript

On November 17, 2008, just after the election that would bring Barack Obama to the White House, the governments of the United States and Iraq signed a Status of Forces Agreement (SOFA) that would govern the withdrawal of American troops from Iraq. Under the terms of this agreement, all U.S. forces "shall withdraw from all Iraqi territory no later than December 31, 2011." The agreement also specifies clearly that "[a]ll United States *combat* forces shall withdraw from all Iraqi cities, villages and localities no later than the time at which Iraqi Security Forces assume full responsibility for security in an Iraqi province, *provided that such withdrawal is completed no later than June 30, 2009*" (emphasis added).[65] In other words, according to the terms of the agreement, while the government of Iraq acknowledges the need to look to the United States to "support" Iraq "in its efforts to maintain security and stability in Iraq," the primary responsibility would fall to the government of Iraq.

As the time got closer for the withdrawal of U.S. forces from Iraq, concerns mounted in both countries. An article in the *New York Times* on June 26, 2009, summarized the ambivalence surrounding this withdrawal. On the one hand, to Iraqi Prime Minister Nuri al-Maliki, the event was seen as a "great victory" and one that "he compares to the rebellion against British troops in 1920." The Americans, for their part, have been willing "to suspend virtually all American operations—even in support roles—for the first few days in July to reinforce the perception that Mr. Maliki desires: that Iraq's security forces are now fully in control of Iraq's cities." However, according to this news report, "the deadline has provoked uncertainty and even dread among average Iraqis, underscoring the potential problems that Mr. Maliki could face if bloodshed intensifies."[66] The concern, clearly, is a return to the sectarian violence that characterized much of the war prior to the increase in the number of American troops, known as "the surge," early in 2007. In light of the violence that has been occurring in Iraq as this goes to press, that concern was prescient.

Under the terms of the Status of Forces Agreement, there would not be a total withdrawal of U.S. troops; thousands would remain in Iraq but with their role shifted from combat to support—primarily training and advising. They would also conduct operations "that the Iraqis could not yet do on their own, like emergency medical evacuation."[67] A paramount goal for both Iraq and the United States was to stress the importance of Iraq as a sovereign nation headed by a democratically elected leader (Mr. Maliki), and to ensure that, eventually, a sense of "normalcy" returns to that country. The SOFA allows for continued U.S. assistance "to strengthen the political and military capabilities of the Republic of Iraq to deter threats against its sovereignty, political independence, territorial integrity, and its constitutional federal democratic system."[68]

The last U.S. combat forces left Iraq prior to the December 2011 date negotiated in the SOFA; although an American military presence remains in that country, sectarian violence continues. Despite the goal of replacing Saddam Hussein with a democratic form of government, that has not yet happened. "By the time the American military left, Iraq had still not passed a major milestone in the life of any successful new democracy: the peaceful handover of power to an opposition party."[69]

In July 2016 the issue of the veracity of the claims of weapons of mass destruction that were the alleged justification for the war in Iraq came to the forefront again, when a British independent Iraq Inquiry Committee released a report that concluded that "Britain, like the United States, used flawed intelligence to justify the invasion, that Iraq posed no immediate national security threat, that the allies acted militarily before all diplomatic options had been exhausted and that there was a lack of planning for what would happen once Mr. Hussein was removed."[70] Despite the fact that Prime Minister Blair was advised by diplomats and ministers of their concern about the U.S. plan, Blair chose to override their objections and support Bush's decision to invade Iraq. The results of the decision to invade Iraq continue to haunt both Britain and the United States, and have affected both countries' foreign policy decisions subsequently. "The legacy of Iraq kept Britain from joining the United States in bombing Syria over its use of chemical weapons. It was also a factor in President Obama's decision to back away from a military strike on Syria's chemical weapons facilities, and to delay military activity there against the Islamic State."[71]

When he came into office in January 2009, President Obama inherited the situation created by Bush: disarray in Iraq, instability in Afghanistan, and the growth of terrorist groups, especially ISIS. How to handle these became part of the discussion and debate in the presidential election of 2008. How to actually address them became part of the foreign policy decisions that the new administration had to make.

If foreign policy is a continuous process, as we indicated in chapter 1, then how could an Obama administration turn aside or reverse the course of Bush administration policy? Or how could the new administration enact policies that would better reflect the changing political and security realities?

In the next chapter, we will explore the policies of the Obama administration in order to draw some lessons for the future of American foreign policy, bearing in mind that it is still too soon to understand the long-term implications of Obama's foreign policy decisions. Then, based on some of the general conclusions about American foreign policy, we will reiterate some of the basic themes and see whether some conclusions can be drawn about the future of U.S. foreign policy.

APPLYING FOREIGN POLICY CONCEPTS: RESPONSE TO SEPTEMBER 11

In this chapter, we looked at the decisions made by the Bush administration based on its understanding of the events of September 11. We now have a more complete understanding of what happened and why, as well as who was behind the awful events. However, at the time, the Bush administration felt that it had to respond, which it did based on what was then known, the advice of those within the administration, and also the underlying ideological perspective that was guiding the administration at that time. If you were an advisor to President Bush, and you knew then what you know now, what would you have recommended, and why?

In order to determine this, you need to identify the critical players at the time (e.g., the terrorist groups involved and the role of Congress, the military, the public, the allies, etc.), what position or positions each of them took on this issue, and what you think was in the national interest at the time. This all must be put into the framework of the proposed Bush administration U.S. foreign policy direction (unilateralist versus expansionist) as well as your own understanding of resources available to the United States, specifically, the use of hard versus soft power. Put another way, would you have resorted to the use of military power against either Afghanistan and/or Iraq or pursued a different option, and why?

The Case

On September 11, 2001, nineteen men hijacked four aircraft. They crashed two into the World Trade Center in New York and one into the Pentagon, and the fourth crashed in Pennsylvania, short of its target in Washington, D.C., when passengers fought back. Approximately three thousand people lost their lives in those attacks. One of the highest priorities of the Bush administration was to find out what happened and then formulate a response to the event.

The United States' allies rallied behind the country and invoked Article 5 of the NATO treaty for the first time in the history of the alliance. But outside of allowing AWACS aircraft to help patrol the skies over the United States in case of further attack, the United States chose not to seek an allied response.

Investigations into the attacks found that the hijackers were all part of the Al Qaeda terrorist network founded and led by Osama bin Laden. The men, all of whom were from the Middle East, were believed to have been part of a group trained in the radical *madrasas* in Pakistan and Afghanistan and to have received their terrorist training at camps in those countries. Through its investigations, the United States also learned that bin Laden probably was in Afghanistan, but the Taliban government refused to turn him over to U.S. authorities.

The period immediately following September 11 was a time of confusion and uncertainty for much of the United States. For the president, however, the attacks "confirmed what Bush already believed: The world was a dangerous place. Terrorists bent on doing harm were not stopped by a smile and an open hand, but by grim determination and a closed fist. International agreements and institutions could not protect the American people; only the might of the American military could." And for President Bush, "foreign policy, or more precisely, the war on terrorism, became the defining mission of his presidency."[72]

President Bush was determined that the United States had to respond forcefully to those attacks. But the question was where and how to respond. Any response would have to send a signal to future groups or even countries that the United States was a major force to be reckoned with. Clearly, the terrorists came from a number of different places and relied on different countries for support. Further, Al Qaeda, a nonstate organization, was the "bad guy" rather than any single country. The American public looked to the president for direction, and the polls showed that he had the support of the public. The Congress understood that this was a direct attack on the country and looked to the executive for a response, albeit with congressional approval. It would be up to the president to determine what to do next and to be sure that Congress and the public supported him.

What Would You Do If . . .

The time is October 2001. George W. Bush has been president for nine months, and he came into office after a disputed election. His priority was to begin to withdraw the United States from some of its commitments abroad and refocus the country's priorities. Rather than looking toward the traditional European allies, Bush felt that the United States should be strengthening its ties to Central and Latin America. Initially Bush was accused of pursuing an isolationist foreign policy, as he refused to endorse the Kyoto Protocol, and he withdrew the United States from the 1972 ABM Treaty as an example of how the United States would chart its own foreign policy course. September 11 changed the direction of U.S. policy, and the responses to that event would define U.S. foreign policy for the Bush administration and beyond.

What would you do if you were a close advisor to President Bush and he looked to you for recommendations about how to respond to the attacks of

September 11? By late September and early October, you have some essential information about the attacks, but there is still a lot that is not yet known. What are the options available to you? You know that you would have the support of the American people and Congress as well as allies for a military response, but against which country should the attack be directed? What should be the short- and long-term goals, and how will you achieve them? Given what you know now, including the consequences (both intended and unintended), what would you recommend that President Bush do, and why? And finally, although we can never know this for certain, speculate as to whether you think the outcome would have been different if Al Gore, Bill Clinton's vice president, had won the contested presidential election of 2000 rather than George W. Bush.

Chapter Seven

Obama and U.S. Foreign Policy

2009–2017 and Beyond

As we consider President Obama and his foreign policy legacy, an article in the *New York Times* published in May 2016 is especially telling: "President Obama came into office seven years ago pledging to end the wars of his predecessor, George W. Bush. On May 6 [2016], with eight months left before he vacates the White House, Mr. Obama passed a somber, little-noticed milestone: he now has been at war longer than Mr. Bush, or any other American president."[1] As a candidate, Obama campaigned on the need to end the war in Iraq. He was awarded the Nobel Peace Prize in 2009 for his desire to rid the world of nuclear weapons. Yet, he has left office with U.S. troops still in Iraq and Afghanistan, instability in the Middle East in general and, in particular, the civil war in Syria still raging, and amid remaining questions about how the United States should address the ongoing, and perhaps rising, threat from terrorism. Some of these events are the result of situations beyond the control of the president and the United States. Yet, ultimately, it was up to Obama to determine what was in the U.S. national interest and changing U.S. priorities during his administration. The full extent of Obama's legacy will not be known for a while, but even in the short term, some assessment is possible.

THE ELECTION OF BARACK OBAMA AND HIS FOREIGN POLICY DIRECTION

The 2008 election brought Barack Obama to office as the first African American president. Candidate Obama distinguished himself by his lofty rhetoric, which the country wanted to hear in the midst of two foreign wars and economic recession. By the election of 2012, the optimism that characterized the 2008 election was replaced by a sense of reality. Those who had supported Obama were disappointed that he did not seem to live up to all his promises, a task made more difficult by a divided government after the election of 2010. Those who did not support Obama felt vindicated when some of his promises were not realized. That said, Obama did manage to put into place the Affordable Care Act ("Obamacare"), which was the first major change in U.S. health policy since the introduction of Medicare in 1965. But it came at the price of political capital.

The start of Obama's second term in 2012 was characterized by increasing partisan gridlock domestically but also by chaos internationally. As of this writing in late 2016, civil war continues in Syria; the situation in Iraq, Afghanistan, and Libya is unstable; and there is danger that the violence could easily engulf the entire region. The resurgence of violence in Iraq raises questions about the long-term future for that country after U.S. involvement and serves as a dire warning regarding what could happen in Afghanistan. The civil war in Syria has created a massive humanitarian crisis while also raising questions about what, if anything, the United States should have/could have done earlier to address the situation. This question—what role *should* the United States play internationally?—became one of the pervading questions of the 2016 presidential election. (See the case at the end of this chapter.)

What has been especially disconcerting about the instability in the Middle East has been the belief (or fear) that it has contributed to the growth of terrorism. Whether rightly or not, many see the issue of terrorism tied directly to issues of immigration in Europe and the United States. What seems to have become a proliferation of terrorist attacks, alleged to have been perpetrated by individuals associated with ISIS, has led to an increasing sense of fear on both sides of the Atlantic. In June 2016, three suicide bombers who had allegedly entered Turkey from the ISIS stronghold of Raqqa, Syria, exploded bombs in the major airport in Istanbul, killing forty-two and wounding scores of others. While no group immediately came forward to take credit, experts believe that ISIS was behind it. This followed other major coordinated attacks in Paris in November 2015 that left 130 dead and many more wounded, and a similar attack in Brussels in March 2016, resulting in thirty-two dead and hundreds wounded. It was believed that at least one person, who was subsequently captured, was involved with both these attacks. Another attack in Nice in July 2016 occurred during Bastille Day celebrations resulting in the death of eighty-four and hundreds wounded. Although the latter attack was believed to have been perpetrated by a "lone wolf" who allegedly had sympathy for ISIS, it contributed to an atmosphere of fear, which is what terrorists hope to achieve.

The United States has not been immune to such attacks and was reminded of the dangers faced at home when forty-nine people were shot to death and scores hospitalized, some in critical condition, following a shooting at a gay nightclub in Orlando, Florida, in June 2016. Although the shooter allegedly pledged allegiance to ISIS, it remains unclear whether ISIS was involved in any way, or whether the shooter was simply stating his political convictions. This followed an attack in San Bernardino, California, in December 2015 when a husband-and-wife team attacked a holiday party, resulting in the deaths of fourteen people. The husband was born in the United States to a Pakistani family while his wife was from Pakistan. They initially connected online and then met in person in Saudi Arabia where they married. As posted online, the pair allegedly had been radicalized and pledged allegiance to the Islamic State.

During a volatile election season, these attacks sparked a major debate within the United States about immigration, access to guns, and what can be done to identify and stop terrorist attacks. The ease with which people can cross borders has been blamed for these attacks and raised fears that other attacks will follow. One result has been a backlash against immigrants and refugees, especially Muslims who are trying to escape the ongoing conflicts in the Middle East and parts of Africa. This anti-Muslim sentiment has been fueled by the growth of right-wing anti-immigrant parties throughout Europe as well as the rhetoric of the U.S. presidential campaign. That sentiment is threatening to obscure the aid and assistance needed not only by the refugees but by the countries that are facing extreme humanitarian crises because of conflict.

As seen by these terrorist attacks, nonstate actors are becoming more prominent players in the international arena; dealing with them is perplexing political leaders as well as contributing to the often-extreme political rhetoric. The most notable of these is ISIS, Islamic State of Iraq and Syria (also known as ISIL, for Islamic State of Iraq and the Levant, and DAESH, which is Arabic for the Islamic State of Iraq and Syria).[2] The structure of the international system has few provisions to deal with nonstate actors, whether nongovernmental organizations (NGOs) working for the common good or terrorist groups that are hoping to foment fear and even revolution. Increasingly, though, they are becoming realities that nation-states need to deal with. What is far more complicated is how to deal with so-called "lone wolf" terrorists, such as the ones believed to be behind the attacks in Nice, Orlando, and San Bernardino, who claim to be allied with a terrorist group, but who act on their own. The only way democracies like the United States can track such individuals would be to impose more draconian surveillance measures, which many oppose. As the Obama administration has struggled, so will the new administration as it balances ways to protect U.S. citizens without infringing on civil liberties.

The situation in other parts of the world is also uncertain amid the dangers posed by an aggressive China, the potential for a nuclear North Korea, and an increasingly assertive Russia, especially in the wake of its annexation of Crimea in 2014. In short, while any of these situations could be resolved peacefully, these, and other possible crises could derail U.S. foreign policy by creating new situations that will require immediate responses.

As we explore Obama's foreign policy and the legacy that he will leave, there are a number of positives that could not have been anticipated when he first came into office. Perhaps one of the most important changes was the Obama administration's decision to establish full diplomatic relations with Cuba. Initially announced by the two countries in December 2014, the move toward "normalization" and full diplomatic recognition culminated in the reopening of the U.S. embassy in Havana in July 2015. The last time there was an embassy in Cuba was January 1961; the embassy was closed and ties between the two countries severed at the height of the Cold War. While there were many within the United States who opposed the decision to change the relationship, many also applauded it as a sign that we were truly moving into a new era.

Similarly, not without controversy was the decision to negotiate a treaty with Iran to limit its development of nuclear weapons in exchange for lifting of economic sanctions. The agreement was negotiated in spring 2015 between Iran, the United States, and the other four permanent members of the Security Council (United Kingdom, France, Russia, China) plus Germany and the European Union. The agreement passed the U.S. Senate in September 2015 when Democrats successfully blocked a Republican resolution to reject the agreement, thus allowing it to go into effect. As of January 2016, the White House issued a statement that touted the successes of the agreement,[3] although this, too, became an issue in the presidential campaign.

In Paris, in December 2015, the successful conclusion of a climate change agreement to limit the growth of greenhouse gas emissions was seen by his supporters as another of Obama's successes as well as a credit to his ability to bring different nations together in pursuit of common goals. His opponents, however, disparaged the agreement, claiming it was another way in which Obama was undercutting U.S. economic growth. The lesson here is that politics can put a distinct spin on something that can be seen as being important for the greater good.

As he left office the lesson for Obama, as was the case for so many presidents before him, has been that despite the greatest plans, events will intervene that take priority and that can easily disrupt proposed foreign and domestic policy agendas. As Obama has been replaced by another president, the issue of his legacy—how he will be remembered—looms large.

CHALLENGES FACING THE OBAMA ADMINISTRATION

It appeared that the major issue of the presidential election campaign of 2008 would be the United States' place in the world in general, and the war in Iraq in particular. Writing in *Foreign Affairs* in 2007, then-candidate Obama confronted what he saw as the failures of American leadership, and he issued a call for the United States to "rebuild the alliances, partnerships, and institutions necessary to confront common threats and enhance common security."[4] Obama echoed many of those themes in a speech in Berlin in July 2008, when he said that "we know that sometimes, on both sides of the Atlantic, we have drifted apart, and forgotten our shared destiny." He then continued, "Just as American bases built in the last century still help to defend the security of this continent, so does our country still sacrifice greatly for freedom around the globe."[5] Once again, the emphasis appeared to be on the ideals of freedom and sacrifice that had been themes in U.S. foreign policy since Woodrow Wilson. But, unlike his predecessor George W. Bush, if elected president, Obama indicated that he was going to do this in a way that was consultative, with an emphasis on building and/or rebuilding the partnerships and alliances that were a mainstay of U.S. foreign policy in the past and that would allow the United States to regain its place as a global leader.

As a candidate in 2008, Obama was criticized during the primaries by his Democratic rivals and then by John McCain, his Republican opponent, for his naiveté in stating that he wanted to reach out to, and negotiate with, hostile countries such as Iran. But Obama remained adamant that the most effective foreign policy would not be based solely on reliance on military might, but must be balanced with cooperation, negotiation, and diplomacy. He remained generally true to these values during his tenure in office.

Going into the 2008 election, the image that had been painted of then-candidate Obama was of someone who was weak on foreign policy, at least compared with his far more experienced opponent, Senator John McCain (R, AZ). Obama's selection of his running mate, Joe Biden (D, DE), a senior senator known for his experience in foreign policy, helped deflect that charge somewhat. But it was assumed that in any McCain-Obama debate on foreign policy, it would be Obama who would be seen as too young and inexperienced to be president in that dangerous time.

However, just a few months prior to the election, the global economic crisis hit and eclipsed all other issues in the campaign. Here the Obama campaign quickly proved to be more adept and was quick to address the situation. Rightly or not, the United States was being blamed for the economic downturn that affected not only it, but also most of the rest of the world. A 2008 Pew poll found that "the U.S. image is suffering almost everywhere," due, at least in part, to the fact that "in the most economically developed countries, people blame America for the financial crisis."[6] Thus, the emphasis of the campaign quickly shifted to economics, although Obama also made it clear that, if elected president, among his first priorities would be foreign policy, specifically ending the war in Iraq, giving renewed attention to the war in Afghanistan, closing the prison camp at Guantanamo Bay, and, in general, working to restore the United States' position in the world. But to the American electorate, foreign policy was a secondary concern compared with the economy, a pattern that seems to be a given. This helped sway the public to elect Obama in an election that also brought a significant Democratic majority to the House and Senate.

Obama and Iraq and Afghanistan

After eight years in which U.S. influence internationally waned and its power—especially soft power—was undermined, many around the world as well as at home were waiting to hear what the new president would say and were eager to learn in what direction he would take the United States. As he made clear in his first inaugural address, Barack Obama came into office facing critical challenges to United States foreign and security policy. In that address on January 20, 2009, Obama identified what his U.S. foreign policy priorities would be as president. To all who were watching and listening, both at home and abroad, he sent these words: "Know that America is a friend of each nation and every man, woman, and child who seeks a future of peace and dignity, and that *we are ready to lead once more*" (emphasis added).[7]

Philip Gordon notes that simply "having a new face in the White House will itself do much to restore many allies' disinclination to work closely with the United States."[8] While that was true initially, the burden has been on the Obama administration to show that it can follow through on its campaign promises and that the United States can lead once again. But this has not proven to be an easy task. As the results of the Pew Global Attitudes Project noted, "When Barack Obama is sworn in as America's new president in January [2009], he will inherit two wars in distant lands, one highly unpopular and the other going badly, along with a worldwide financial crisis that is being measured against the Great Depression. He will confront the prospect of destructive global climate change and the spread of nuclear weapons to rogue states."[9] In short, President Obama began his presidency facing a number of challenges, both domestic and international.

Before his first year in office had ended, Obama set out his priorities clearly in a speech that he gave at West Point in December 2009: "In early 2003, the decision was made to wage a second war, in Iraq. The wrenching debate over the Iraq war is well-known and need not be repeated here. It's enough to say that for the next six years, the Iraq war drew the dominant share of our troops, our resources, our diplomacy, and our national attention—and that the decision to go into Iraq caused substantial rifts between America and much of the world." Obama then went on to note that while the war in Iraq was coming to a close, "the situation in Afghanistan has deteriorated" thereby allowing Al Qaeda and the Taliban to gain control over more parts of Afghanistan. And then he announced the "surge" of 30,000 additional troops to be deployed to Afghanistan for eighteen months in order "to seize the initiative, while building the Afghan capacity that can allow for a responsible transition of our forces out of Afghanistan."[10]

In this speech in the first year of his presidency, Obama made a few important points: not only was leaving Iraq and Afghanistan an important goal, but the United States simply could no longer afford to stay. Iraq and Afghanistan had already cost one trillion dollars but he also suggested "that some conflicts, no matter how morally worthy, are simply not worth the cost."[11]

In some ways, the course for the U.S. withdrawal from Iraq was set by the outgoing Bush administration. According to Leslie Gelb, when he was running for president "Barack Obama proposed a fixed deadline for withdrawing U.S. combat troops from Iraq, though few experts considered this a realistic proposal." Bush claimed that such a plan would lead to certain defeat in Iraq while the Democrats continued to press for a withdrawal. However, in November 2008, before leaving office Bush agreed to "a three-year deadline for the withdrawal of all U.S. troops after having insisted during the campaign that such a deadline would be totally irresponsible." It was that Status of Forces (SOFA) Agreement that became the starting point for the new Obama administration. What is especially important to note about the agreement was that neither this, nor any of the other proposals suggested, "linked withdrawals to an Iraqi political settlement, even though every counterinsurgency expert argued that this linkage was absolutely essential."[12]

Clearly, Iraq was not a war of Obama's making, and his administration consistently made it clear that it was not a war that he would have chosen to fight. That decision was made by his predecessor, leaving the United States committed for a number of years but now with an apparent end point. However, as Obama learned, withdrawing combat troops from Iraq does not equate with the end of conflict. Despite Obama's desire to negotiate a way to maintain a small military presence in order to ensure some stability in the country after U.S. troops left, talks between the U.S. and Iraq collapsed, and, consistent with the agreement, U.S. combat forces withdrew as of December 2011. "Without American forces to train and assist Iraqi commandos, the insurgent group Al Qaeda in Iraq is still active in Iraq and is increasingly involved with Syria."[13]

Obama had also made it clear that his focus would be on the war in Afghanistan, which he felt suffered under the Bush administration's attention to Iraq. In one of many speeches that he gave on the subject as a candidate for office, Obama claimed that by focusing on Iraq, "[w]e did not finish the job against al Qaeda in Afghanistan. We did not develop new capabilities to defeat a new enemy, or launch a comprehensive strategy to dry up the terrorists' base of support. We did not reaffirm our basic values, or secure our homeland." And he outlined the direction that his administration would take, emphasizing his main points: "The first step must be getting off the *wrong battlefield* in Iraq, and taking the fight to the terrorists in Afghanistan and Pakistan" (emphasis added). [14]

As president, as promised, Obama turned his attention to Afghanistan. In remarks he made on March 27, 2009, shortly after taking office, Obama made it clear that there would be a new direction in U.S. foreign policy: "So I want the American people to understand that we have a clear and focused goal: to disrupt, dismantle, and defeat al Qaeda in Pakistan and Afghanistan, and to prevent their return to either country in the future." He framed the changes in policy by noting that "our troops [in Afghanistan] have fought bravely against a ruthless enemy . . . . Afghans have suffered and sacrificed for their future. But for six years, Afghanistan has been denied the resources that it demands because of the war in Iraq. Now, we must make a commitment that can accomplish our goals." And in words that harkened back to the idealism of the past, he continued, *"That is a cause that could not be more just"* (emphasis added). [15]

With that, he announced the deployment of additional U.S. troops to Afghanistan to engage in direct combat with the Taliban and to help secure the borders, but also to train the Afghan forces specifically for the purpose of building an Afghan army. Clearly the goal was to strengthen the Afghan military "as our plans to turn over security responsibility to the Afghans go forward." [16] His hope was that the United States would be involved with Afghanistan for a limited amount of time and with specific goals in mind, and then leave. This initial deployment was to be followed up by the surge of troops announced in December 2009.

At the end of May 2016, the United States had more than 4,000 troops in Iraq and about 9,800 in Afghanistan, far fewer than the 200,000 American troops in the two countries at the start of the Obama administration. [17] Obama had authorized air strikes against terrorist groups in Libya, Pakistan, Somalia and Yemen, but Libya and Yemen as well as Iraq and Afghanistan remain politically unstable.

By targeting the military focus Obama was able to accomplish something that the Bush administration could not do: locate and kill Osama bin Laden. On Sunday, May 2, 2011, President Obama made the following announcement: "Tonight, I can report to the American people and to the world, the United States has conducted an operation that killed Osama bin Laden, the leader of al Qaeda, and a terrorist who's responsible for the murder of thousands of innocent men, women, and children." In his brief statement Obama also made it clear that "we must also reaffirm that the United States is not—and never will be—at war with Islam. I've made clear, just as President Bush did shortly after 9/11, that our war is not against Islam."[18] However, he also noted that the raid took place in Abbottabad, Pakistan, and in so doing, the United States was engaged in a military action in Pakistan, an erstwhile ally. The result was strained relations with that country at a time when the United States was still engaged in conflict in neighboring Afghanistan.

The civil war in Syria exacerbated an already uncertain situation in the Middle East. Unlike the uprisings in Tunisia, Libya, and Egypt that collectively formed what has become known as "The Arab Spring," the outbreak of violence in Syria in 2011 did not result in the overthrow of ruler Bashar al-Assad but rather led to an all-encompassing civil war. By 2012, fighting had reached the capital city of Damascus and the major commerce center of Aleppo, as the rebel forces battled the military arm of the government. According to a BBC news report, "The conflict is now more than just a battle between those for or against Mr. Assad. It has acquired sectarian overtones, pitching the country's Sunni majority against the president's Shia Alawite sect, and drawn in regional and world powers. The rise of the jihadist group Islamic State (IS) has added a further dimension."[19] How to respond to this created a dilemma for the Obama administration.[20]

In August 2014 the imminent genocide of thousands of Yazidis, who had fled their villages for the Sinjar mountains near the Iraq-Syria border to escape ISIS fighters who had threatened to kill them unless they converted to their brand of Islam, prompted U.S. action. Obama authorized air strikes against ISIS with assistance by Kurdish forces, Britain, and a number of other countries, which saved thousands of lives. Obama also made it clear, however, that he would not deploy American ground forces to fight in Syria.

Despite the success of this as a humanitarian mission, what remains controversial is that Obama mounted these attacks without congressional authorization. As air attacks continued against ISIS forces in Syria as well as Iraq, justified on humanitarian grounds as well as the need to send a signal to the terrorist group, questions remained as to whether the president needed congressional authorization, a delicate political issue domestically. This issue surfaced in the run-up to the presidential election of 2016, and will continue to be contentious for the new president.

Ties to the Islamic World

From the time that he came into office Obama understood that diminished relations with the Islamic world was one of the major results of the Bush administration policies and that he was in a unique position to try to heal that. Although he is a Christian, he had spent some of his childhood in Indonesia, the world's most populous Islamic country. Outreach to the Islamic world was important to mend fences as well as to establish credibility among the Islamic nations as they hoped to move past conflict. He began the process by making a speech about U.S. relations with the Islamic world in June 2009, about five months after taking office, and did so in a Muslim country, Egypt. Hence, the content of the speech had far-reaching consequences.

The decision to give the speech at Cairo University in Egypt was, in itself, fraught with symbolism. While some were puzzled by his choice of Egypt, which had been less than democratic in presidential elections as well as having a relatively poor human rights record, the White House stressed the importance of Cairo as the "heart of the Muslim world." Furthermore, the speech in Cairo would virtually guarantee a Palestinian audience, important if negotiations between Israel and the Palestinians were to succeed, as well as send an important symbolic message by choosing the first country to sign a peace agreement with Israel as the venue.

The speech itself was closely watched and parsed not only for what it did say, but also for what it did not. Obama began by recognizing the tensions that emerged between the United States and the Muslim world in general as well as acknowledging the need for a "new beginning between the United States and Muslims around the world: one based upon mutual interest and mutual respect." Then Obama outlined what he called "specific issues that . . . we must finally confront together," beginning with the need "to confront violent extremism in all of its forms."[21] In saying this, Obama echoed a point that he had made during a speech in Ankara, Turkey, a few months prior and that he would reprise in his statement following the death of bin Laden: *"America is not—and never will be—at war with Islam* (emphasis added).[22] We will, however, relentlessly confront violent extremists who pose a grave threat to our security. Because we reject the same thing that people of all faiths reject: the killing of innocent men, women, and children. And it is my first duty as President to protect the American people."[23]

In saying this, President Obama drew an important distinction between the Islamic people and the terrorists or extremists that attacked and threatened the United States and its allies. Obama made it clear that he understood the difference between a war of necessity (Afghanistan) and war of choice (Iraq), and that he would engage in the latter only when it becomes necessary. In saying this, however, he also stressed that his emphasis would be on the use of diplomacy and soft power: "I believe that events in Iraq have reminded America of the need to use diplomacy and build consensus to resolve our problems whenever possible."[24]

In identifying the issues that countries need to address together, Obama focused on many that were of special interest to his audience in the Middle East and Islamic world, including the countries of Iraq and Israel and the Palestinian people. And in a point directed especially to Iran, he spoke of the need to stop the spread of nuclear weapons. In a clear criticism of Egyptian

President Mubarak as well as other autocratic leaders, Obama also spoke of those who "once in power . . . are ruthless in suppressing the rights of others" and of how "you must maintain your power through consent, not coercion. . . . Without those ingredients, elections alone do not make a true democracy."[25] Implied in his words was not the rhetoric of "regime change" or "axis of evil," but rather, the recognition that ultimately it must be up to the people of the state to make decisions about their form of government. Clearly, the United States would help promote the ideals that are important by providing economic aid and assistance, expanding access to education, technological development, and so on. But to be effective, it would have to be a partnership, and the goals that he outlined could be achieved only if countries work together.

In retrospect, it is possible to ponder whether those words helped foment the nascent rebellion that led to the Arab Spring and the Egyptian uprising and overthrow of Mubarak in February 2011. What Obama could not have anticipated was the subsequent election of Mohamed Morsi from the Muslim Brotherhood and his ouster by the military in July 2013, leading to political chaos and violence in Egypt.

The United States and Israel

In going to Cairo and also in a separate meeting with Israeli Prime Minister Netanyahu, Obama also made it clear that the United States would again be an active participant in peace talks between Israel and the Palestinians. Working toward Middle East peace had been a priority of the United States in the past but had languished under the Bush administration. In contrast, Obama signaled early on that the United States would be actively engaged in the peace process once again. The decision to appoint George Mitchell as special envoy to the Middle East was another sign of the seriousness with which this administration took the Middle East negotiations. Mitchell, the former Senate majority leader, had been appointed by President Clinton to help negotiate a settlement in Northern Ireland, which resulted in the signing of the Good Friday Agreement in 1998. Appointing Mitchell was proof positive of this administration's commitment to the peace process.

Obama also made clear that the position of the United States is that Israel would have to freeze all settlement activities, a point that was reiterated by Secretary of State Clinton. After both Mrs. Clinton's meetings and President Obama's with both Netanyahu and Palestinian President Mahmoud Abbas, George Mitchell began negotiating with Israel and its neighbors. Despite these good intentions, however, Obama also learned that wanting something to happen in the world of foreign policy is not the same as making it happen. In May 2011 the White House announced that Mitchell was resigning his position "as the chief United States envoy to the Israelis and Palestinians amid growing frustration over the impasse in peace talks."[26] Not only did this put a temporary halt to the negotiations, but years of tense relations between the United States and Israel followed due, in part, to the difficult personal relationship between Obama and Israel's Prime Minister Netanyahu. With the appointment of John Kerry as Secretary of State at the start of the second Obama administration following the resignation of Hillary Clinton, resuming negotiations between Israel and the Palestinians became a high priority once again, as did "resetting" the relationship between the United States and Israel. Once again, these good intentions did not come to fruition.

In January 2015, in violation of established protocol, then-Speaker of the House John Boehner issued an invitation to Israel's Prime Minister Benjamin Netanyahu to address a joint session of Congress specifically about the negotiations between the United States and Iran. The speech was scheduled for March 3, two weeks before Israel's elections, thus making it a highly charged political event in both the United States and Israel. Obama refused to schedule a formal meeting with Netanyahu, and a number of primarily Democratic members of Congress refused to attend the congressional session. Although the two leaders did meet subsequently, a successful negotiation to the Israeli-Palestinian issue will not be part of Obama's legacy.

The "Arab Spring" and Civil War in Syria

Ensuring a more stable relationship between the United States and Israel for Obama's second term became even more important in the wake of the revolutions and unrest that swept the Middle East. A rebellion that began in Tunisia in December 2010 led to the ouster of that country's president, Zine El Abidine Ben Ali, in January 2011. Thanks to technology and the ease with which information could be transmitted, the popular uprising against autocratic leaders quickly spread to other countries in the region, including Libya, where fighting continued through the summer, ending in October 2011 when Gaddafi was captured and then killed.

Egypt, an important ally of the United States, was another country affected by the revolutions of the Arab Spring. In the midst of the political unrest, on February 11, 2011, Hosni Mubarak stepped down after more than thirty years as president, to be replaced initially by the military and then by Muslim Brotherhood candidate Mohammed Morsi following elections in June 2012. Morsi subsequently was deposed in a coup in July 2013 and was replaced as president by Abdul Fattah al-Sisi, the former head of Egypt's armed forces. He resigned from the military in March 2014 and ran successfully for president of Egypt. As Egypt is a major recipient of U.S. foreign and military aid, the instability posed a problem initially for the Obama administration. As implied by the president and explicitly noted by members of Congress, the more than one billion dollars a year in military aid that the

United States gives to Egypt would be cut off if Morsi's overthrow was deemed a military coup. Despite the violent way that the current government in Egypt came into office, at the end of 2016, it appears that the current government of al-Sisi has been accepted as legitimate by the people of Egypt and the international community and relative stability appears to have returned to that country.

In late 2016, it is the civil war in Syria that continues to bedevil the United States and its allies. What began in March 2011 as a popular uprising against the Assad regime has grown into a bloody civil war that had claimed the lives of more than 470,000 people as of February 2016, with the death toll rising daily.[27] In addition, the UN High Commissioner for Refugees has estimated that almost five million people have fled Syria, with almost nine million displaced within the country.[28] The ancient city of Aleppo has become a major battleground, divided between government and rebel forces since the summer of 2012. Seen as a major prize, it has been the focus of attacks that have resulted in the deaths of thousands of civilians, with hundreds of thousands more at risk. The situation is considered a humanitarian crisis, especially as fighting escalated in the wake of a failed cease-fire effort in fall 2016.

In July 22, 2013, the House and Senate both voted to approve the Obama administration's plans to initiate a CIA operation to send weapons shipments to opposition fighters in Syria. But this decision was not without controversy and it reflected the partisan politics already playing out in Washington, as well as illustrating clearly the complexity of the situation. On the one hand, Democratic members of Congress as well as those in the administration claimed that this would give the United States a position in the conflict and that "it will allow the administration to exert leadership and coordinate the many streams of aid flowing to the rebels from other countries, including sophisticated surface-to-air missiles coming from Saudi Arabia and other countries in the Persian Gulf."[29] They also claimed that this involvement would ensure that the arms would go to members of the Free Syrian Army rather than extremists fighting on behalf of President Bashar al-Assad and that it would help establish U.S. ties with the opposition movement. On the other hand, Republican members of Congress argued that this proposal did not do enough and that the United States should be taking a stronger stand. At a time when the United States was finally extricating itself from the wars in Iraq and Afghanistan, few members of Congress or the public would be willing to risk U.S. involvement in another war in the Middle East without any clearly defined national interest. Yet as the bloodshed and humanitarian crisis caused by the war continues, it raises questions about whether the United States and/or its European allies should have been more actively involved.

Writing in the *Wall Street Journal* in 2012 columnist Gerald F. Seib poses two important questions that continue to be worth thinking about not only for the Obama administration but also for the Trump administration that follows: "Does the U.S., with a shrunken checkbook and a weary military, have the power to steer events [in the Middle East]? And does the U.S., tired after a decade of war in Iraq and happy to be growing less dependent on Middle East oil, even care enough to try?"[30] The reality remains that the growing instability in the region threatens to spread unless the United States can find a way to work with other countries in the region and to do so without committing U.S. forces. Will this be possible? Too soon to tell. But what is clear is that the region cannot be ignored and that there are no easy answers that can be tied to U.S. national interest. Nonetheless, this, too, became grist for the presidential campaign in 2016.

Relations with Russia

Relations between the United States and Russia have been difficult, especially following Russia's 2014 invasion of Ukraine and subsequent takeover of Crimea. Nonetheless, the two countries tried to work together to address the crisis in Syria caused by the lengthy civil war. Despite differences as to the desired outcome—Russia supports Assad while the United States and other Western countries would like to see him gone—the members of the UN Security Council all agreed that the highest priority is negotiating and implementing a cease-fire. "'This council is sending a clear message to all concerned that the time is now to stop the killing in Syria and lay the groundwork for a government that the long-suffering people of that battered land can support,' U.S. Secretary of State John Kerry told the 15-nation council after the vote [in December 2015]. The resolution also calls for the U.N. to present the council with options for monitoring a ceasefire [*sic*] within one month."[31]

Following up on that starting point, early in February 2016, diplomats from more than a dozen countries, including the United States and Russia, met in Munich and agreed to a "cessation of hostilities," a temporary halt in fighting while peace talks continued. Unfortunately, this partial truce did not last and fighting resumed. Months of talks continued sporadically and then in September 2016, the United States and Russia brokered another pause in the fighting. That lasted approximately seven days before the Syrian military declared it over and resumed attacks on the rebel-held parts of Aleppo. Secretary Kerry was planning to meet with the members of the International Syria Support Group, the international body that has assumed responsibility for finding a way to limit the violence and to arrive at a peace agreement, but this meeting and the possibility of arriving at any agreement that would last has been met with skepticism. The cease-fire negotiated between the United

States and Russia initially was seen as a confidence-building measure between the two countries; instead, it has become another source of acrimony.[32]

While any agreement as to the future of the Assad regime is far from certain, as noted in the quote by Secretary Kerry above, countries are shocked by the killing of innocent civilians as well as being overwhelmed by the number of refugees who are fleeing the civil war and seeking asylum elsewhere.

It seems clear that President Putin is trying to chart an independent path for Russia even though that puts it in direct conflict with the countries of the West in general and the United States in particular. In March 2016, facing mounting international pressure, President Putin announced that "the main part" of Russia's forces would leave Syria having accomplished their mission—framing the intervention as a battle of good versus evil. Although Russia did recall a handful of aircraft, the reality is that it remains a major presence in Syria. In fact, additional attack helicopters were deployed for closer air support and antiaircraft missiles maintain a perimeter in the eastern Mediterranean. According to one analysis, on the ground "Russia seems to be running the show," with Russian and Syrian forces operating "on Russian terms."[33] In addition to bringing discipline to the haphazard Syrian military forces, Russian forces are involved in intelligence and targeting operations, Russian instructors train their Syrian counterparts, and Russian officers have been involved with brokering cease-fires at the local level. In short, Russia seems to be in Syria for the long haul.[34]

Russia's presence in Syria on the part of Assad not only complicates the situation politically and militarily, but also has created a real military threat to the anti-Assad forces. In November 2015, Turkish jets shot down a Russian fighter-bomber near the Syrian border, arguing that the plane had violated Turkish air space and that the pilot had been warned. One pilot survived but the other was killed as was a Russian soldier involved in the rescue mission. Putin accused the Turkish government of protecting ISIS and of allowing its oil trade to flourish across the Turkish border. Clearly, this incident shows how volatile the situation is, bearing in mind that Turkey is a NATO partner and any military confrontation between Turkey and Russia risks getting the Alliance involved.

Underlying all this is the significant difference in perspective, with Russia backing Assad and Turkey siding with the United States and the West. Other factors come into play on both sides, though. Turkey also has a vested interest in keeping Syria's Kurds from gaining territory that could be used against Turkey while Russia wants to protect Assad, a long-time ally. Turkey's ire has been further stoked by Russian air strikes against Turkomen (Syrians of Turkish origin) villages, which Russia says harbor Islamist terrorists. Turkey brought the issue to the UN Security Council. The reality is that neither side wants the situation to escalate any further. However, the situation caused increased tensions not only between the two countries, but with the NATO allies as well at a time when tensions with Russia were already high.

According to a BBC analysis of the situation,

> What began as another Arab Spring uprising against an autocratic ruler has mushroomed into a brutal proxy war that has drawn in regional and world powers.
>
> Iran and Russia have propped up the Alawite-led government of President Assad and gradually increased their support. Tehran is believed to be spending billions of dollars a year to bolster Mr. Assad, providing military advisers and subsidised weapons, as well as lines of credit and oil transfers. Russia has meanwhile launched an air campaign against Mr Assad's opponents. . . .
>
> The Sunni-dominated opposition has, meanwhile, attracted varying degrees of support from its international backers—Turkey, Saudi Arabia, Qatar and Jordan, along with the US, UK and France.[35]

Some argue that relations with Russia have become as tense as at any point since the Cold War. This, too, was played out in the presidential election campaign with Republican contender Donald Trump saying complimentary things about Russian President Putin, while Democrat Hillary Clinton said that the relationship between the two countries is a complicated one. Like many other areas in the 2016 campaign, how to approach Russia and Putin was one of the major policy differences between the two candidates.

Relations with Europe

Relations between the United States and its European allies were strained severely because of the U.S. decision to go to war with Iraq in 2003. The enmity that many in Europe felt toward the United States was heightened by the onset of the economic crisis, which, correctly or not, was blamed on the United States.[36] Obama initially met with many European leaders either individually or as part of summits, and he came into office wildly popular in Europe. Nonetheless, the lesson that Obama learned is that Europe is no longer an unquestioning ally, willing to go along with whatever the United States wants or wherever the United States leads. Knowing that, Obama has worked hard to reestablish relationships with the European allies.

Relations between the United States and its European allies, however, were strained again relatively early in Obama's second term when information was leaked that the National Security Agency (NSA) had been collecting phone and data records of millions of Americans. Added to that, it was revealed that the United States had also bugged EU offices, which drew criticism from European leaders and cast a pall over Obama's trip to Berlin following the G8 summit in Northern Ireland in June 2013. Pressed by German Chancellor Angela Merkel, on June 19, 2013, Obama said that "terrorist threats in her country [Germany] were among those foiled by such intelligence operations worldwide—a contention that Ms. Merkel seemed to confirm."[37] At a news conference with the two leaders, Merkel said that "she and Mr. Obama had discussed the surveillance issue at length, indicating that it took precedence over subjects like the global economy and conflicts in Syria and Afghanistan."[38] This latest issue in many ways overshadowed what the administration hoped would be Obama's successful reemergence on the world stage. His audience for remarks in Berlin on June 19, 2013, was far smaller than then-candidate Obama's trip to Germany in 2008, and while he remains popular in Europe, he has not lived up to the expectations that were imposed on him from the time he was initially elected.

The results of a Pew Global Attitudes poll show that in 2012, near the end of his first term in office and despite Obama's desire to distance himself from Bush administration policies, concerns remained about the ways in which the United States uses its military power. These concerns were exacerbated by news about the U.S. use of drone strikes to target perceived extremist groups in countries such as Pakistan and Yemen.[39] Also contributing to this has been the administration's inability to live up to its promise to close the prison at Guantanamo Bay in Cuba.

There are important lessons to be learned from the U.S. relationship with its European allies and the interaction between and among them. First is the fact that the individual president, in this case Barack Obama, has a direct impact on perceptions that other countries have of the United States. We can see this clearly with the change in attitudes toward the United States from the period of the Bush presidency to Obama's. Second, even though many both at home and abroad disagreed with some of the administration's policies, other countries still have confidence in the United States and in this president to lead. And third, even though there might be a decline in his overall popularity, there is still a belief in the importance of the relationships—political, military, economic—between the United States and the countries of Europe. That relationship, however, was threatened once again during the 2016 presidential campaign. Where candidate Clinton spoke of the importance of such relationships, candidate Trump disparaged them, thereby sowing seeds for the possibility of future mistrust.

The European allies have their own issues to deal with, as they have to determine how to respond to the results of the "Brexit" vote in June 2016 and the British decision to leave the European Union. Although it might appear that this has little to do with the United States, the reality is that the United States is tied to the European Union as a bloc economically; it is the largest trading partner that the United States has. Plus the possible break-up of the European Union raises questions about European security and what this might mean for NATO. During the campaign candidate Trump raised questions about the relevance of NATO in the wake of the Cold War, claiming that the United States is bearing too much of the burden for Europe's security. In contrast, candidate Clinton talked about the importance of NATO, especially in the face of a resurgent Russia. This difference in approach also reflects the divergence between the two candidates about Russia in general, with Trump talking about Putin in complimentary terms and hinting that the United States and Russia could (and should) work together to address the crisis in Syria and elsewhere, while Clinton called Putin a "bully." Prior to the end of her tenure as Secretary of State she warned Obama about Russia, claiming that relations between the two countries (Russia and the United States) were at a low point. This is another example of the difference in perspective between the two candidates, and also illustrates why the rest of the world watches U.S. elections, especially presidential ones, so closely. Clearly there is a difference between the rhetoric of the campaign and what Trump will do as president. Nonetheless, Trump's dismissal of NATO during the campaign and his assertions that U.S. support of the NATO allies would be contingent on their willingness to increase their financial contribution to the alliance have raised concerns among the European allies who are also facing their own issues. Uncertainty regarding the future of NATO and the strength of the partnership is causing consternation on both sides of the Atlantic and contributing to concerns about a resurgent Russia.

"Pivot to the Pacific"

China's rise as a major regional, if not global, power is perhaps one of the major challenges to the United States for any number of reasons. China is highly integrated into the global economy in general, and the U.S. economy in particular, which, to a large extent, constrains the policy options available to the United States. On the one hand, a sound argument can be made that China's integration into and role in the world economy suggest that it is unlikely to engage in any armed conflict that would disturb that balance. On the other hand, China's aggressive actions in Asia, and especially in the South and East China Seas since 2013, have resulted in tensions between China and the United States and its allies in the region, including Japan and the Philippines, but have also led to the question of whether China's continued ascendency can remain peaceful.

Hence, U.S. relations with China seem to be especially problematic. As the 2010 *Nuclear Posture Review Report* notes, "The United States and China's Asian neighbors remain concerned about China's current modernization efforts, including its qualitative and quantitative modernization of its nuclear arsenal." Moreover, "the lack of transparency surrounding its nuclear programs—their pace and scope, as well as the strategy and doctrine that guide them—raises questions about China's future intentions."[40] It is this uncertainty that is so problematic for the United States, but also for other states in the region that wonder about China's intentions. As a result, President Obama announced a shift in U.S. policy that has become known as "the pivot to the Pacific." Obama took the opportunity of a visit to Australia in November 2011 to announce an agreement that would expand military cooperation between the two allies and would enhance U.S. military presence in the region by deploying U.S. marines to a base in Darwin in the northern part of Australia. By framing the increased U.S. presence in the Asia-Pacific region as a cooperative agreement between the United States and Australia, a traditional ally, analysts said that it would appear to be a less-confrontational policy than the United States might otherwise have pursued, although clearly it sends a message to China as well as to other U.S. allies in the region and beyond that the United States will stand by its security agreements.

A Pew Global Attitudes poll revealed an interesting, and also problematic, shift in global perceptions about both the United States and China. According to the report, general publics around the world see a shift in the global balance of power, with China's economic might on the rise. They perceive that China will eventually surpass the United States as the world's dominant superpower. But overall, more people perceive the United States more favorably than they do China due in part to the belief that the United States is a better partner and more willing than China to consider other countries' interests.[41] That perception continues to bode well for the United States.

One of the highlights of the Obama administration was the successful completion of the Trans-Pacific Partnership (TPP), a free trade agreement that links the United States, Canada, and Mexico with nine other countries that border the Pacific Ocean. According to the Office of the Trade Representative, if approved this agreement would result in a number of benefits for the United States, including eliminating a number of taxes and tariffs that work against the United States, incorporating protections for U.S. workers, and adding environmental protections.[42] Nonetheless, pressure from Democratic presidential contender Bernie Sanders resulted in candidate Clinton's pledge not to put the agreement forward for approval, a position shared by Trump. Thus, at this time it seems unlikely that President Trump will submit the TPP to the Senate for ratification.

Relations with Africa

In addition to dealing with the changing power balance in Asia, the United States has been working hard to establish a role in Africa, a region that has long been neglected by the United States. Many countries are starting to recognize the important contributions that Africa can make internationally in a globalized world. However, Sub-Saharan Africa had generally not been a primary area of focus of U.S. foreign policy. Even during periods of civil war and genocide in countries such as Rwanda and Sudan, the United States remained removed from any active policies beyond verbally condemning the acts. Because Africa was seen as outside the U.S. sphere of influence, successive presidents, including Clinton and Bush, could not justify U.S. military intervention. As the first African American president and with a Kenyan father, Obama has stronger ties to Africa than any previous president. His decision to visit Ghana following the G8 summit in July 2009 was seen as an indicator that U.S. policy toward Africa might become more proactive in an Obama administration. And the visit of the First Lady to South Africa in June 2011 was also seen as a positive step. But the reality is that little has changed thus far in the way of U.S. foreign policy toward the continent.

That point became clear when Obama and his family visited three African countries, Senegal, South Africa, and Tanzania, at the end of June 2013. That visit was overshadowed by the illness of Nelson Mandela, who was then hospitalized in critical condition. Throughout his trip, in his various speeches, Obama paid homage to Mandela, although he did not make a visit to the ailing leader. He did take the opportunity to unveil what he called "a new partnership with Africa, one that would help sustain its recent run of tremendous economic growth while broadening the rewards to help as many people as possible."[43] Sub-Saharan Africa experienced 5.1 percent economic growth in 2015, and the IMF predicts 5.4 percent in 2016, and up to 5.7 percent in 2017. This is at a time of economic slowdown for both Europe and the United States. Trade between the United States and Africa has more than doubled in the past decade and Obama used the visit to stress the economic partnership between the United States and the countries of Africa.[44]

By coincidence, former-President George W. Bush was in Tanzania at the same time as the Obama visit, which could not help but create comparisons between the two administrations. While in office, Mr. Bush started the Millennium Challenge Corporation to direct aid to African states that tried to reform corrupt and undemocratic governments. He also initiated the President's Emergency Plan for AIDS Relief, or PEPFAR, which invested tens of billions of dollars to fighting HIV, and later tackled malaria and tuberculosis. Thus, while the policies of the Bush administration continue to remain suspect at home, his work with Africa has been applauded. In contrast, Obama's critics claim that Obama has not done enough for and with Africa. In response to that implicit charge, Obama has sought "to demonstrate his own commitment to improving the lives of Africans, announcing plans to bolster trade and investment, improve the delivery of electricity and expand PEPFAR to combat other diseases."[45] And Obama promised to return to the continent before his second term ended, which he did. In addition to his visit in 2013, in 2015 he visited Kenya and Ethiopia. Nonetheless, especially since 2014, with the rapid economic growth of some of the countries of Africa as well as the increased interest that China has shown to the continent, the United States has embraced Africa as an area that lies within its national interest.[46]

Other Challenges to the United States

As Obama looks toward his legacy, it is clear that the idealistic views he put forward at the start of his first term, to "rebuild alliances, partnerships, and institutions," would neither be as easy nor as predictable as he had thought or hoped. Rather, events intervened that deflected the path that he had hoped to take. Making Obama's task even more challenging has been an intransigent House of Representatives with a Republican majority that took power in 2010. While the country's founders advocated for divided government as a form of protection against tyranny of the government, they could not have anticipated the gridlock in Washington that has made it even more difficult to get legislation passed. The economic crisis that broke just before the November 2008 election had to take priority over all else. As promised, Obama ended the war in Iraq, although instability continues in that country. While the U.S. combat role in Afghanistan formally ended in 2014, a small American military presence has remained (although done without congressional authorization) primarily to provide air support for Afghan forces who continue to fight the Taliban and ISIS forces. What Obama could not have been imagined or anticipated were the revolutions that swept the Middle East and that continue to cause havoc in Egypt and Syria.

Furthermore, Obama has had to confront new threats: cyberterrorism and cybersecurity have become major factors in ensuring the security of the United States in a way that could not have been imagined even in 2008 when Obama was first running for office. Yet now this is a fact of life during an age in which technology is ubiquitous. Similarly, climate change presents an ongoing concern as changing weather patterns have contributed not only to major storms but also to unprecedented heat, drought, and floods in parts of the country. Issues of what feminist authors call "human security"—protecting health and preventing disease, access to clean water, equal educational opportunity, for example—also have been surfacing as more important globally as well as being challenging to deal with.

OBAMA'S LEGACY: THE FUTURE OF U.S. FOREIGN POLICY

The presidential election campaign of 2016 offered very different and conflicting views of the role of the United States and the future of U.S. foreign policy. While some of this was alluded to in the Republican primaries especially—the Democratic race focused more on competing economic visions—by the time of the major party conventions in July 2016, the differences were apparent. Republican candidate Donald Trump offered a dark vision of an America under threat, a claim aided by the various attacks that had taken place earlier in the summer. In contrast, Democratic candidate Hillary Clinton presented a picture of a strong country made stronger by decisions made by President Obama. The reality is probably a little of each.

In fact, there is little debate that there has been a resurgence of apparently terrorist violence, although as of this writing it still remains unclear whether some of these were "lone wolf" attacks or part of a larger plan perpetrated by ISIS. The Middle East remains in chaos, with the civil war in Syria a critical factor for both security and humanitarian reasons. The Israeli-Palestinian situation is no closer to resolution and the future of both Afghanistan and Iraq remains uncertain. A general election held in South Africa in August 2014 and then local elections held in 2016 raise questions about the stability that followed the end of apartheid and, as one of the continent's largest and most stable countries, there are questions about the country's future. The rise of the terrorist group Boko Haram has made the situation in Nigeria, an oil-producing country and member of OPEC, unstable. Refugees fleeing conflict as well as environmental issues in Africa continue to flood into Europe, raising questions about the responsibilities of individual countries as well as the international system toward these people who have fled their homeland. And while many of these issues and problems seem to be removed from the United States, the reality is that countries still look to the United States to provide guidance and leadership. The challenge for the new president will be how to address this range of international challenges without neglecting the many domestic priorities that will need attention. As candidates, Trump laid out a vision that would significantly change the direction of U.S. foreign policy, while Clinton focused on what should be continued even if tweaked a bit. There is a direct relationship between the domestic political situation and international issues and, as we have seen in a number of cases, regardless of how well or carefully a president lays out both a domestic and international course of action, events can intervene.

Foreign policy is not made in a vacuum. Rather, it is a response to events that have occurred while also trying to anticipate what might take place. As we consider Obama's legacy and what the new president has inherited, we must also be aware that despite the best planning, things happen that cannot be anticipated and that will come to the top of the foreign policy agenda. It is how a president deals with those that shape the legacy and how the president ultimately will be judged.

APPLYING FOREIGN POLICY CONCEPTS:
U.S. RESPONSE TO CIVIL WAR IN SYRIA

In this chapter, we looked at the foreign policy situation that the Obama administration inherited and the ways in which the president chose to respond. While in many ways the direction regarding Iraq was set by the previous Bush administration, the decision to initiate a military surge regarding Afghanistan was made by Obama and his advisors. Similarly, the administration's decision to authorize air strikes against terrorist groups in Libya, Pakistan, Somalia, and Yemen, was a show of U.S. military force as well as resolve. However, how to respond to the ongoing civil war in Syria has been a contentious issue both within the White House and during the 2016 presidential race. While some applauded Obama's cautious approach and restraint in deploying U.S. forces, especially in contrast to the previous Bush administration, others argued that there was an excess of caution that sent a message about U.S. weakness.

As Obama's time in office has ended, the next president will inherit this conflict. Regardless of the outcome of the election, both campaigns had to think about and address what they would do as of January 20, 2017, upon taking office. In many ways, the outcome of the election here was less important than the type of planning that both sides had to engage in *prior to* taking office so that they would be prepared on day one to begin to implement their agreed-upon policy.

If you were a foreign policy/national security advisor to one of the campaigns (Trump or Clinton), you know that one of your roles is to outline the options that would be available to your candidate regarding the situation in Syria. On Clinton's side, there is an extensive record of what she recommended when she was Secretary of State. We know that in the past, as far back as 2012, she advocated funneling weapons to the Syrian rebels, something that President Obama initially resisted but later authorized on a limited basis. She wanted to create no-fly zones and to implement humanitarian corridors as a way to protect the civilians on the ground. Again, this was opposed by the president, who did not want the United States involved in what could become another large-scale military involvement.[47] On the other hand, although Trump has often said that he was against the war in Iraq because he thought it would destabilize the situation in the Middle East, during the campaign he did say that he would deploy U.S. troops to the region specifically to fight ISIS. He also indicated his willingness to work with Russia in this area, especially as the United States escalates the fighting in Syria against ISIS. So each of the two candidates indicated that s/he would take a very different approach toward Syria. It is also clear that what is said in the heat of a campaign is not the same thing as what each would do should s/he be elected president. But it did give an indication as to the direction that each might take on this particular issue.

The Case

As of fall 2016, going into the presidential election, the civil war in Syria continued with no end in sight despite various attempts by the international community to negotiate a settlement. The war has brought with it a great deal of death and destruction; more than 480,000, many of whom are civilians, were estimated to have been killed as of February 2016, with the death toll raising daily.[48] Similarly, the number fleeing Syria or displaced within the country is in the millions and continues to grow. The virtual siege of the city of Aleppo, an ancient city in the northern part of Syria as well as the largest city in the country, has created a humanitarian disaster as the civilians trapped in the city have little food, little or no water, and limited access to medical care. And that situation has been repeated in any number of places throughout the country as the military forces of the government continue to fight with the rebel forces who seek to overthrow the Assad regime.

At various points since the war started in March 2011, the international community has attempted to mediate a peace between the warring factions. Under the leadership of UN Special Envoy Lakhdar Brahimi, talks were initiated in early 2014 but they broke down when according to Brahimi, the Syrian government refused to discuss opposition demands.[49] Brahimi's successor, Staffan de Mistura, focused on establishing a series of local cease-fires rather than seeking a comprehensive peace plan. His proposal for a "freeze zone" in Aleppo was rejected, but a three-year siege of the Homs suburb of al-Wair was successfully brought to an end in December 2015.[50]

The situation became even more difficult with the growth of ISIS forces in parts of Syria but also Russia's and Iran's intervention on the part of the Assad regime. Underlying all this is the significant difference in perspective with Russia backing Assad and Turkey, a NATO ally, siding with the United States and the West. The reality is that neither side wants the situation to escalate any further; the situation has caused increased tensions not only between the two countries, but with the NATO allies as well at a time when tensions with Russia were already high.

In January 2016, the United States and Russia led efforts to get representatives of the government and the opposition to attend "proximity talks" in Geneva to discuss a Security Council–endorsed road map for peace, including a cease-fire and a transitional period ending with elections.[51] The idea of "proximity talks" means that the two sides will be in different rooms with Staffan de Mistura, the UN Special Envoy for the Syrian crisis, going between them. The primary issue is whether Assad should remain in power (which clearly is the position of the government) or whether negotiations can result in a way for him to leave office. If the latter, then the question of what happens next remains. None of the options suggested thus far (i.e., handing power over to some of Assad's deputies, creating a ruling council, hoping a new leader would emerge), seems to satisfy all sides.[52] The situation has become even more complicated as the Trump administration takes office. The hard-line rhetoric of the campaign coupled with candidate-Trump's statements about working with Russia have created uncertainty about what U.S. policy is likely to be toward Syria both militarily and diplomatically. Meanwhile, as talks continue in fits and starts, the situation continues to fester with civilians bearing the brunt of the ongoing conflict.

What Would You Do If . . .

Going into the 2016 presidential election you are an advisor to one of the two major presidential campaigns (Trump versus Clinton). You know what your candidate has said in the past, but that is not the same thing as preparing a policy position that could be implemented as Friday, January 20, 2017, Inauguration Day. With the war in Syria continuing and negotiations faltering, growing tensions between the United States and Russia, each of which has a different perspective on the conflict and backs a different side, and with the growing number of civilian losses and ongoing humanitarian crisis, your job is to outline a strategy that will be acceptable to your candidate but also to Congress and the American people.

What would you do if you were an advisor charged with outlining that policy during the campaign? You know what the criticisms have been of the Obama administration, and you are also aware of the fact that as a new president, virtually the entire world will be looking to your candidate to see what kind of signal his or her response to Syria will send. Your job is to lay out the various options that are available, determine not only what will make the most sense militarily and politically, but also what type of signal the various options will send to the rest of the world, and draw a conclusion as to which is the most viable. As you explore the various options, you will need to draw on what each of the candidates said during the campaign but also prior to that. Recommending a particular option will also mean determining how you would present the desired outcome to Congress, which technically should approve any military option, and also to the American public.

Chapter Eight

The Future of U.S. Foreign Policy

Chapter 1 posed several questions about U.S. foreign policy, starting with why it is important to learn about the subject. The goal of this chapter is to tie together the themes and ideas raised throughout the book so that you can begin to answer some of those questions for yourself. Remember that in many cases there are no clear-cut answers, nor are there always objective "right" or "wrong" answers. Rather, the main point is that you need to know how to gather and analyze information so that you have the tools to better understand U.S. foreign policy.

It is beyond the scope of this book to try to speculate or predict the shape of U.S. foreign policy in the future. However, by looking at the past and understanding the ideas that have governed its development, you will be in a better position to understand what *might* happen in the future and why, as well as to evaluate what *did* happen in the past.

THE COLD WAR AS A FRAMEWORK FOR U.S. FOREIGN POLICY

The Cold War provided a clear framework for guiding U.S. foreign policy.[1] According to the realist theorists, power is the ability of one country to influence another to do what it wants or to influence the outcome of events. During the Cold War, "power" was thought of primarily as hard power (i.e., tied to military might), and foreign policy was based on the belief that it was necessary to maintain a balance of power between the United States and the Soviet Union. This did not mean that both sides needed to have exactly the same number of weapons; rather, it meant that there had to be a sense that if one side attacked, the other side had the capability to respond, at least enough so that it would not be worth it for either side to attack first (i.e., deterrence).

While it is not often placed in the same category as military might, economic power also has been used to leverage the outcome of events. The decision to "reward" a country by giving it financial aid or other assistance was one economic approach used during and after the Cold War to sway countries to a particular side. Conversely, imposing economic sanctions or tariffs to "punish" countries is an approach that is still used; removing those tariffs is another way to reward a country. For example, agreeing to lift economic sanctions was among the incentives for Iran to agree to the nuclear deal and for Cuba to open diplomatic relations with the United States. Hence, economic tools can be used to influence a country's position. In a world that has become increasingly interdependent, economic power is an important commodity.

The Cold War provided a framework that guided much of U.S. foreign policy. However, absent that framework, policy-making has often floundered with no clear direction. As we learned in chapter 1, foreign policy decisions should further the national interest. During the Cold War, it was relatively easy to determine what that was. After the Cold War ended, and prior to 9/11, it was much more difficult to identify "national interest." The events of 9/11 offered some clear direction but, as we have also seen, the subsequent emergence of new threats and challenges has made it even more difficult to steer a course for the future.

The Changing Notion of Power

One of the things that has changed most dramatically since the Cold War ended has been the very notion of what "power" is or means as well as discussions and disagreements about how the United States should wield the power that it has. It still is important to have economic power as well as enough military power to deter, defend, and protect as necessary, and both are considered examples of "hard power." As noted in the overview in chapter 1, the concept of power can be broadened to include "soft power." According to Joseph Nye, "Hard power rests on inducements (carrots) or threats (sticks)," whereas "soft power rests on the ability to set a political agenda in a way that shapes the preferences of others."[2] While soft power has always been a component of U.S. foreign policy, it has become more prominent since the end of the Cold War.

However, soft power carries with it dangers, some of which have become apparent in the wake of September 11, 2001. Where "soft power arises in large part from our values" and from the desire for other countries or for people in other countries to want to emulate the United States,[3] it also carries with it the risks that those values are, or are perceived to be, antithetical to the core values of another country or culture. The imposition of one country's values on another is known as "cultural imperialism," something that the United States has been accused of.

As noted above, Nye divides power into two broad categories, hard and soft, while Walter Russell Mead makes a further distinction when he divides American power in particular into four types: sharp (military), sticky (economic), sweet (culture and ideals), and hegemonic.[4] His point is that power can be looked at in any number of ways; American power is hegemonic because when the various types of power are applied together, as they have been since the end of World War II, they allow the United States to grow in strength and importance in the international arena. In his estimation, the United States has been so effective because of the use of the *full range* of the power that it has and has used.

Nye, Mead, and others who try to categorize power would affirm that there is a time and situation within which applying one or the other type in pursuit of national interest would be most appropriate. A major foreign policy challenge facing the United States is how to use its hegemonic power— the application of its military, economic, and "soft" power of culture, ideals, and values—and to what ends. Or, put another way, how and when should the United States assume that soft power is the best option versus resorting to the use of hard power, which is, by its nature, a less cooperative and more conflictual option? That is the challenge that the Obama administration faced and is something that future leaders will confront. After years of resorting to primarily hard (military) power with little success, should the country rethink its approach to power? This question becomes especially relevant in the face of an ascendant China, the rise of nonstate actors, especially terrorist groups, fraying security relationship with some of our allies, a Middle East in turmoil, and a host of other issues that the United States is confronting well into the twenty-first century.

U.S. Power and National Interest

By 1991, the Cold War was over. Since that time the United States has yet to develop a cohesive foreign policy framework that can guide the country through the many challenges it faces in the twenty-first century. Much as George H. W. Bush advocated for a new world order, Bill Clinton shifted the focus to the economy and globalization, and George W. Bush stressed the imposition of freedom and democracy, the reality is that U.S. foreign policy in the twenty-first century will be as much a product of reactions to various events as it will be the result of proactive decisions. As Meade notes, "Each generation of Americans must reinvent its country and its foreign policy to meet the demands of a world that, thanks in large part to our own success, is perpetually more complex and more explosive."[5] Barack Obama discovered that reality during his eight years as president.

As we look to the future of U.S. foreign policy, it is essential to go back to first principles and ask what policies are in the national interest and how that is determined. How should the United States use its power and its superpower status? Is the goal of U.S. power, as President Bush outlined in his second inaugural address, "to seek and support the growth of democratic movements and institutions in every nation and culture, with the ultimate goal of ending tyranny in our world"?[6] Is the goal, as Mead suggests, that the United States act as "the chief agent in a global revolutionary process through which liberal capitalism and liberal democracy are sweeping the world"?[7] Or is the goal "to join with citizens and governments; community organizations, religious leaders, and businesses . . . around the world to help our people pursue a better life," as President Obama stated in his address in Cairo?[8] All of these represent a liberal/idealist interpretation of the role of the United States, one tied to values and cooperation for mutual good. If those are the priorities, then U.S. foreign policy should be directed toward achieving those goals using the appropriate type and amount of power to achieve them.

The divergent views about the role of the United States and its use of power in a changing world can be seen clearly in the uncertain response to the civil war in Syria. Obama "generally does not believe a president should place American soldiers at risk in order to prevent humanitarian disasters, unless those disasters pose a direct security threat to the United States." In contrast, Samantha Power, the U.S. Ambassador to the UN appointed by Obama, believes in the "responsibility to protect" especially in cases where a state is slaughtering its own citizens.[9] Then-Secretary of State Hillary Clinton also believed in the need for an early and assertive response to Assad's violence.[10] Ultimately, though, the decision was the president's and, right or wrong, will affect Obama's legacy as well as international perceptions of the United States.

The Changing Notion of Threat

A "threat" is anything that endangers or potentially could endanger a country or its people. Since the end of the Cold War, U.S. foreign policy has had to confront the changing perception of threat. Traditionally, threat has been tied to military might, as threats were generally perceived as the dangers from one country attacking another. But in the twenty-first century, a threat could emerge from situations other than military attack or an attack from one country against another. It is not necessary to belabor the impact of September 11, 2001. Suffice it to say that the attacks of that day were one example of a direct threat coming from a nonstate actor—in this case an Islamic fundamentalist group. But other threats need to be considered as well, for they too pose a threat to the security of the people of the United States and will—or should—influence American foreign policy decisions.

The changing nature of the threat and the unknown dangers that can emerge in this technological and globalized age became especially clear with the leak and subsequent publication of hundreds of thousands of military and diplomatic documents by Pvt. Bradley (Chelsea) Manning. The release of those documents to WikiLeaks, an online international organization that publishes secret information generally obtained from anonymous sources, illustrates clearly how easy it is to obtain and publicly post information in this technological age. Even though Manning was subsequently found "not guilty" of the charge of "aiding the enemy," he was convicted of violating six counts of the Espionage Act of 1917. And this was only one of a number of cases of leaking classified information that has come to light during the Obama administration. As one news account of this case notes, "Private Manning's actions lifted a veil on American military and diplomatic activities around the world, and engendered a broad debate over what information should become public, how the government treats leakers, and what happens to those who see themselves as whistle-blowers."[11] Or, put another way, how much *should* the public know versus how much information is truly proprietary and essential to ensuring U.S. security? And who is to decide?

In a globalized world, as American companies such as Starbucks or McDonald's open stores in more countries, they bring with them the perception of American dominance. McDonald's is ubiquitous, and Starbucks has been able to make inroads in China and Japan, both tea-drinking countries.[12] On the one hand, this means that people in those countries are accepting the image that Starbucks is selling, which is tied closely to American culture. On the other hand, that success also represents an assertion of American cultural values that not everyone in those countries likes or accepts. It is also an indirect and very visible assertion of American power and influence—that is, soft power. And, as a result, has made the United States and its citizens targets for those who oppose our values.

Clearly, then, one of the characteristics of the globalized world in which we now live is a breakdown in national borders, as people, products, and ideas are transmitted easily from one country to another—communication between and among countries is virtually seamless. One can travel around the world in less than a day. Ideas and knowledge are shared easily, as scientists collaborate with colleagues in other countries using e-mail and computer technology or as information is published online. A globalized world means that contraband materials, such as weapons and drugs, can be shipped from one place to another virtually undetected. Illegal immigrants can move from one country to another, some seeking economic opportunity, others intent on terrorism. Infectious diseases, such as Ebola, can spread quickly as one person who is unknowingly carrying the disease gets on a plane and spreads it among fellow passengers, who then disperse and spread it still further.[13] Advances in technology mean that an individual or a group can hack into corporate or government computers, resulting in breaches of privacy at the least, or even chaos and extreme disruptions; we saw this in the summer of 2016 when the computers of the Democratic National Committee were hacked, allegedly by Russia. Each of these examples represents a security threat that can be addressed by a foreign policy response. For example, the decision to close a border or make it more difficult to enter a country, imposing stricter controls at entry areas (such as ports), and screening passengers for health problems are possible responses to the health challenges noted above. However, while such policies might be designed to protect the population, they are also subject to cries of human rights abuses, depending on the application of the policies.

It also should be noted that the traditional approaches to American foreign policy decision-making are not necessarily able to deal with these new and emerging threats; U.S. foreign policy is still premised on a threat coming from a country and taking a particular form. However, as the examples above show, the nature of the threat has changed. Although the Bush administration created the Department of Homeland Security in 2002 to try to address the terrorist threat (a threat by a nonstate actor) and restructured the intelligence community in 2008, no administration to date has arrived at a way to create U.S. foreign policy that can anticipate and respond to the changing nature of the threats or the full range of potential dangers that this country now faces. The inability to confront these threats and the difficulty in even identifying the sources of such threats are among the foreign policy challenges that the United States and other countries face in the twenty-first century.

Identifying threats from nonstate actors does not mean that other nation-states do not also pose a threat to the United States. In his State of the Union address in January 2002, then-President Bush identified three countries he called an "axis of evil"—Iraq, Iran, and North Korea. "States like these, and their terrorist allies, constitute an axis of evil, arming to threaten the peace of the world. By seeking weapons of mass destruction, these regimes pose a grave and growing danger."[14] Since the time he made that speech, the government in Iraq has changed, although the situation is far from stable. We have subsequently learned that Iraq did not possess weapons of mass destruction that could threaten the United States.

In 2015 Iran and the United States signed an agreement that would limit Iran's ability to build a nuclear weapon for at least the next fifteen years. Only North Korea remains a threat, if not to the United States directly, then certainly to U.S. allies and potentially the world, if it continues to pursue the development of nuclear weapons. In an indicator of how relationships can shift, Pakistan, a country that had been a strong ally of the United States in its war on terror, has become increasingly unstable as Taliban and other militant factions have become active around the border between Pakistan and Afghanistan. As U.S. forces withdraw from Afghanistan, there are questions about the future of that country after more than a decade of war. Under the leadership of Vladimir Putin, Russia has become more militant and aggressive in its foreign policy, resulting in growing tensions between the United States and Russia once again. China is another country currently vying for major-power status, a perspective that will certainly affect U.S. foreign policy. It has become the second-most-important country in the world economically and militarily, adding a wholly new element to the international system.

What this all suggests is that the United States is confronting more and different types of threats and challenges from other nation-states as well as nonstate actors or even individuals than it did in the past. This suggests that the United States needs to develop a foreign policy better suited to the challenges that the country is facing. This might mean injecting more diplomacy, thereby balancing soft with hard power. Or it may mean more reliance on allies or even military might once again. The critical factor should be to ensure that the foreign policy is appropriate to the situation and existing political and economic realities.

THE ACTORS AND THE DOMESTIC BALANCE OF POWER

In the first chapter, we talked about the actors who make foreign policy and the constitutional framework that was to guide this process. However, in the wake of 9/11 we once again see the emergence of a strong executive. Under George W. Bush Congress was willing to allow the administration to pursue policies that, in retrospect, might be seen as questionable. Among these policies were the circumvention of the Foreign Intelligence Surveillance Act (FISA) and authorization of wiretaps on American citizens by the NSA; the use of torture, such as waterboarding, on terrorism suspects; and the use of "extraordinary rendition" to send suspects to other countries for extreme forms of interrogation. These policies were all enacted in the name of national security and were justified as essential to safeguarding the security of the United States. What emerged subsequently have been charges and counter-charges about what information Congress was given, how much members of Congress actually knew and when they knew it, and what their role should be. Note that these policies are not confined to one administration. In 2013 it was revealed that the Obama administration had authorized the NSA to monitor phone and data records of U.S. citizens as well as allies, most notably Germany, building on policies put into place under Bush but also raising questions about the range and reach of the government. And as noted in chapter 7, the Obama administration's decision in 2014 to authorize air strikes in Syria and parts of Iraq was made without congressional authorization.

What history has shown is a pendulum swinging between the assertion of presidential authority and congressional prerogatives given in the Constitution if not to oversee that authority, at least to balance presidential power. The last time the perception arose that the pendulum had swung too far and that the president was abusing his power was during the administration of Richard Nixon. This resulted in passage of the War Powers Resolution and a belief in the need to check the power of the president. What followed was a series of fairly weak presidents (Ford and Carter), until Reagan once again started asserting executive power. What we saw subsequently under George W. Bush was an unapologetic assertion of executive power justified by events of the time.

Obama had the advantage of coming into office as a popular president and with a strong Democratic majority in Congress. Like Johnson before him, he also had a robust domestic agenda that he wanted to accomplish, including addressing the economic downturn and the crisis in health care. However, a political shift in 2010 brought to power a Republican majority in the House with a strongly conservative focus. Even the then–minority leader of the Senate, Republican Mitch McConnell, noted that his goal was to make Obama a one-term president.[15] Although this did not happen, the partisan politics of Washington made it much harder for Obama to enact the policies that he had hoped to. In addition to affecting his domestic agenda, it also made it much more difficult for Obama's foreign policy agenda, although Obama has become very effective at using executive action as a way to circumvent Congress.[16] This led to questions during the 2016 presidential campaign about "overreach," although Obama would contend that that was the only way in which he could ensure the implementation of some of his priority issues. However, this also set a precedent for future presidents.

ONGOING CHALLENGES TO U.S. FOREIGN POLICY

As we have seen, at the end of 2016, the United States faces a number of foreign policy challenges. The decisions made by Obama to respond to those challenges during his two terms in office have far-reaching implications for the future of U.S. foreign policy. It is clear that major events, such as 9/11, can dramatically alter the direction of U.S. foreign policy. Those are events that cannot be anticipated but, as we have seen, can alter the direction of U.S. foreign policy for decades.

As the United States inaugurates another president, the challenges remain and, in many ways, are even more difficult because of the range of domestic and international actors involved. As noted above, the very nature of the threat has changed, which, in turn, has affected the types of responses available.

One point that has been made throughout this book is that many of the issues that the United States will face are beyond the control of the country or its leaders. For example, few could have anticipated the Brexit vote; nor, as of this writing, is it clear when this exit will take place or what it might mean for the future of the United Kingdom, one of the most important allies of the United States. Although this will not directly affect NATO or U.S. security ties, the reality is that the exit will have an impact on all countries with which the EU interacts as that bloc struggles to determine its own future. This was completely unexpected and yet will force the United States to reassess its relationship with the countries of Europe both individually and as parts of both the EU and NATO.

The world of the twenty-first century is a difficult and complicated place, and it will be up to present, as well as future, decision-makers to determine how to frame foreign policy that will meet those challenges and also serve U.S. national interest.

Suggested Readings

BOOKS

A more detailed list of readings can be found in the notes for each chapter. Among the books that are especially recommended and are cited in the text are the following:

Allison, Graham T. *The Essence of Decision: Explaining the Cuban Missile Crisis.* Boston: Little, Brown, 1971. This is the classic book explaining the Cuban Missile Crisis.

Bacevich, Andrew. *The Limits of Power: The End of American Exceptionalism.* New York: Henry Holt and Company, 2008. This is one of two relatively recent books by Andrew Bacevich that offers a critique of current U.S. foreign policy for what he sees as the errors in many of the decisions that have been made.

Gaddis, John Lewis. *Strategies of Containment: A Critical Appraisal of American National Security Policy during the Cold War.* New York: Oxford University Press, 2005. Gaddis is one of the preeminent historians of the Cold War and all of his books are well researched and documented. This is one of the ones cited in the text.

Gall, Carlotta. *The Wrong Enemy: America in Afghanistan, 2001–2014.* New York: First Mariner Books, 2015. A reporter for the *New York Times* who was based in Afghanistan, Gall offers a very readable although disturbing account of the fighting in Afghanistan as well as the impact that the war had on the people.

Gordon, Michael R., and General Bernard E. Trainor, *The Endgame: The Inside Story of the Struggle for Iraq, from George W. Bush to Barack Obama.* New York: Vintage Books, 2012. This is a very comprehensive book that reviews U.S. policy regarding Iraq from the Bush administration to the present.

Gordon, Philip H. *Winning the Right War: The Path to Security for America and the World.* New York: Times Books, 2007. This relatively short book identifies parallels between the war on terror and the Cold War to draw conclusions about the future direction of U.S. foreign policy.

Herring, George C. *America's Longest War: The United States and Vietnam, 1950–1975.* New York: McGraw-Hill, 1996. This classic and concise description of the Vietnam War and U.S. involvement in Vietnam is straightforward and relatively easy to read and understand.

Ikenberry, G. John, Thomas J. Knock, Anne-Marie Slaughter, and Tony Smith. *The Crisis of American Foreign Policy: Wilsonianism in the Twenty-First Century.* Princeton, N.J.: Princeton University Press, 2009. Four scholars look at and compare the foreign policies of

George W. Bush and Woodrow Wilson to arrive at some conclusions about Bush's foreign policy decisions.

Judis, John B. *The Folly of Empire: What George W. Bush Could Learn from Theodore Roosevelt and Woodrow Wilson.* New York: Scribner, 2004. Judis puts the policies of George W. Bush into a historical framework by contrasting them with the policies of Theodore Roosevelt in his quest for American empire and with Woodrow Wilson's idealism.

Landler, Mark. *Alter Egos: Hillary Clinton, Barack Obama, and the Twilight Struggle Over American Power.* New York: Random House, 2016. This book spans virtually all of Obama's two terms in office addressing the major foreign policy and national security issues that the administration had to confront. It provides insight into not only Obama and his decision-making, but also Clinton during her time as Secretary of Defense, which has also helped inform her subsequent policy decisions. It also offers an interesting perspective into the decision-making process.

Mandelbaum, Michael. *Mission Failure: America and the World in the Post–Cold War Era.* New York: Oxford University Press, 2016. This book offers a comprehensive assessment of the United States and the foreign policy decisions that it made in a world that has changed quickly. Mandelbaum describes the U.S. penchant for nation-building, despite the apparent failures of this policy. While one could take issue with his thesis, the book makes a strong and well-argued case.

McDougall, Walter A. *Promised Land, Crusader State.* New York: Houghton Mifflin, 1997. McDougall is a diplomatic historian who frames the evolution of U.S. foreign policy in broadly conceptual terms, including what he sees as the role that religion has played in influencing many of the country's leaders.

Mead, Walter Russell. *Special Providence: American Foreign Policy and How It Changed the World.* New York: Alfred A. Knopf, 2002. Mead believes that Americans, and especially American leaders, are ahistorical. He goes back to the start of the country to arrive at some important and general conclusions about the reasons for some U.S. foreign policy decisions.

———. *Power, Terror, Peace, and War: America's Grand Strategy in a World at Risk.* New York: Alfred A. Knopf, 2004. In this book Mead elaborates further on some of the ideas raised in *Special Providence,* including further distinctions on the concept of "power" and what these mean for U.S. foreign policy.

Mearsheimer, John. *The Tragedy of Great Power Politics.* New York: W. W. Norton, 2001. Mearsheimer puts U.S. foreign policy and the emergence of the United States as a great power into a broad historical context that takes into account the emergence of other major powers. He takes us to the start of the twenty-first century to assess the major threats/ dangers facing the United States today and how the country is likely to meet those threats. Although more than a decade old, this book puts China's rise and what that means to the United States into some context.

Nye, Joseph S. *The Future of Power.* New York: PublicAffairs, 2011. In this update of his earlier work, *The Paradox of American Power,* Nye elaborates on and broadens his definitions of power, and what these changes mean for the future of U.S. foreign policy.

Sanger, David E. *The Inheritance: The World Obama Confronts and the Challenges to American Power.* New York; Three Rivers Press, 2009. David Sanger is a respected journalist for the *New York Times* based in Washington. Even though this book was published in 2009, it does an excellent job of laying out the foreign policy/national security challenges that Obama inherited and how Obama started to address them in his first year in office.

WEBSITES

Be aware that the specifics of a site can change, but you can go to the main page and navigate from there or use a search engine to find a site. The websites listed were current and active as of October 2016.

Government sites are particularly important for accessing primary source documents. Among the most helpful to navigate is the State Department site, http://www.state.gov. See the U.S. House of Representatives site at http://www.house.gov for the Constitution and other documents.

Copies of presidential speeches (especially recent ones) and related documents can be found at https://www.whitehouse.gov. This site then requires additional navigation to get to the particular places that are most relevant.

The main site for the North Atlantic Treaty Organization (NATO) is http://www.nato.int. From that point, it is possible to navigate through all important NATO documents, including the NATO Treaty. The main United Nations site is http://www.un.org/en/index.html.

News organizations are an important source for current information, including recent poll numbers. Some news sites require navigation to get to the desired story or information. Helpful sites are http://www.cnn.com; http://www.pbs.org; https://www.c-span.org/; http://www.cbsnews.com; and http://www.nytimes.com. Most reports from the Pew Research Center can be accessed through http://www.pewresearch.org, and global attitudes polls can be accessed through http://www.pewresearch.org/search/ with the search words "Pew+global+attitudes." Also see http://www.gallup.com for Gallup organization polls.

One of the most valuable sites is accessible through Yale University's Avalon Project. It contains a host of primary source documents often cited in this text. The general URL is http://avalon.law.yale.edu/.

Presidential libraries and universities with presidential papers are an important source for primary documents. For example, the Kennedy Library home page, https://www.jfklibrary.org, allows you to navigate through the various documents and digital archives for this president. The Johnson Library home page is http://www.lbjlibrary.org. Reagan's library home page is http://www.reaganfoundation.org. All of these require some navigation to get to the parts that are most valuable and germane. Specific sites for documents referenced can be found in the text, and all of them can easily be accessed through a search engine. The library then provides access to documents, digital recordings, and other materials through their own search engines. For a guide to different types of presidential documents, including website links, see the National Archives, "Presidential Documents Guide," which can be accessed at http://www.archives.gov/presidential-libraries/research/guide.html. The American Presidency Project, of the University of California, Santa Barbara, is also a wonderful source for presidential documents going back to the beginning of the nation. The site also contains a search engine. The home page is available at http://www.presidency.ucsb.edu/index.php.

Notes

PREFACE TO THE FOURTH EDITION

1. Walter Russell Mead, *Special Providence: American Foreign Policy and How It Changed the* World (New York: Alfred A. Knopf, 2002), 7.

2. John B. Judis, *The Folly of Empire: What George W. Bush Could Learn from Theodore Roosevelt and Woodrow Wilson* (New York: Scribner, 2004), 46.

1. SETTING THE STAGE FOR UNDERSTANDING U.S. FOREIGN POLICY

1. For a more complete description of these different approaches to American foreign policy, see Walter Russell Mead, *Special Providence: American Foreign Policy and How It Changed the World* (New York: Alfred A. Knopf, 2002).

2. For more detail on accessing specific websites see chapter endnotes and also the section on "Suggested Readings," especially the reference to specific web pages. Bear in mind that specific URLs can change. However, most of the primary sources are readily available through Google or other search engines.

3. See, for example, Don Oberdorfer, "Cuban Missile Crisis More Volatile than Thought," *Washington Post*, January 14, 1992; and Martin Tolchin, "U.S. Underestimated Soviet Force in Cuba during '62 Missile Crisis," *New York Times*, January 15, 1992. Both these articles describe what became known as the result of a conference held in 1992, thirty years after the Cuban Missile Crisis. For a more comprehensive and relatively recent book that includes new information about this event, see Michael Dobbs, *One Minute to Midnight: Kennedy, Khrushchev, and Castro on the Brink of Nuclear War* (New York: Alfred A. Knopf, 2008).

4. Mead, in *Special Providence*, notes that "foreign policy and domestic politics were inextricably mixed throughout American history" (26). That said, throughout the book he also condemns Americans, even those in positions of leadership and responsibility, for their "lack of interest in the history of American foreign policy" (7).

5. While many political science texts refer to the early period of U.S. foreign policy as "isolationist," diplomatic historians, such as Walter McDougall, make the point that the period is better described as "unilateralist." According to McDougall, "the essence of Unilateralism was to be *at Liberty* to make foreign policy independent of the 'toils of European ambition.'

Unilateralism never meant that the United States should, or for that matter could, sequester itself or pursue an ostrich-like policy toward all foreign countries. It simply meant . . . that the self-evident course for the United States was to avoid permanent entangling alliances and to remain neutral in Europe's wars." Walter A. McDougall, *Promised Land, Crusader State* (New York: Houghton Mifflin, 1997), 40. The concept of *unilateralism* thus describes a foreign policy through which the United States is engaged with the world although steering clear of formal alliances or political obligations.

6. "The National Security Strategy of the United States of America," http://georgewbush-whitehouse.archives.gov/nsc/nssall.html.

7. As we will see in chapter 6, the Bush administration justified the decision to go to war in Iraq based on alleged evidence that Saddam Hussein had weapons of mass destruction, an allegation that was subsequently disproved. A relatively new book, *Bush,* by John Edward Smith, makes the case that Bush's decision to invade Iraq was one of the worst foreign policy decisions made by an American president (New York: Simon & Schuster, 2016).

8. John B. Judis makes the case that "the end of the Cold War created the conditions for finally realizing the promise of Wilson's foreign policy." John B. Judis, *The Folly of Empire: What George W. Bush Could Learn from Theodore Roosevelt and Woodrow Wilson* (New York: Scribner, 2004), 7. In many ways, it also set the stage for the policies of George W. Bush, specifically the idealistic desire to spread democracy worldwide, which in many ways harkens back to the idealism of Wilson.

9. For a detailed description of the ways in which an American corporation affects other countries, see the three articles on "the Walmart effect" in the *Los Angeles Times*: Abigail Goldman and Nancy Cleeland, "An Empire Built on Bargains Remakes the Working World," November 23, 2003; Nancy Cleeland, Evelyn Iritani, and Tyler Marshall, "Scouring the Globe to Give Shoppers an $8.63 Polo Shirt," November 24, 2003; Nancy Cleeland and Abigail Goldman, "Grocery Unions Battle to Stop Invasion of the Giant Stores," November 25, 2003. Although the articles are relatively old, they do a great job of describing the relationship between Walmart and individuals in this country and other countries, and a range of other critical actors. The series won a Pulitzer Prize in 2004.

10. Joseph Nye, *The Paradox of American Power: Why the World's Only Superpower Can't Go It Alone* (Oxford: Oxford University Press, 2002), 9.

11. Walter Russell Mead, *Power, Terror, Peace and War: America's Grand Strategy in a World at Risk* (New York: Alfred A. Knopf, 2004).

12. Hans J. Morgenthau, *Politics among Nations: The Struggle for Power and Peace* (Boston: McGraw-Hill, 1993), 5.

13. According to Barry Hughes, core interests "flow from the desire [of the state] to preserve its essence: territorial boundaries, population, government, and sovereignty." Barry Hughes, *Continuity and Change in World Politics: The Clash of Perspectives*, 2nd ed. (Englewood Cliffs, N.J.: Prentice Hall, 1994), 79.

14. Cynthia Enloe makes a persuasive argument about the need to take women's experiences in foreign policy and international relations seriously. For example, she writes about why and how "Carmen Miranda's movies helped make Latin America safe for American banana companies at a time when U.S. imperialism was coming under wider regional criticism." This is but one example of the ways in which women's images have been used to shape international business and economics as well as foreign policy. Cynthia Enloe, *Bananas, Beaches, and Bases* (Berkeley: University of California Press, 2000), 124.

15. See J. Ann Tickner, *Gendering World Politics* (Cambridge: Cambridge University Press, 2001).

16. John Shattuck, "Human Rights and Humanitarian Crises: Policy-Making and the Media," in *From Massacres to Genocide: The Media, Public Policy, and Humanitarian Crises*, ed. Robert I. Rotberg and Thomas G. Weiss (Washington, D.C.: Brookings Institution, 1996), 174.

17. A series of polls released in June 2005 showed that public support for the conflict in Iraq was dropping. One poll found that 37 percent of those polled approved of the president's handling of the situation in Iraq, down from 45 percent in February (Robin Toner and Marjorie Connelly, "Bush's Support on Major Issues Tumbles in Poll," *New York Times*, June 17, 2005). A *Washington Post*–ABC News poll found that 50 percent of the respondents "now disapprove

of the way Bush is handling both the economy and the situation in Iraq." This poll also found that "support for the war is the lowest yet recorded in this poll" (David Broder, "A Growing Public Restlessness," *Washington Post*, June 12, 2005, B9). Also see "Bush's Approval Ratings Stay Low," CBS News, http://www.cbsnews.com/news/bushs-approval-ratings-stay-low/.

18. "Less Optimism about Iraq," Pew Research Center for People and the Press, May 1, 2008, http://www.people-press.org/2008/05/01/section-5-less-optimism-about-iraq.

19. Many foreign policy texts refer to the early period of U.S. foreign policy as a period of "isolationism," meaning that the United States was "isolated" (removed) from the rest of the world, preferring to focus within. In fact, I would argue that the United States was involved in a limited way of its own choosing, thereby making the word *unilateralist* more appropriate, consistent with the point made by McDougall (note 5). However, in contrast, Mearsheimer makes the case that U.S. foreign policy in the period between the two world wars really was isolationist, in that "the United States made no serious move toward a continental commitment when the war [World War II] broke out." In fact, he notes, from the period from 1923 to the summer of 1940, the "United States committed no forces to Europe," suggesting a return to the policy advocated by George Washington of remaining "aloof from" the wars in Europe. John Mearsheimer, *The Tragedy of Great Power Politics* (New York: W. W. Norton, 2001), 254. For purposes of this text, each term will be used to describe policies that are slightly different, as appropriate at various periods in U.S. history.

20. Eugene R. Wittkopf, Charles W. Kegley, Jr., and James M. Scott, *American Foreign Policy*, 6th ed. (Belmont, Calif.: Wadsworth/Thomson Learning, 2003), 27.

21. "George Washington's Farewell Address," September 17, 1796, http://avalon.law.yale.edu/18th_century/washing.asp.

22. Charles Francis Adams, *The Works of John Adams, Second President of the United States*, Kindle edition (Amazon Digital Services), 2010.

23. Mead, *Special Providence*, 14.

24. Mead, *Special Providence*, 17.

25. Mearsheimer writes that "the United States achieved great-power status in about 1898" and that "the United States was no ordinary great power by 1900. It had the most powerful economy in the world and it had clearly gained hegemony in the Western Hemisphere." Mearsheimer, *The Tragedy of Great Power Politics*, 234–35.

26. A joint U.S.-Soviet commission was established as part of the 1972 summit, when the two countries also initialed the SALT I agreement. The purpose of this commission was to begin the process for granting most favored nation trade status to the Soviet Union by the United States. The trade patterns between the two countries ebbed and flowed throughout the Cold War.

27. The U.S.-North Korean Agreed Framework of 1994 allowed for the export of U.S. oil to North Korea as well as assistance in dismantling its graphite-moderated nuclear reactors to replace them with water-moderated reactors, which is a safer method of nuclear power production. See "Agreed Framework of 21 October 1994 between the United States of America and the Democratic People's Republic of Korea," https://www.iaea.org/sites/default/files/publications/documents/infcircs/1994/infcirc457.pdf.

28. For a more detailed explanation of the various actors and their relationship to one another and to the "rings" of power, see Roger Hilsman (with Laura Gaughran and Patricia A. Weitsman), *The Politics of Policy Making in Defense and Foreign Affairs: Conceptual Models and Bureaucratic Politics*, 3rd ed. (Englewood Cliffs, N.J.: Prentice Hall, 1993).

29. See the Constitution of the United States, which can be found at the following website, among others: http://www.archives.gov/exhibits/charters/constitution_transcript.html.

30. For more detail as to the relationships among the various branches of government specifically regarding war powers, see Donald L. Westerfield, *War Powers: The President, the Congress, and the Question of War* (Westport, Conn.: Praeger, 1996). Westerfield goes through a number of cases and reviews issues of constitutionality as well as how "the sense of the Congress" plays a role in limiting the power of the president.

31. Article II, Section 2, Clause 2, Constitution of the United States, http://www.archives.gov/exhibits/charters/constitution_transcript.html.

32. Article II, Section 2, Clause 1, Constitution of the United States, http://www.archives. gov/exhibits/charters/constitution_transcript.html.

33. Article I, Section 8, Clause 11, Constitution of the United States, http://www.archives. gov/exhibits/charters/constitution_transcript.html.

34. "Truman's Korean War Statement," June 27, 1950, http://www.presidency.ucsb.edu/ws/ ?pid=13538.

35. The Tonkin Gulf Resolution is described and explored in more detail in chapter 4, "The Making of a Superpower: Cold War Foreign Policy, 1946–1980."

36. The Constitution made Congress the branch of government that is closest to the people. This is especially true of the House of Representatives, where all members must stand for election every two years. This means that they are most sensitive to public opinion.

37. The term *military-industrial complex* was coined by President Eisenhower in his farewell address, delivered on January 17, 1961, in which he said, "We must guard against the acquisition of unwarranted influence, whether sought or unsought, by the military-industrial complex. The potential for the disastrous rise of misplaced power exists and will persist." "Military-Industrial Complex Speech, Dwight D. Eisenhower, 1961," http://avalon.law.yale. edu/20th_century/eisenhower001.asp.

38. Article 5 states that "an armed attack against one or more of them [the parties to the treaty] in Europe or North America shall be considered an attack against them all." The full text of the North Atlantic Treaty can be found at the NATO website, http://www.nato.int/cps/en/ natolive/official_texts_17120.htm.

39. A report released by the United Kingdom in July 2016 by an Iraq Inquiry Committee found that "the decision to go to war had been based on flawed intelligence, and that the threat of unconventional weapons used to justify military intervention had been presented with a certainty that was not justified by the evidence," as noted by John Chilcot who led the inquiry. This has opened old wounds in the United Kingdom, as well as led to a scathing indictment of then–Prime Minister Tony Blair for his judgment. See Dan Bilefsky, "Chilcot Report Reopens Wounds for Relatives of Fallen British Soldiers, *New York Times,* July 6, 2016, http://www. nytimes.com/2016/07/07/world/europe/chilcot-report-families-british-soldiers.html.

40. Avery Johnson, "Sticker Shock at the Lumberyard," *Wall Street Journal*, August 11, 2004, D1.

41. "Twenty-Sixth Amendment: Reduction of Voting Age Qualification," https://www.law. cornell.edu/constitution/amendmentxxvi.

2. UNILATERALISM TO ENGAGEMENT

1. Mark Binelli, "'Hamilton' Creator Lin-Manuel Miranda: The Rolling Stone Interview," *Rolling Stone,* June 1, 2016, http://www.rollingstone.com/music/features/hamilton-creator-lin-manuel-miranda-the-rolling-stone-interview-20160601#ixzz4DwpmWUx1.

2. Jean E. Smith, *The Constitution and American Foreign Policy* (St. Paul, Minn.: West Publishing, 1989), 14.

3. Quoted in Smith, *The Constitution and American Foreign Policy*, 16–17.

4. Charles Tilly makes the point that the evolution of the European state system was tied, in large measure, to war (i.e., the means of coercion), especially at a time when the United States was being created and established. "As European states moved into the phase of nationalization (especially between 1700 and 1850 . . .) dynasties lost much of their ability to make war on their own behalf, and something we call vaguely 'national interest' came to dominate states' involvement or non-involvement in wars. National interest synthesized the interests of the dominant classes, but compounded them with a much stronger drive to control contiguous territories and populations within Europe, as well as a fiercer competition for land outside Europe." Charles Tilly, *Coercion, Capital, and European States: AD 990–1990* (Cambridge, Mass.: Basil Blackwell, 1990), 185. It appears that Washington and some of the other founders of the country saw what was going on in Europe and, understanding that drive for competition leading to war, wanted to keep the United States removed from it as much as possible.

5. Alexander Hamilton, *The Federalist Papers*, No. 24 (New York: Mentor, 1961), 160–61, and online at https://www.congress.gov/resources/display/content/The+Federalist+Papers.

6. James Madison, *The Federalist Papers*, No. 41 (New York: Mentor, 1961), 256–57, and online at https://www.congress.gov/resources/display/content/The+Federalist+Papers.

7. Walter A. McDougall, *Promised Land, Crusader State* (New York: Houghton Mifflin, 1997), 31–32.

8. See full text of George Washington's Farewell Address, September 17, 1796, http://avalon.law.yale.edu/18th_century/washing.asp.

9. The Farewell Address is well worth reading in its entirety for the way in which Washington perceived the country at that time, as well as for the argument that he made about what U.S. foreign policy should be.

10. Eugene R. Wittkopf, Charles W. Kegley, Jr., and James M. Scott, *American Foreign Policy*, 6th ed. (Belmont, Calif.: Wadsworth/Thomson Learning, 2003), 28.

11. Mearsheimer makes the point that "the phrase 'Manifest Destiny' was not actually coined until 1845." John Mearsheimer, *The Tragedy of Great Power Politics* (New York: W. W. Norton, 2001), 487, fn. 11. By that time, the United States was well into its westward expansion and had already acquired the Louisiana Purchase and the Texas territories.

12. "The Monroe Doctrine," http://avalon.law.yale.edu/19th_century/monroe.asp.

13. James Buchanan, quoted in McDougall, *Promised Land, Crusader State*, 92.

14. T. Harry Williams, *The History of American Wars: From Colonial Times to World War I* (New York: Alfred A. Knopf, 1981), 144–45.

15. Robert Ryal Miller, "The War between the United States and Mexico," http://www.pbs.org/kera/usmexicanwar/aftermath/war.html.

16. Mearsheimer, *The Tragedy of Great Power Politics*, 244.

17. Walter Russell Mead, *Special Providence: American Foreign Policy and How It Changed the World* (New York: Alfred A. Knopf, 2002), 14. In the first chapter of his book, Mead makes the case that U.S. economic interests were directly tied to other parts of the world through interlinked financial markets. This meant not only that "foreign money dug the canals, built the railroads and settled much of the West" but also that "domestic prosperity was threatened or ruined by financial storms that originated overseas" (15–16). We see many of these same patterns today.

18. Mead, *Special Providence*, 26.

19. Paul Kennedy, *The Rise and Fall of the Great Powers* (New York: Vintage, 1987), 180.

20. The Treaty of Chemulpo between the United States and Korea begins by stating that "there shall be perpetual peace and friendship between the President of the United States and the King of Chosen [Korea] and the citizens and subjects of their respective Governments." "Treaty of Peace, Amity, Commerce and Navigation Between Korea (Chosen) and the United States of America," http://photos.state.gov/libraries/korea/49271/June_2012/1-1822%20Treaty.pdf. This treaty also provided for trade on a most-favored-nation basis, established diplomatic relations between the two countries, allowed for the immigration of Koreans to the United States, and established mutual defense in case of foreign invasion. According to George Herring, although this agreement was part of the United States' search for markets, trade between the two countries was "negligible." George C. Herring, *From Colony to Superpower: U.S. Foreign Relations since 1776* (Oxford: Oxford University Press, 2008), 287.

21. The DeLome letter can be found at http://www.ourdocuments.gov/doc.php?flash=true&doc=53.

22. Note that there are parallels between the sinking of the *Maine*, which contributed to the outbreak of war with Spain, and the Gulf of Tonkin incident, which led to the resolution passed in 1964 that gave Lyndon Johnson the excuse to escalate the war in Vietnam. In the latter case, the U.S. destroyers *Maddox* and *Turner Joy* allegedly came under attack while patrolling the Gulf of Tonkin off the coast of North Vietnam, although at the time, they were in international water. This was seen as an act of war and gave President Johnson the rationale to go to Congress to secure passage of a resolution authorizing him to take "all necessary measures to repel any armed attacks against the forces of the United States and to prevent further aggression." (See chapter 4 for more detail about this incident.) The commander of the *Maddox*

indicated that "freak weather effects" and "overeager" sonar operators might have been to blame, rather than an actual attack. But it was clear that Johnson, who had the resolution already prepared, and Secretary of Defense Robert McNamara were ready to escalate the conflict, and this incident provided the opportunity for them to do so. See George C. Herring, *America's Longest War: The United States and Vietnam, 1950–1975* (New York: McGraw-Hill, 1996), 133–37.

23. "Not for Cuba Only," *New York Times*, July 30, 1891, http://timesmachine.nytimes.com/timesmachine/1898/07/30/105963836.html?pageNumber=6 .

24. The first Open Door note was sent on September 6, 1899, to Germany, Russia, and England. The second Open Door note, which was similar, was sent later to Japan, Italy, and France. Russia and Japan did not comply but went to war in 1904–1905 over control of Manchuria and Korea (the Russo-Japanese War).

25. "The Roosevelt Corollary to the Monroe Doctrine," Theodore Roosevelt's Annual Message to Congress, December 6, 1904, https://www.ourdocuments.gov/doc.php?flash=true&doc=56&page=transcript.

26. Work on the Panama Canal started in 1907, and it was opened in 1914. Its completion meant that the United States could move warships quickly between the Atlantic Ocean and the Pacific, which "transformed naval strategy" and, in fact, "changed hemisphere policy." But it also meant that "a deep distrust had been sown . . . in the minds of Latin Americans, about the ambitions and lack of scruple of American foreign policy." J. M. Roberts, *Twentieth Century: A History of the World, 1901–2000* (New York: Viking, 1999), 105.

27. Robert B. Marks, *The Origins of the Modern World: A Global and Ecological Narrative from the Fifteenth to the Twenty-First Century*, 3rd ed. (Lanham, Md.: Rowman & Littlefield, 2015), 127.

28. "Wilson's First Inaugural Address," March 4, 1913, http://avalon.law.yale.edu/20th_century/wilson1.asp.

29. The First *Lusitania* Note, May 13, 1915, https://wwi.lib.byu.edu/index.php/Wilson's_First_Lusitania_Note_to_Germany.

30. Daniel J. Boorstin and Brooks Mather Kelley, *A History of the United States* (Lexington, Mass.: Ginn, 1981), 448.

31. "Peace without Victory," address of President Wilson to the U.S. Senate, January 22, 1917, http://www.firstworldwar.com/source/peacewithoutvictory.htm.

32. Office of the Historian, U.S. Department of State, "U.S. Entry into World War I, 1917," https://history.state.gov/milestones/1914-1920/wwi.

33. "Wilson's Speech for Declaration of War against Germany," address delivered at joint session of Congress, April 2, 1917, http://millercenter.org/president/speeches/detail/4722. It is also important to note that in this speech, Wilson stated, "We have no quarrel with the German people. We have no feeling toward them but one of sympathy and friendship. It was not upon their impulse that their government acted in entering this war." In this speech, his words were very similar to words George Kennan later used in his "Long Telegram," sent from Moscow in 1946, in which he, too, drew a distinction between the outlook of the Russian people, and that of their government. This point is developed in chapter 4.

34. "President Woodrow Wilson's Fourteen Points," Wilson's address to Congress, January 8, 1918, http://avalon.law.yale.edu/20th_century/wilson14.asp.

35. According to John B. Judis, "Wilson understood that the war itself [World War I] was rooted not just in Prussian militarism but in a flawed international system that had encouraged and would continue to encourage war." Judis continues: "Wilson also understood that the United States would have to abandon its isolationist and imperialist approaches to foreign policy. . . . For Wilson, America's mission was not to create an empire, but a global democracy of equal and independent nations." To do so, the United States would have to be prepared "to abandon forever Washington and Jefferson's injunctions against 'entangling alliances.'" John B. Judis, *The Folly of Empire: What George W. Bush Could Learn from Theodore Roosevelt and Woodrow Wilson* (New York: Scribner, 2004), 96–97.

36. The Covenant of the League of Nations can be found at http://avalon.law.yale.edu/20th_century/leagcov.asp. This principle of "collective defense" the idea that all are bound together in the event of an attack on any one, is the cornerstone of Article 5 of the North Atlantic Treaty

that created NATO (the North Atlantic Treaty Organization) in 1949, after World War II. Article 5 states, "The parties agree that an armed attack against one or more of them in Europe or North America shall be considered an attack against them all and consequently they agree that, if such an armed attack occurs, each of them, in exercise of the right of individual or collective self-defense . . . will assist the Party or Parties attacked." The full text of the treaty is available at the NATO web page, http://www.nato.int/cps/en/natolive/official_texts_17120. htm.

37. Mead, *Special Providence*, 8–9.

38. For example, see Nancy F. Cott, *Public Vows: A History of Marriage and the Nation* (Cambridge, Mass.: Harvard University Press, 2000); Linda K. Kerber, *No Constitutional Right to Be Ladies* (New York: Hill & Wang, 1998); and Joyce P. Kaufman and Kristen P. Williams, "United States and Derivative Citizenship," in *Women, the State, and War: A Comparative Perspective on Citizenship and Nationalism* (Lanham, Md.: Lexington Books, 2007), 41–77.

39. Judis, *The Folly of Empire*, 37.

40. Judis, *The Folly of Empire*, 39.

41. Judis, *The Folly of Empire*, 46.

42. Herring, *From Colony to Superpower*, 367.

3. FROM ISOLATIONISM TO SUPERPOWER

1. Although the early period might be called unilateralist, I concur with John Mearsheimer, who makes it clear that "isolationism was the word commonly used to describe American policy during the years between the world wars." John Mearsheimer, *The Tragedy of Great Power Politics* (New York: W. W. Norton, 2001), 254. In this case, the distinction between unilateralism and isolationism is that during the period from about 1920 to 1940, the United States really did try to stay removed from the political and military events—especially conflicts—outside its borders. Although the United States did have some gunboats patrolling Asia at this time, their role was limited. A further indicator of the policy of isolationism during this period was that the United States chose not to respond militarily in the 1930s when Japan conquered Manchuria, nor when Japan and the Soviet Union clashed later in that decade (258).

2. According to Paul Kennedy, by 1917 the United States "produced half of the world's food exports, which could now be sent to France and Italy as well as to its traditional British market." Paul Kennedy, *The Rise and Fall of the Great Powers* (New York: Vintage, 1987), 271. Thus, the United States played an important role in sustaining the Allies' war effort far beyond just military support.

3. Quoted in John B. Judis, *The Folly of Empire: What George W. Bush Could Learn from Theodore Roosevelt and Woodrow Wilson* (New York: Scribner, 2004), 120.

4. J. M. Roberts, *Twentieth Century: The History of the World, 1901 to 2000* (New York: Viking, 1999), 333–34.

5. The Immigration Act was a direct reaction to the influx of immigrants that had risen to approximately one million per year prior to World War I. Unlike the welcoming notion of America as a "melting pot" that characterized an earlier immigration pattern, the new law tied immigration to country of origin and, according to Robert Ferrell, limited immigration to "3 percent of the number of foreign-born of each nationality residing in the United States in 1910. This reduced European immigrants to a maximum of 355,000 a year. . . . Congress passed it [the act] in the belief that millions of Europeans . . . were about to descend on the United States. By this time, the notion of a melting pot was in disrepute, and there was talk about 'alien indigestion.'" Robert H. Ferrell, *The Presidency of Calvin Coolidge* (Lawrence: University Press of Kansas, 1998), 113–14. Although the law restricted the number of people who could enter the country from Europe and parts of Asia, it did not place restrictions on immigration from the Western Hemisphere or the Philippines. As a result, there was an influx of immigrants from Mexico and the Philippines.

6. Clive Ponting notes that the act stopped the "very low level of black immigration" by prohibiting "aliens ineligible for citizenship." Since 1790, only whites could become natural-

ized citizens, thereby precluding nonwhite immigrants from entering the country. Clive Ponting, *The Twentieth Century: A World History* (New York: Henry Holt, 1999), 475.

7. The Washington Conference resulted in a number of treaties. Under the Four Power Treaty, signed in December 1921, the United States, Britain, France, and Japan agreed to respect one another's possessions in the Pacific. The Five Power Treaty of February 1922 committed Great Britain, France, Italy, Japan, and the United States to limit the number of their ships with more than 10,000 tons displacement. And the countries agreed not to build any more military forts or naval bases on their possessions in the Pacific. "Although the agreement gave Britain and the United States overall superiority, it allowed Japan local dominance in the Pacific." Ponting, *The Twentieth Century*, 256. A Nine Power Treaty was signed in February 1922, protecting Western interests by binding all countries to respect the Open Door in China as well as China's integrity and not to seek land or special privileges there. The result of these treaties was to head off a naval arms race and to stabilize the situation in the Pacific in the short term, although, as Kennedy notes, while Britain and the United States "economized during the 1920s and early 1930s, Japan built right up to the treaty limits—and secretly went far beyond them." Kennedy, *The Rise and Fall of the Great Powers*, 300.

8. In this phrase, the pact draws on the work of Carl von Clausewitz, who defined war as "a mere continuation of policy by other means." But Clausewitz concludes his treatise *On War* this way: "War is an instrument of policy; it must necessarily bear its character, it must measure its scale: the conduct of War, in its great features, is therefore policy itself, which takes up the sword in place of the pen, but does not on that account cease to think according to its own laws." Carl von Clausewitz, *On War*, ed. Anatol Rapoport (Baltimore, Md.: Penguin, 1968), 410.

9. "Kellogg-Briand Pact 1928" (The Kellogg Peace Pact, August 27, 1928), http://avalon. law.yale.edu/20th_century/kbpact.asp.

10. It should be noted that technically the pact remains in force today.

11. F. D. Roosevelt's first inaugural address, March 4, 1933, http://avalon.law.yale.edu/ 20th_century/froos1.asp.

12. Roberts, *Twentieth Century*, 367.

13. Roberts, *Twentieth Century*, 367

14. The entire speech is relatively short and well worth reading. F. D. Roosevelt's first inaugural address, March 4, 1933, can be found at http://avalon.law.yale.edu/20th_century/ froos1.asp.

15. All quotes taken from Roosevelt's first inaugural address. F. D. Roosevelt's first inaugural address, March 4, 1933, http://avalon.law.yale.edu/20th_century/froos1.asp.

16. In 1938, Mexico nationalized all foreign oil companies, about 60 percent of which were British and 40 percent American. Needless to say, this directly affected American interests. But by that point, U.S. concerns were elsewhere. Roberts, *Twentieth Century*, 375.

17. Roberts, *Twentieth Century*, 421.

18. Roosevelt's address at Charlottesville, Virginia, June 10, 1940, http://www. americanrhetoric.com/speeches/fdrthefourfreedoms.htm. Note that this link also has an audio version.

19. Roberts, *Twentieth Century*, 421.

20. Roosevelt's "Four Freedoms" speech, January 6, 1941, http://www.americanrhetoric. com/speeches/fdrthefourfreedoms.htm.

21. Roosevelt's "Four Freedoms" speech, January 6, 1941, http://www.americanrhetoric. com/speeches/fdrthefourfreedoms.htm.

22. See the "Atlantic Charter, August 14, 1941," http://avalon.law.yale.edu/wwii/atlantic. asp.

23. President Roosevelt's message asking for war against Japan, December 8, 1941, http:// docs.fdrlibrary.marist.edu/tmirhdee.html.

24. See Kennedy, *The Rise and Fall of the Great Powers*, 202.

25. Under political pressure, Roosevelt issued Executive Order 8802 affirming the policy of the United States that there shall be "no discrimination in the employment of workers in defense industries or government because of race, creed, color, or national origin." The full text of Executive Order 8802 can be found at http://docs.fdrlibrary.marist.edu/odex8802.html.

However, members of the military resisted the call for integration of the armed forces out of concern that this change in policy would affect military readiness. President Harry Truman formally ended segregation in the military in 1948 by "Executive Order 9981, . . . on Equality of Treatment and Opportunity in the Armed Forces," http://www.trumanlibrary.org/9981a.htm.

26. Executive Order 9066, signed February 19, 1942, states that "the successful prosecution of the war requires every possible protection against espionage and against sabotage to national-defense material, national-defense premises and national defense utilities." As such, it authorizes the secretary of war and the military commanders to designate areas from which "persons" may be excluded and, similarly, areas to which those people can be relocated. It is important to note that this order does not specifically name Japanese, but it was applied against that group of people, as well as some of German and Italian descent. "Executive Order 9066," http://historymatters.gmu.edu/d/5154.

27. Roosevelt's annual message to Congress, titled "An Economic Bill of Rights," January 11, 1944, http://www.fdrlibrary.marist.edu/archives/address_text.html.

28. It is important to note that Japanese cities were constructed largely of wood, so fire-bombing literally incinerated them. The city of Kyoto, the original capital of Japan (Heian), was spared specifically because of its historical importance.

29. See, for example, work done at the Ohio University Contemporary History Institute, a summary of which was published as "The Great Atomic Bomb Debate," by Bryan McNulty, in *Perspectives* (Spring–Summer 1997).

30. White House press release, August 6, in Robert H. Ferrell, ed., *Harry S. Truman and the Bomb: A Documentary History* (Worland, Wyo.: High Plains Publishing, 1996), 48; for the full text of the release, see 47–52. The text can be found online at http://www.trumanlibrary.org/whistlestop/study_collections/bomb/large/documents/pdfs/59.pdf#zoom=100.

31. White House press release, August 6, https://www.trumanlibrary.org/whistlestop/study_collections/bomb/large/documents/index.php?documentid=59&pagenumber=1.

32. Paul Kennedy notes that a "mix of motives" pushed the United States "toward the decision to drop the bomb—the wish to save allied casualties, the desire to send a warning to Stalin, the need to justify the vast expenses of the atomic project," all of which are still debated. What is not debated is that dropping the atomic bombs "marked the beginning of a new order in world affairs." Kennedy, *The Rise and Fall of the Great Powers*, 356–57. And Bill Gordon, scholar of Japanese history and culture, writes, "The concerns of top American leaders about the Soviet Union's future actions had the most significant influence on President Truman's deliberations on whether or not to drop the atomic bomb on Japan. If America did not drop the bomb in order to demonstrate its military superiority, American leaders had concerns that the Soviet Union would occupy Manchuria and would share the occupation of Japan with the U.S. . . . In addition, American leaders believed that dropping of the bomb would strengthen their position in future dealings with the Soviet Union concerning their sphere of influence in Eastern Europe." Bill Gordon, "Reflections on Hiroshima," http://wgordon.web.wesleyan.edu/papers/hiroshim.htm.

33. Townsend Hoopes and Douglas Brinkley, *FDR and the Creation of the U.N.* (New Haven, Conn.: Yale University Press, 1997), 9.

34. The Atlantic Charter reaffirms that "all nations of the world, for realistic as well as spiritual reasons must come to the abandonment of the use of force. Since no future peace can be maintained if land, sea or air armaments continue to be employed by nations which threaten, or may threaten, aggression outside of their frontiers, they believe, *pending an establishment of a wider system of general security, that the disarmament of such nations is essential*" (emphasis added). Atlantic Charter, August 14, 1941, http://avalon.law.yale.edu/wwii/atlantic.asp.

35. Quoted in Hoopes and Brinkley, *FDR and the Creation of the U.N.*, 40.

36. See "Declaration of the United Nations," http://avalon.law.yale.edu/20th_century/decade03.asp.

37. Chiang Kai-shek was the leader of China at the time. Prior to World War II, Chiang had been fighting a civil war against Mao Tse-tung (Mao Zedong), the leader of the communist forces. The civil war resumed after World War II ended and resulted in Mao's victory over the nationalist forces led by Chiang. In 1949, Chiang Kai-shek and his troops fled mainland China

for the island of Taiwan, and on October 1, Mao and the communists declared the creation of the People's Republic of China.

38. Franklin D. Roosevelt, "Fireside Chat," December 24, 1943, online at Gerhard Peters and John T. Woolley's *The American Presidency Project*, http://www.presidency.ucsb.edu/ws/index.php?pid=16356.

39. "Proposals for the Establishment of a General International Organization," Dumbarton Oaks, October 7, 1944, http://www.unmultimedia.org/searchers/yearbook/page.jsp?volume=1946-47&bookpage=4.

40. Bill Gordon, "Reflections on Hiroshima," http://wgordon.web.wesleyan.edu/papers/hiroshim.htm.

41. Bill Gordon, "Reflections on Hiroshima," http://wgordon.web.wesleyan.edu/papers/hiroshim.htm.

42. McNulty, "The Great Atomic Bomb Debate," *Perspectives* (Spring-Summer 1997).

43. Bruce Stokes, "70 Years after Hiroshima, Opinions Have Shifted on Use of Atomic Bomb," *Pew Research Center*, August 5, 2015, http://www.pewresearch.org/fact-tank/2015/08/04/70-years-after-hiroshima-opinions-have-shifted-on-use-of-atomic-bomb/.

44. Arthur H. Vandenberg, Jr., quoted in George C. Herring, *From Colony to Superpower: U.S. Foreign Relations since 1776* (Oxford: Oxford University Press, 2008), 538–39.

45. "The Manhattan Project: Making the Atomic Bomb," *Atomic Archive*, http://www.atomicarchive.com/History/mp/introduction.shtml.

46. "The Manhattan Project: Making the Atomic Bomb," *Atomic Archive*, http://www.atomicarchive.com/History/mp/introduction.shtml.

47. "Potsdam Declaration: Proclamation Defining Terms for Japanese Surrender," issued at Potsdam, July 26, 1945, *Atomic Archive*, http://www.atomicarchive.com/Docs/Hiroshima/Potsdam.shtml.

48. "Potsdam Declaration: Proclamation Defining Terms for Japanese Surrender," issued at Potsdam, July 26, 1945, *Atomic Archive*, http://www.atomicarchive.com/Docs/Hiroshima/Potsdam.shtml.

49. "White House Press Release on Hiroshima: Statement by the President of the United States," http://www.atomicarchive.com/Docs/Hiroshima/PRHiroshima.shtml.

50. "White House Press Release on Hiroshima: Statement by the President of the United States," http://www.atomicarchive.com/Docs/Hiroshima/PRHiroshima.shtml.

4. THE MAKING OF A SUPERPOWER

1. According to John Mearsheimer, "When the Third Reich finally collapsed in April 1945, the Soviet Union was left standing as the most powerful state in Europe. Imperial Japan collapsed four months later (August 1945) leaving the Soviet Union also as the most powerful state in Northeast Asia. . . . The United States was the only state powerful enough to contain Soviet expansion." John Mearsheimer, *The Tragedy of Great Power Politics* (New York: W. W. Norton, 2001), 322.

2. On the role of economics as part of the U.S. policy of containment, Walter Russell Mead notes, "The progress toward free trade and the development of an international legal and political system that supported successive waves of expansion and integration across the entire world economy is one of the great (and unheralded) triumphs of American foreign policy in the second half of the twentieth century." He considers this policy "very much an element of the overall grand strategy of containing communism in part through creating a prosperous and integrated noncommunist world." Walter Russell Mead, *Power, Terror, Peace, and War: America's Grand Strategy in a World at Risk* (New York: Alfred A. Knopf, 2004), 33–34.

3. See Roosevelt's "The Four Freedoms" speech, January 6, 1941, http://www.americanrhetoric.com/speeches/fdrthefourfreedoms.htm.

4. Harry S. Truman: "Address on Foreign Policy at the Navy Day Celebration in New York City.," October 27, 1945, online at Gerhard Peters and John T. Woolley's *The American Presidency Project*, http://www.presidency.ucsb.edu/ws/?pid=12304.

5. Truman: "Address on Foreign Policy at the Navy Day Celebration in New York City.," October 27, 1945, http://www.presidency.ucsb.edu/ws/?pid=12304.

6. "Speech Delivered by J. V. Stalin at a meeting of Voters of the Stalin Electoral District, Moscow," February 9, 1946, http://www.marx2mao.com/Stalin/SS46.html.

7. Referring to Kennan, John Lewis Gaddis writes, "Rarely in the course of diplomacy does an individual manage to express within a single document, ideas of such force and persuasiveness that they immediately change a nation's foreign policy. That was the effect, though, of the 8,000-word telegram dispatched from Moscow by Kennan on February 22, 1946." John Lewis Gaddis, *Strategies of Containment: A Critical Appraisal of American National Security Policy during the Cold War* (New York: Oxford University Press, 2005), 18–19.

8. All quotes here and in the following paragraphs are taken from George Kennan, "861.00/2 - 2246: Telegram," "The Long Telegram," February 22, 1946, http://nsarchive.gwu.edu/coldwar/documents/episode-1/kennan.htm.

9. Kennan included in the list of potentially vulnerable countries Germany, Argentina, and parts of the Middle East. He also identified Iran as one of the countries of "strategic necessity" to the United States. See George Kennan, "861.00/2 - 2246: Telegram," "The Long Telegram," February 22, 1946, http://nsarchive.gwu.edu/coldwar/documents/episode-1/kennan.htm.

10. On September 27, 1946, Soviet ambassador to the United States Nikolai Novikov sent a cable back to Moscow in which he described U.S. foreign policy as expansionistic and part of a drive for world hegemony. Although parts of Novikov's analysis were questioned and Novikov apparently also was dissatisfied with the result of the document, as one observer notes, "The general picture of the world they [Novikov and Kennan] painted was essentially the same: a dichotomous cleavage—on one side the powers of good, on the other, evil." Viktor L. Mal'kov, "Commentary," in *Origins of the Cold War: The Novikov, Kennan, and Roberts "Long Telegrams" of 1946*, ed. Kenneth M. Jensen (Washington, D.C.: United States Institute of Peace Press, 1993), 75. It is well worth reading the three telegrams, by Kennan, Novikov, and Frank Roberts (British chargé d'affaires in Moscow) for the picture each paints of the emerging Cold War.

11. George Kennan, "The Sources of Soviet Conduct," originally in *Foreign Affairs*, July 1947, found in its entirety at https://www.foreignaffairs.com/articles/russian-federation/1947-07-01/sources-soviet-conduct. All quotes from this article in the following paragraphs are from this source.

12. Kennan, "The Sources of Soviet Conduct."

13. Harry S. Truman, "Special Message to the Congress on Greece and Turkey," "Truman Doctrine," March 12, 1947, http://avalon.law.yale.edu/20th_century/trudoc.asp. All quotes in the paragraphs that follow are also from this source.

14. The structure of the Department of Homeland Security was outlined by President Bush in June 2002. The legislation formally creating the agency was passed by the U.S. Congress and signed by the president in November 2002. The text of the act (Public Law 107-296) that created the Department of Homeland Security can be found at http://www.dhs.gov/xlibrary/assets/hr_5005_enr.pdf. This change was followed by sweeping changes to the intelligence community with congressional passage of the Intelligence Reform and Terrorism Prevention Act of 2004 (IRTPA). "The IRTPA created the Office of the Director of National Intelligence (ODNI) to oversee a 17-organization Intelligence Community (IC) and improve information sharing, promote a strategic, unified direction, and ensure integration across the nation's IC." ODNI Fact Sheet, https://www.dni.gov/files/documents/ODNI%20Fact%20Sheet_2011.pdf.

15. The full text of the National Security Act of 1947 (Public Law 80-253) with some supporting documentation can be found at http://global.oup.com/us/companion.websites/9780195385168/resources/chapter10/nsa/nsa.pdf.

16. The National Security Act of 1947 gave each of the three military branches (Army, Navy, and newly created Air Force) its own civilian service secretary. In 1949, the National Security Act was amended "to give the Secretary of Defense more power over the individual services and their secretaries." U.S. Department of State, National Security Act of 1947, http://global.oup.com/us/companion.websites/9780195385168/resources/chapter10/nsa/nsa.pdf.

17. See the full text of the "Marshall Plan" speech, given on June 4, 1947, at Harvard University, http://www.oecd.org/general/themarshallplanspeechatharvarduniversity5june1947. htm.

18. The full text of the North Atlantic Treaty can be found at the NATO website, http://www.nato.int/cps/en/natolive/official_texts_17120.htm. When the treaty was drafted, the stipulation of collective security/defense outlined in Article 5 was assumed to be directed at a Soviet attack from the east on Western Europe, probably an attack on Germany through the Fulda Gap. However, the only time in its history that NATO invoked Article 5 was on September 12, 2001, in response to the September 11 attacks on the United States.

19. As noted in chapter 2, Article 10 of the League charter was the focus of much of the concern by congressional opponents of the League. Their fear was that if the United States signed the charter, Article 10 could have the effect of drawing the United States into wars that did not directly involve the country and, therefore, were not in U.S. national interest.

20. Article 2, the North Atlantic Treaty, http://www.nato.int/cps/en/natolive/official_texts_17120.htm.

21. This is also one of the reasons that the former communist countries of Eastern Europe, such as Poland, Hungary, the Czech Republic, and others, were so eager to join NATO when it enlarged initially in the 1990s, and why the countries of Eastern Europe and the former Soviet Union have wanted to join as NATO continued to enlarge. To them, this served as a way of formally recognizing that they, too, are members of that democratic capitalist group of countries tied to the West. It was also recognition that the old days of Soviet domination had ended.

22. Soviet communism was based on the idea of a planned economy that had at its hub centralized state planning with large urban bureaucracies/ministries to manage it. The central state made the decisions and choices about the allocation of resources. In contrast, in China, Mao's model relied on the mass mobilization of rural labor as central to his idea of communism. His model was based on the voluntary collectivization of agriculture and the full employment of peasant labor found in a more rural country. Each of the two versions of communism was designed for the needs of the particular country as envisioned by its leaders. Ultimately, the two versions were seen by each country as being at odds with each other.

23. John B. Judis, *The Folly of Empire: What George W. Bush Could Learn from Theodore Roosevelt and Woodrow Wilson* (New York: Scribner, 2004), 142.

24. The entire document of NSC 68, while quite lengthy, lays out in detail U.S. perceptions of the Soviet Union and its intentions, the goals of the United States, and why the two were in conflict. It also describes Soviet military capabilities as then known and a range of options available to the United States to successfully deter and counter the Soviet Union. While it recognizes the "heavy responsibility" placed on the United States, the document also makes clear the need to "organize and enlist the energies and resources of the free world" in support of this effort. NSC 68 also notes the importance of keeping "the U.S. public fully informed and cognizant of the threats to our national security so that it will be prepared to support the measures which we must accordingly adopt." National Security Council, NSC 68: "United States Objectives and Programs for National Security," April 14, 1950, http://www.fas.org/irp/offdocs/nsc-hst/nsc-68-cr.htm.

25. This is an important point because the United States was aware that if the vote had come when the Soviet ambassador was present, he probably would have exercised the veto, thereby killing the motion. It is also important to note that the Security Council seat held by "China" at that time was actually held by the government of Taiwan, not the PRC, which was allied with North Korea. It was not until October 1971 that the UN General Assembly voted to seat the PRC in place of Taiwan, which resulted in removing Taiwan from the UN.

26. "Truman's Statement on the Korean War," "Statement by the President on the Situation in Korea," June 27, 1950, https://www.trumanlibrary.org/publicpapers/index.php?pid=800&st=&st1=. According to political scientist Peter Irons, President Truman specifically circumvented Congress in authorizing U.S. troops into Korea without asking for approval or a formal declaration of war. Irons also makes the case that Truman violated the provisions of the UN charter by taking unilateral action prior to a UN Security Council call for assistance. Thus, Irons concludes, "Truman had no legal or constitutional authority for his actions at the outset of the Korean War. He ordered U.S. forces to undertake acts of war in Korea, despite his claim at a

June 29 press conference, that 'we are not at war.'" Peter Irons, *War Powers: How the Imperial Presidency Hijacked the Constitution* (New York: Metropolitan Books, 2005), 171.

27. On April 11, 1951, President Truman called a press conference to announce that General MacArthur had been removed from the command of the forces in Korea. Truman believed that MacArthur had overstepped his bounds when he launched an attack into North Korea that pushed the enemy back toward the Yalu River, bordering China. MacArthur requested support to blockade the Chinese coast and bomb the mainland, which was denied by Washington. MacArthur was then warned to restrict the fighting to the area south of the thirty-eighth parallel, so as not to incite China. When MacArthur spoke out against what he saw as this strategy of "limited war," Truman saw this as a direct challenge to him as president and commander in chief, and he responded by firing MacArthur.

28. Quoted in Paul Kennedy, *The Rise and Fall of the Great Powers* (New York: Vintage, 1987), 382.

29. According to J. M. Roberts, "This was to turn out to be one of the most influential acts by a statesman of any nationality since 1945. It shook the monolithic front communism had hitherto presented." J. M. Roberts, *Twentieth Century: A History of the World, 1901–2000* (New York: Viking, 1999), 649. Excerpts of Khrushchev's speech can be found at https://www.marxists.org/archive/khrushchev/1956/02/24.htm.

30. In his memoirs, Khrushchev reflected, "For some time the United States lagged behind us. We were exploring space with our Sputniks. People all over the world recognized our success. Most admired us; the Americans were jealous." Nikita Khrushchev, *Khrushchev Remembers: The Last Testament*, trans. Strobe Talbott (Boston: Little, Brown, 1974), 54.

31. Under President Eisenhower's leadership, spy and intelligence technology made great advances in the 1950s. Specifically designed to monitor the Soviet Union and protect the United States from surprise nuclear attack, the U.S. intelligence apparatus came to depend increasingly on reconnaissance aircraft and spy satellites. For the background story of many of these developments, see Philip Taubman, *Secret Empire: Eisenhower, the CIA, and the Hidden Story of America's Space Espionage* (New York: Simon & Schuster, 2003).

32. For a fascinating and detailed account of the U-2 incident, see Michael R. Beschloss, *Mayday: Eisenhower, Khrushchev, and the U-2 Affair* (New York: Harper & Row, 1986).

33. Quoted in James MacGregor Burns, *The Crosswinds of Freedom* (New York: Alfred A. Knopf, 1989), 262.

34. The news conference of Friday, April 21, 1961, can be found at http://www.jfklibrary.org/Asset-Viewer/Archives/JFKPOF-054-012.aspx.

35. Resentment and tensions had been building between the Soviet Union and China. Since the 1950s, China had implemented policies to reduce its dependence on the USSR. The tensions between the two countries grew until the Soviet Union withdrew its economic and technical aid and advisors in 1960. Concurrent with that, the two countries engaged in countercharges about border violations, with shots fired across the border as early as 1963. In 1964, China exploded its first nuclear weapon, becoming the fifth country to acquire this technology (following the United States, Soviet Union, Britain, and France). Subsequently, the two countries pursued very different policies, undermining the notion of monolithic communism.

36. Upon hearing that Soviet ships bearing missiles heading to Cuba had stopped and then turned around at sea, then–Secretary of State Dean Rusk was quoted as saying, "We're eyeball to eyeball and I think the other fellow just blinked." This statement is quoted in any number of places as indicative of the tensions that existed at this time. This one was taken from an article by Michael Dobbs, "The Price of a 50-Year Myth," *New York Times,* October 15, 2012, http://www.nytimes.com/2012/10/16/opinion/the-eyeball-to-eyeball-myth-and-the-cuban-missile-crisiss-legacy.html. The article itself deals with this as just one example of a foreign policy decision based on misunderstanding.

37. See, for example, Graham T. Allison, *Essence of Decision: Explaining the Cuban Missile Crisis* (Boston: Little, Brown, 1971). This is perhaps the classic book on the missile crisis. Also see Raymond L. Garthoff, *Reflections on the Cuban Missile Crisis* (Washington, D.C.: Brookings Institution, 1989); and Robert F. Kennedy, *Thirteen Days: A Memoir of the Cuban Missile Crisis* (New York: W. W. Norton, 1969) for a fascinating first-person account of the event by someone intimately involved. For a work that draws on previously secret documents

from Russian and U.S. archives to offer further insights into the crisis, see Aleksandr Fursenko and Timothy Naftali, *"One Hell of a Gamble": Khrushchev, Castro, and Kennedy, 1958–1964* (New York: W. W. Norton, 1997). Also see Michael Dobbs, *One Minute to Midnight: Kennedy, Khrushchev, and Castro on the Brink of Nuclear War* (New York: Alfred A. Knopf, 2008) for a detailed account of the crisis that draws on exhaustive and relatively new research.

38. Don Oberdorfer, "Cuban Missile Crisis More Volatile than Thought," *Washington Post*, January 14, 1992, A1.

39. Quoted in Martin Tolchin, "U.S. Underestimated Soviet Force in Cuba during '62 Missile Crisis," *New York Times*, January 15, 1992.

40. Michael Dobbs, in his 2008 book about the Cuban Missile Crisis, notes that there were many "unintended consequences" of the event, some of which are just being realized. For example, he quotes Clark Clifford, who served as secretary of defense after Robert McNamara, as saying that "the architects of the Vietnam War were 'deeply influenced by the lessons of the Cuban missile crisis.' They thought that concepts like 'flexible response' and 'controlled escalation' had helped Kennedy prevail over Khrushchev—and would work equally well in Vietnam." Dobbs also asserts that a "somewhat different—but equally mistaken—lesson from the Cuban missile crisis was drawn by modern-day neoconservatives. In planning for the war in Iraq, they shared the conceit that the political will of the president of the United States trumps all other considerations." Dobbs, *One Minute to Midnight*, 346–47.

41. Quoted in George C. Herring, *America's Longest War: The United States and Vietnam, 1950–1975* (New York: McGraw-Hill, 1996), 38.

42. Quoted in Herring, *America's Longest War*, 78.

43. Statement by President Kennedy on the importance of Laos, at a news conference March 23, 1961, http://www.mtholyoke.edu/acad/intrel/pentagon2/ps5.htm.

44. For more detail about Laos and its relationship to Vietnam, see Norman B. Hannah, *The Key to Failure: Laos and the Vietnam War* (Lanham, Md.: Madison Books, 1987). Hannah makes the argument that not only were the situations in Laos and Vietnam related, which seems apparent, but in chapter 2, "The Bay of Pigs and Indochina," he makes the case that "the pattern of our failure in Indochina was set at the Bay of Pigs" (9).

45. Roberts, *Twentieth Century*, 673.

46. According to Doris Kearns Goodwin, "Johnson did worry about the loss of his domestic programs. As a boy of five, he had heard his Populist grandfather describe the devastating impact of the Spanish-American War on social reform. He had lived through the periods of reaction following World War I and World War II, seen a virtual paralysis of domestic action in the aftermath of Korea. And one cannot doubt the intensity of this concern." Doris Kearns Goodwin, *Lyndon Johnson and the American Dream* (New York: Harper & Row, 1976), 259.

47. Goodwin, *Lyndon Johnson and the American Dream*, 251–52.

48. For a broader discussion of the events in the Gulf of Tonkin during that period in early August, including questions about what really happened on August 4 and references to declassified documents, see John Prados, "Essay: 40th Anniversary of the Gulf of Tonkin Incident," National Security Archive, http://nsarchive.gwu.edu/NSAEBB/NSAEBB132/essay.htm.

49. The Southeast Asia Collective Defense Treaty that established the Southeast Asia Treaty Organization (SEATO) was signed in 1954 and entered into force in 1955. It joined the United States and the countries of Australia, France, New Zealand, Pakistan, Philippines, Thailand, and United Kingdom. Article 4 of this treaty is the collective defense provision similar to the one in Article 5 of the NATO treaty. The goal of the treaty and of SEATO was to oppose communist gains in Southeast Asia after the withdrawal of the French. The organization was divided by the U.S. role in Vietnam and was officially disbanded in 1977.

50. "President Johnson's Message to Congress, Joint Resolution of Congress, H.J. RES 1145," http://avalon.law.yale.edu/20th_century/tonkin-g.asp.

51. "Joint Resolution of Congress, H.J. RES 1145," http://avalon.law.yale.edu/20th_century/tonkin-g.asp.

52. Donald L. Westerfield, *War Powers: The President, the Congress, and the Question of War* (Westport, CT: Praeger Press, 1996), 53. Article I, Section 8, of the Constitution explicitly grants to Congress the power to declare war.

53. Herring, *America's Longest War*, 136.

54. Quoted in Westerfield, *War Powers*, 84.

55. Herring, *America's Longest War*, 167.

56. Herring, *America's Longest War*, 173.

57. Herring, *America's Longest War*, 173.

58. Walter Cronkite, "We Are Mired in Stalemate," broadcast, February 27,1968, https://facultystaff.richmond.edu/~ebolt/history398/cronkite_1968.html. It can also be seen at various postings on YouTube. When Lyndon Johnson heard Cronkite's commentary on the news, he was reported to have said, "If I've lost Cronkite, I've lost Middle America."

59. Burns, *The Crosswinds of Freedom*, 412.

60. Burns, *The Crosswinds of Freedom*, 413.

61. The full text of Lyndon Johnson's announcement of March 31, 1968, can be found at http://www.lbjlib.utexas.edu/johnson/archives.hom/speeches.hom/680331.asp. The video of the last critical minutes of this announcement can be seen at http://abcnews.go.com/Archives/video/march-31-1968-lbj-seek-election-9626199.

62. Quoted in Goodwin, *Lyndon Johnson and the American Dream*, 343.

63. For more detail about this and other related events during this period see Office of the Historian, "Ending the Vietnam War, 1969–1973," https://history.state.gov/milestones/1969-1976/ending-vietnam.

64. Richard Nixon, "Address to the Nation on the War in Vietnam," November 3, 1969, https://www.nixonlibrary.gov/forkids/speechesforkids/silentmajority/silentmajority_transcript.pdf.

65. Gallup, "Presidential Approval Ratings—Gallup Historical Statistics and Trends," http://www.gallup.com/poll/116677/presidential-approval-ratings-gallup-historical-statistics-trends.aspx.

66. Roberts, *Twentieth Century*, 675.

67. War Powers Resolution, Public Law 93-148, 93rd Congress, H.J.Res. 542, November 7, 1973, "War Powers Resolution: Joint Resolution Concerning the War Powers of Congress and the President," http://avalon.law.yale.edu/20th_century/warpower.asp.

68. War Powers Resolution, Public Law 93-148, 93rd Congress, H.J.Res. 542, November 7, 1973, "War Powers Resolution: Joint Resolution Concerning the War Powers of Congress and the President," http://avalon.law.yale.edu/20th_century/warpower.asp.

69. Despite the caveats built into the War Powers Resolution, in October 2002 Congress gave President George W. Bush virtually the same authority regarding the conduct of the war with Iraq. Congress gave the president authorization "to use the Armed Forces of the United States as he determined to be necessary and appropriate in order to (1) defend the national security of the United States *against the continuing threat posed by Iraq*; and (2) enforce all relevant United Nations Security Council Resolutions regarding Iraq" (emphasis added). Like the Tonkin Gulf Resolution, this resolution was premised upon a case that has since been disproved. "Joint Resolution to Authorize the Use of United States Armed Forces against Iraq," October 2, 2002, http://georgewbush-whitehouse.archives.gov/news/releases/2002/10/20021002-2.html.

70. For a more detailed discussion of the constitutionality of the resolution and these parts in particular, see Westerfield, *War Powers*, 90–92, and many of the sources that he cites. Peter Irons raises an interesting point when he notes that "rather than limiting the president's war-making powers, as its sponsors intended, the War Powers Resolution of 1973 actually expanded them by failing to include any enforcement provisions." This leads him to state that, therefore, "presidents could—and most often did—ignore the resolution's consulting and reporting provisions, or comply in the most perfunctory manner." Irons, *War Powers*, 219. However, as desired, the act has forced presidents to report to Congress. Whether, when, and how Congress responds is a different question.

71. In addition to the United States and the Soviet Union, the United Kingdom became nuclear in 1956, France in 1960, and China in 1964. India conducted its first nuclear test in 1974, and by the 1980s it was clear that Pakistan had nuclear weapons as well. In addition, Argentina, Brazil, and South Africa all had a nuclear capability but chose not to build nuclear weapons. It is an open secret that Israel has nuclear weapons, and North Korea and Iran have both made it clear that each would be pursuing its own nuclear weapons program. In July 2015,

the United States, China, France, Germany, the Russian Federation, the United Kingdom, and representatives of the European Union signed a "Comprehensive Plan of Action" with Iran to limit its nuclear program only for peaceful purposes. See "Joint Comprehensive Plan of Action," July 14, 2015, https://assets.documentcloud.org/documents/2165399/full-text-of-the-iran-nuclear-deal.pdf.

72. Quoted in Eugene R. Wittkopf, Charles W. Kegley, Jr., and James M. Scott, *American Foreign Policy*, 6th ed. (Belmont, Calif.: Wadsworth/Thomson Learning, 2003), 51.

73. Wittkopf, Kegley, and Scott, *American Foreign Policy*, 51.

74. For a fascinating and brief description of Nixon's position on China, including short excerpts of some of his writings on the topic, see "Finding China," in Burns, *The Crosswinds of Freedom*, 468–75.

75. "Joint Communiqué of the People's Republic of China and the United States of America," February 28, 1972, http://www.china-embassy.org/eng/zmgx/zywj/t36255.htm.

76. Ford's statement about the pardon can be found in the *New York Times*, "Statement by the President in Connection with his Proclamation Pardoning Nixon," September 9, 1974, http://timesmachine.nytimes.com/timesmachine/1974/09/09/99181264.html?pageNumber=24.

77. For a detailed first-person account of the events leading up to the Iranian hostage crisis, the U.S. attempts at diplomatic solution, the failed rescue attempt, and the implications of the crisis, see Gary Sick, *All Fall Down: America's Tragic Encounter with Iran* (New York: Random House, 1985).

78. Memorandum From the President's Assistant for National Security Affairs (Kissinger) to President Ford, May 12, 1975, https://history.state.gov/historicaldocuments/frus1969-76v10/d280.

79. "President Johnson's Message to Congress; Joint Resolution of Congress, H.J. RES 1145," http://avalon.law.yale.edu/20th_century/tonkin-g.asp.

5. THE COLD WAR AND BEYOND

1. What Kennedy meant was that he, too, is a citizen of Berlin. Although most people knew what he was trying to say, the colloquial translation of this statement is, "I am a jelly-filled donut," since a "Berliner" is a popular type of pastry. This is one example of how language, especially in translation, can confound international relations. This example is cited in Raymond Cohen, *Negotiating Across Cultures* (Washington, D.C.: United States Institute of Peace Press, 1992).

2. President Reagan delivered the speech on June 12, 1987, at the Brandenburg Gate in West Berlin. It is important to note that the speech could be heard on the eastern side of the Berlin Wall and sent an important message. About halfway through the speech, Reagan directed his comments not only to the people of Berlin but also to Mikhail Gorbachev in the Soviet Union when he said, "General Secretary Gorbachev, if you seek peace, if you seek prosperity for the Soviet Union and Eastern Europe, if you seek liberalization: Come here to this gate! Mr. Gorbachev, open this gate! Mr. Gorbachev, tear down this wall!" The transcript of the speech with video can be found at http://www.americanrhetoric.com/speeches/ronaldreaganbrandenburggate.htm.

3. The beginning of the end of the Cold War started in 1989 when "the Soviet Union suddenly reversed course . . . and abandoned its empire in Eastern Europe." John Mearsheimer, *The Tragedy of Great Power Politics* (New York: W. W. Norton, 2001), 201–2. In the most tangible example of the changes taking place, in November 1989 the Berlin Wall came down. Two years later, in 1991, the Soviet Union broke apart and became fifteen separate states. With that, the Cold War ended.

4. Zbigniew Brzezinski and Brent Scowcroft, *America and the World: Conversations on the Future of American Foreign Policy,* moderated by David Ignatius (New York: Basic Books, 2008), 3.

5. J. M. Roberts, *Twentieth Century: A History of the World, 1901–2000* (New York: Viking, 1999), 742.

6. For a detailed discussion of "soft" and "hard" power and the role that each has played in American foreign policy, see Joseph S. Nye, Jr., *The Paradox of American Power: Why the World's Only Superpower Can't Go It Alone* (New York: Oxford University Press, 2002). Nye later built on that by adding in the concept of "smart power," which he defines as "the ability to combine hard and soft power resources into effective strategies." Joseph S. Nye, Jr., *The Future of Power* (New York: PublicAffairs, 2011), 22–23.

7. President Reagan delivered the first "evil empire" speech, as it came to be known, to the British House of Commons on June 8, 1982. Although Reagan did not label the Soviet Union the "evil empire" per se, in speaking to the British people about the contest of democracy versus communism and West versus East, he did say, "Given strong leadership, time, and a little bit of hope, the forces of good ultimately rally and triumph over evil," http://people. hofstra.edu/alan_j_singer/242%20Course%20Pack/3.%20Tenth/136.pdf. Reagan reprised many of these themes in a speech he gave on March 8, 1983, to the National Association of Evangelicals in Florida. However, he was even more blunt this time, given his audience: "So, in your discussions of the nuclear freeze proposals, I urge you to beware the temptation of pride— the temptation of blithely declaring yourselves above it all and label both sides equally at fault, to ignore the facts of history and the aggressive impulses of an *evil empire*, to simply call the arms race a giant misunderstanding and thereby remove yourself from the struggle between right and wrong and good and evil" (emphasis added), http://www.reagan.utexas.edu/archives/ speeches/1983/30883b.htm.

8. Roberts, *Twentieth Century*, 747.

9. The arms control process did continue under Reagan, but unsuccessfully, at least initially. For more detail about the progress of some of the negotiations, see Strobe Talbott, *Deadly Gambits* (New York: Alfred A. Knopf, 1984). Especially instructive is chapter 6, "A Walk in the Woods" (117–51), describing the informal talks that took place between U.S. negotiator Paul Nitze and Soviet negotiator Yuli Kvitsinsky, and why those negotiations were doomed to fail.

10. Jack F. Matlock, Jr., *Reagan and Gorbachev: How the Cold War Ended* (New York: Random House, 2004), 302. This is an example of how a powerful individual actor can play an important role in international relations and the direction of a particular nation-state. As a post-script to this, in reflecting on what happened during this period, Brent Scowcroft claims that Gorbachev is "one of the most detested people in Russia. . . . Because he destroyed the glory of Russia." Brzezinski and Scowcroft, *America and the World*, 162. Some argue now that it is that glory that Russian current-President Putin is trying to regain.

11. In Gorbachev's first meeting with a Western leader, Prime Minister Margaret Thatcher reported that she was impressed and described Gorbachev as someone she could work with. Further, Gorbachev articulated his apparently forward-looking ideas about glasnost (openness) and perestroika (economic restructuring away from a command economy) in his book *Perestroika*, which was published in the West. Mikhail Gorbachev, *Perestroika: New Thinking for Our Country and the World* (New York: Harper & Row, 1987). He also stressed the idea of a "common European home" in a speech that he gave in July 1989 in Strasbourg to the Council of Europe titled "Europe as a Common Home," https://chnm.gmu.edu/1989/archive/files/ gorbachev-speech-7-6-89_e3ccb87237.pdf.

12. See Matlock, *Reagan and Gorbachev*. One of the more interesting insights that can be seen in this book is the role played by both Raisa Gorbachev and Nancy Reagan. In a number of places, Matlock describes the important behind-the-scenes roles that the two wives had in influencing their husbands at this critical point. If one is looking at foreign policy through "gender-sensitive lenses," although the two women had the traditional role of wife, in both cases they were extremely important in influencing the outcome of events.

13. See Howard Zinn, *The Twentieth Century* (New York: HarperCollins, 2003), 355–57. The "Boland Amendment" was the name given to three congressional amendments sponsored by Congressman Edward Boland (D-MA) between 1982 and 1984, all of which dealt with limiting U.S. assistance to the Contras. The first one, passed in 1982, was an amendment to the Defense Appropriations Act. The second one was an amendment to the Intelligence Authoriza-tion Act for Fiscal Year 1983 and was passed on November 3, 1983. It was initially introduced as a House resolution "to prohibit United States support for military or paramilitary operations

in Nicaragua." It also amended the Intelligence Authorization Act "to prohibit the Central Intelligence Agency or any other agency involving intelligence operations from using FY 1983 or FY 1984 appropriations to support military or paramilitary operations in Nicaragua" (http://www.milnet.com/boland.htm). The third was passed as part of a defense appropriations bill in 1984 for fiscal year 1985, again limiting funding for Nicaragua.

14. *The Tower Commission Report: The Full Text of the President's Special Review Board* (New York: Random House, 1997), 6.

15. *The Tower Commission Report*, 87.

16. "Toward a New World Order," President George H. W. Bush's address to a joint session of Congress and the nation, September 11, 1990, http://www.sweetliberty.org/issues/war/bushsr.htm.

17. Text of UN Security Council Resolution 660, http://www.un.org/en/ga/search/view_doc.asp?symbol=S/RES/660%281990%29.

18. The text of Resolution 678 can be found at http://www.un.org/en/ga/search/view_doc.asp?symbol=S/RES/678%281990%29. Twelve of the fifteen members of the Security Council voted in favor of the resolution. Two countries, Cuba and Yemen, voted against it; China, one of the permanent members and therefore with veto power, chose to abstain. It is interesting to note that the resolution referred to "member states" at a time when one of the major changes in the international system was the emergence and predominance of nonstate actors. This, too, created a dilemma for U.S. foreign policy, since policy had always been premised on nation-to-nation interaction. This issue of how to deal with nonstate actors became especially acute after September 11, 2001, and the attack that was mounted by Al Qaeda, a terrorist organization.

19. In his memoirs, George H. W. Bush notes that while preparing to go to Congress, he studied the way in which Johnson "had handled Congress at the time of the Gulf of Tonkin Resolution in 1964." Bush acknowledges that "the Vietnam War was different, but his effort made a big impression on me, and I began to think about seeking a similar congressional vote of support." George Bush and Brent Scowcroft, *A World Transformed* (New York: Alfred A. Knopf, 1998), 371.

20. Bush and Scowcroft, *A World Transformed*, 446.

21. In 1995, Andrew Kohut and Robert Toth of the Pew Center for People and the Press issued a report that stated, "Until a generation ago, elites were probably the only Americans interested in foreign news. . . . Today, much broader and less sophisticated U.S. audiences are exposed to the world, but because most Americans lack much knowledge about international affairs, they can be easily stirred to demand action by dramatic stories that they read and that they see." What they are describing is what we have come to know as "the CNN effect." Andrew Kohut and Robert C. Toth, "A Content Analysis: International News Coverage Fits Public's Ameri-Centric Mood," http://www.people-press.org/files/legacy-pdf/19951031.pdf.

22. Brzezinski and Scowcroft, *America and the World*, 12–13.

23. Roberts, *Twentieth Century*, 775.

24. Leslie H. Gelb, *Power Rules: How Common Sense Can Rescue American Foreign Policy* (New York: HarperCollins, 2009), 62–63.

25. For an excellent history of Yugoslavia leading up to the breakup, see John R. Lampe, *Yugoslavia as History: Twice There Was a Country*, 2nd ed. (Cambridge: Cambridge University Press, 2000). Also see Susan L. Woodward, *Balkan Tragedy: Chaos and Destruction after the Cold War* (Washington, D.C.: Brookings Institution, 1995).

26. The country of Yugoslavia was a federation of six republics: Serbia, Croatia, Bosnia-Herzegovina, Montenegro, Macedonia, and Slovenia. With the exception of Bosnia, the other five were fairly homogeneous, that is, Serbia was primarily Serb, Croatia was primarily Croat, and so on. In general, all the groups are ethnically similar. The main difference is religion. Serbs tend to be Eastern Orthodox, Croats are generally Catholic, and Bosnians are generally Muslim. Prior to the war, intermarriage among the groups, especially in Bosnia, was not unusual. (In Bosnia, prior to the war, as many as 30 percent of marriages were between different groups.) The emergence of leaders such as Slobodan Milosevic in Serbia and Franjo Tudjman in Croatia fueled the nationalist fervor within each group and led directly to ethnic conflict. The most destructive and longest war was in Bosnia, and it involved fighting among the Serbs, Croats, and Bosnian Muslims.

27. Roper Public Opinion Archives, "George H. W. Bush Presidential Approval," https://presidential.roper.center.

28. Eugene R. Wittkopf, Charles W. Kegley, Jr., and James M. Scott, *American Foreign Policy*, 6th ed. (Belmont, Calif.: Wadsworth/Thomson Learning, 2003), 452–53.

29. Elizabeth Drew, *On the Edge: The Clinton Presidency* (New York: Simon & Schuster, 1994), 323.

30. For a harrowing description of the battle in Mogadishu, Somalia, and the issues surrounding it, see Mark Bowden, *Black Hawk Down* (London: Corgi Books, 1999).

31. Drew, *On the Edge*, 318.

32. Quoted in Fraser Cameron, *American Foreign Policy after the Cold War: Global Hegemon or Reluctant Sheriff?* (New York: Routledge, 2002), 22.

33. The fact that the United States chose not to intervene in genocide in various places has been condemned by a number of authors who felt that an important role that the United States could and should play in the post–Cold War world was as a moral leader. For example, one journalist who covered the wars in the Balkans told me that, in her opinion, the lack of action by the Bush administration meant that the United States exercised no "moral authority" regarding policies in Bosnia, and that this lack of action set a precedent that would hamper the Clinton administration's ability to take action. (Interview with the author in December 2000.) For more detail about specific cases, see Samantha Power, *"A Problem from Hell": America and the Age of Genocide* (New York: HarperCollins, 2002).

34. "A Joint Resolution regarding United States Policy toward Haiti," S.J. Res 229, October 6, 1994, https://www.govtrack.us/congress/bills/103/sjres229/text.

35. Quoted in Woodward, *Balkan Tragedy*, 6.

36. According to a Pew poll, Clinton's approval rating in September 1994 was 41 percent, and disapproval was at 52 percent. "Americans Unmoved by Prospect of Clinton, Lewinsky Testimony," Pew Research Center for People and the Press, August 4, 1998, http://www.people-press.org/1998/08/04/americans-unmoved-by-prospect-of-clinton-lewinsky-testimony.

37. A number of books deal with the war in Bosnia and the negotiations surrounding the Dayton peace agreement. See, for example, Ivo H. Daalder, *Getting to Dayton: The Making of America's Bosnia Policy* (Washington, D.C.: Brookings Institution, 2000); Saadia Touval, *Mediation in the Yugoslav War: The Critical Years, 1990–1995* (London: Palgrave, 2002); and Joyce P. Kaufman, *NATO and the Former Yugoslavia: Crisis, Conflict, and the Atlantic Alliance* (Lanham, Md.: Rowman & Littlefield, 2002).

38. "National Security Strategy for a New Century," 1997, http://clinton2.nara.gov/WH/EOP/NSC/Strategy.

39. In an interview in Washington, D.C., in August 2000, one high-level official in the Clinton administration told me that the United States should not have publicly taken the position that it did about its unwillingness to use ground forces. He claimed that doing so clearly sent the wrong signal to Milosevic, limited negotiating options, and further damaged relations within NATO and between the United States and its NATO allies.

40. Roper Public Opinion Archives, "Bill Clinton Presidential Approval," https://presidential.roper.center/.

41. Wittkopf, Kegley, and Scott, *American Foreign Policy*, 265. The Roper Archives, which compiled a series of polls in December 2000 just before Clinton left office, listed his approval ratings at between 65 and 67 percent. Roper Public Opinion Archives, "Bill Clinton Presidential Approval," https://presidential.roper.center/.

42. When George W. Bush became president in 2001, he defied convention because the first foreign leader he met with was President Vicente Fox of Mexico, rather than one of the leaders of Canada or Europe, which had been the tradition.

43. It is important to remember that terrorist attacks against the United States or Americans abroad were not limited to the Clinton administration. The suicide bombing of the U.S. Marine barracks in Beirut, Lebanon, in October 1983, under Reagan resulted in the deaths of 241 marines and other U.S. personnel. In fact, a State Department survey of international terrorist attacks for the period 1981 through 2000 showed a decline in the overall number of attacks, down from a high of 666 in 1987. However, what has changed has been an increase in the intensity of attacks directed specifically at U.S. citizens or interests. While the overall number

of attacks might have declined, the loss of life from attacks such as those in Beirut, the USS *Cole* in Yemen (2000), the American embassies in Kenya and Tanzania (1998), the first World Trade Center bombing (1993), and, of course, September 11 all have resulted in a significant increase in the number of American lives lost. Statistics are drawn from Wittkopf, Kegley, and Scott, *American Foreign Policy*, 193.

44. In an op-ed piece in the *New York Times* following the terrorist bombs detonated in London on July 7, 2005, Robert A. Pape makes the point that since 1990, most of the suicide terrorists "came from America's closest allies in the Muslim world—Turkey, Egypt, Pakistan, Indonesia and Morocco—rather than from those the State Department considers 'state sponsors of terrorism,' like Iran, Libya, Sudan and Iraq." Robert A. Pape, "Al Qaeda's Smart Bombs," *New York Times*, July 9, 2005, A29.

45. Gelb, *Power Rules,* 65.

46. "Remarks of President Clinton to the UN General Assembly," September 21, 1998 http://avalon.law.yale.edu/20th_century/t_0026.asp.

47. Despite Clinton's willingness to deploy U.S. forces in support of humanitarian missions, Samantha Power claims that the United States waited too long to act in many of these cases, which resulted in further acts of genocide. She is one of the most outspoken critics of U.S. foreign policy for its apparent hesitancy to use military force in order to address—and halt—genocide. See Power, *"A Problem from Hell."* Interestingly, early in his second term President Obama named Samantha Power to serve as U.S. Ambassador to the United Nations to replace Susan Rice, who became his National Security Advisor.

48. Steven W. Hook, *U.S. Foreign Policy: The Paradox of World Power*, 2nd ed. (Washington, D.C.: CQ Press, 2008), 57.

49. Hook, *U.S. Foreign Policy*, 56.

50. Quoted in David Owen, *Balkan Odyssey* (New York: Harcourt Brace, 1995), 14.

51. Ivo H. Daalder, *Getting to Dayton: The Making of America's Bosnia Policy* (Washington, D.C.: Brookings Institution, 2000), 150.

52. Peter Irons, *War Powers: How the Imperial Presidency Hijacked the Constitution* (New York: Metropolitan Books, 2005), 212.

53. See chapter 11, "We Were Going to War," in Irons, *War Powers*, 204–20. Irons argues that in the cases of Somalia, Haiti, and eventually Bosnia, "Clinton failed to comply with the War Powers Resolution; he claimed that he was acting according to his powers as commander in chief, not as a result of Congressional approval. His assertions, in fact, provoked a response in the Senate" (211).

6. GEORGE W. BUSH

1. ISIS is an acronym for the terrorist group, Islamic State of Iraq and Syria. The U.S. government often refers to the group as ISIL, Islamic State of Iraq and the Levant, and it is also referred to by its Arabic language acronym, DAESH. For simplification, we will simply refer to it here as ISIS.

2. Jean Edward Smith, *Bush* (New York: Simon & Schuster, 2016), xv.

3. Smith, *Bush*, 660.

4. In addition to the new biography of Bush, there are a plethora of books that have examined this decision from a number of political and policy perspectives, many of which came out during or shortly after the end of the Bush administration. Among those are Thomas Ricks, *Fiasco: The American Military Adventure in Iraq, 2003–2005* (New York: Penguin Press, 2006); Todd S. Purdum, *A Time of Our Choosing: America's War in Iraq* (New York: Times Books, 2003); and Michael R. Gordon and General Bernard E. Trainor, *The Endgame: The Inside Story of the Struggle for Iraq, from George W. Bush to Barack Obama* (New York: Vintage Books, 2012). All three of these rely on interviews and documents to tell the story of the war with Iraq and how it evolved. See also Carolotta Gall, *The Wrong Enemy: America in Afghanistan, 2001–2014* (New York: Mariner Book, 2014), which addresses the impact of the U.S. invasion on Afghanistan and its people; and Rajiv Chandrasekaran, *Imperial Life in the*

Emerald City: Inside Iraq's Green Zone (New York: Vintage Books, 2006), which looks at Iraq in the immediate aftermath of the U.S. invasion in 2003.

5. Condoleezza Rice, "Promoting the National Interest," *Foreign Affairs*, January/February 2000, 45.

6. Rice, "Promoting the National Interest," 53.

7. In her article, "Promoting the National Interest," Rice also states that "a Republican administration should refocus the United States on the national interest and the pursuit of key priorities" (46). She then outlines what these should be. But even more instructive now, she foreshadowed what became a Bush administration priority of spreading and promoting democracy: "America is blessed with extraordinary opportunity. It has had no territorial ambitions for nearly a century. Its national interest has been defined instead by a desire to foster the spread of freedom, prosperity, and peace. Both the will of the people and the demands of modern economies accord with that vision of the future" (62). See Condoleezza Rice, "Promoting the National Interest," 45–62. That same issue included a companion piece, "A Republican Foreign Policy," by Robert Zoellick, who became deputy secretary of state in Bush's second term and then director of the World Bank. He was quite blunt that "a primary task for the next president of the United States is to build public support for a strategy that will shape the world so as to protect and promote American interests and values for the next 50 years" (63). Zoellick was very critical of Clinton and his foreign policy, particularly the fact that he "failed to define a new internationalism for the United States" (64). He outlined a "modern Republican foreign policy" built on five principles. The last of these is recognition of the fact that "there is still evil in the world—people who hate America and the ideas for which it stands" (70). One of his proposed solutions included the need to "deter and even replace" their brutal regimes, and it assumed that the United States will have a strong military—and use it when necessary. Although Zoellick warned that "[i]t is a mistake for the United States simply to react to events," the reality is that the events of September 11, 2001, overshadowed all other aspects of U.S. foreign policy and redefined the policy direction. Robert B. Zoellick, "A Republican Foreign Policy," *Foreign Affairs*, January/February 2000, 63–78.

8. Rice, "Promoting the National Interest," 62.

9. There is a great deal of documentation suggesting that there were some in the Bush administration, generally grouped under the heading of the "neocons," as well as Bush himself, who were looking for ways to invade Iraq even before the 9/11 attacks. For example, Godfrey Hodgson notes that "from the very first days of his administration, well before 9/11, George Bush showed an interest in attacking Iraq." Godfrey Hodgson, *The Myth of American Exceptionalism* (New Haven, Conn.: Yale University Press, 2009), 169. He continues that "Bush had been preoccupied with the danger from Iraq long before 9/11" (170). Hodgson builds a case that for some in the administration, especially Paul Wolfowitz, concern about Iraq goes back to the Cold War, especially concern about control of Iraq's oil fields. Judis also notes that "the nationalists and neoconservatives had begun to call for Saddam Hussein's ouster in the late 1990s after the UN inspectors left Iraq. In 1998, Rumsfeld joined Wolfowitz and other conservatives in signing the Project for the New American Century's open letter to [President] Clinton calling for Saddam's ouster." John B. Judis, *The Folly of Empire: What George W. Bush Could Learn from Theodore Roosevelt and Woodrow Wilson* (New York: Scribner, 2004), 175. Philip Gordon is another author who also identifies both the individuals and the policies, going back to the 1990s, who made the case for war against Iraq way before 9/11. Philip H. Gordon, *Winning the Right War* (New York: Times Books, 2007).

10. "President Bush Discusses Global Climate Change," press release, June 11, 2001, http://georgewbush-whitehouse.archives.gov/news/releases/2001/06/20010611-2.html.

11. According to the terms of the 1994 U.S.-North Korean Agreed Framework, North Korea was required to freeze and eventually dismantle its nuclear facilities that could be used to manufacture fuel for nuclear weapons. In exchange, North Korea was promised light-water reactors (which could not be used for nuclear weapons) and the U.S. promise to send tons of heavy fuel to the country. As a result of these talks, North Korea was encouraged to engage in negotiations with Asian countries as well. One effect has been increased trade between North Korea and South Korea, China, and Japan. "The U.S.-North Korean Agreed Framework at a Glance," https://www.armscontrol.org/factsheets/agreedframework.

12. "Statement by the North Atlantic Council," September 12, 2001, http://www.nato.int/docu/pr/2001/p01-124e.htm.

13. There were some in the Bush administration who had been looking for an excuse to invade Iraq and to get rid of Saddam Hussein since the end of the first Persian Gulf War, explored in the section on the "Neocons" in this chapter. Although there was never any proof that Iraq had anything to do with 9/11, that attack became part of the justification for the invasion and subsequent "regime change."

14. Peter Irons, *War Powers: How the Imperial Presidency Hijacked the Constitution* (New York: Metropolitan Books, 2005), 217–18.

15. Irons, *War Powers*, 218.

16. Irons, *War Powers*, 218.

17. *War Powers Resolution*, Public Law 93-148, November 7, 1973, http://avalon.law.yale.edu/20th_century/warpower.asp.

18. The lone "no" vote in the House was cast by Barbara Lee, Democrat of California. For the full text of S.J. Res 23 see, "Authorization for Use of Military Force," http://www.govtrack.us/congress/bills/107/sjres23/text.

19. Richard F. Grimmett, "Authorization for Use of Military Force in Response to the 9/11 Attacks (P.L. 107-40): Legislative History," CRS Report for Congress, Order Code RS22357, Updated January 16, 2007, CRS-3, http://www.fas.org/sgp/crs/natsec/RS22357.pdf.

20. Grimmett, "Authorization for Use of Military Force," CRS-3.

21. S.J. Res. 23, passed September 14, 2001, http://www.govtrack.us/congress/bills/107/sjres23/text.

22. "President Signs Authorization for Use of Military Force Bill," Statement by the President, September 18, 2001, http://avalon.law.yale.edu/sept11/ president_022.asp.

23. Irons, *War Powers*, 219.

24. "September 11, 2001: Attack on America—S.J. Resolution 23 - Authorization for Use of Military Force (Enrolled Bill); September 18, 2001," http://avalon.law.yale.edu/sept11/sjres23_eb.asp.

25. For the actual data see "Presidential Approval Ratings—George W. Bush," http://www.gallup.com/poll/116500/presidential-approval-ratings-george-bush.aspx.

26. Alan Cowell, "A Nation Challenged: Britain; Blair Declares the Airstrikes Are an Act of Self-Defense," *New York Times*, October 8, 2001, http://www.nytimes.com/2001/10/08/world/nation-challenged-britain-blair-declares-airstrikes-are-act-self-defense.html.

27. As of January 2009, when Obama took office, there were 33,000 U.S. troops in Afghanistan, 15,000 troops with the NATO ISAF mission, and 18,000 fighting insurgents and training the Afghan army and police. By contrast, there were 144,000 U.S. troops in Iraq. The White House, "Facts and Figures on Drawdown in Iraq," August 2, 2010, https://www.whitehouse.gov/the-press-office/facts-and-figures-drawdown-iraq.

28. George W. Bush, "State of the Union Address," January 29, 2002, http://georgewbush-whitehouse.archives.gov/news/releases/2002/01/20020129-11.html. A video of the address is available at the same site.

29. George W. Bush, "President Thanks World Coalition for Anti-Terrorism Effort: Remarks on the Six-Month Anniversary of the September 11 Attacks," https://georgewbush-whitehouse.archives.gov/news/releases/2002/03/20020311-1.html.

30. "The National Security Strategy of the United States of America," September 2002, http://www.state.gov/documents/organization/63562.pdf.

31. Ilan Peleg, *The Legacy of George W. Bush's Foreign Policy: Moving Beyond Neoconservatism* (Boulder, Colo.: Westview Press, 2009), 49–50.

32. Peleg, *The Legacy of George W. Bush's Foreign Policy*, 106–9.

33. Todd S. Purdum, *A Time of Our Choosing: America's War in Iraq* (New York: Times Books, 2003), 4.

34. Purdum, *A Time of Our Choosing*, 41–42.

35. Purdum, *A Time of Our Choosing*, 52.

36. "H.J.Res. 114 (107th): Authorization for Use of Military Force Against Iraq Resolution of 2002," http://www.govtrack.us/congress/bills/107/hjres114/text.

37. "H.J.Res. 114 (107th): Authorization for Use of Military Force Against Iraq Resolution of 2002," http://www.govtrack.us/congress/bills/107/hjres114/text.

38. Public Law 107-40, September 18, 2001, http://avalon.law.yale.edu/sept11/sjres23_eb.asp.

39. Purdum, *A Time of Our Choosing*, 55.

40. UN Security Council Resolution 1441, adopted November 8, 2002, http://www.un.org/Depts/unmovic/documents/1441.pdf.

41. George W. Bush, "State of the Union Address, January 28, 2003, http://www.washingtonpost.com/wp-srv/onpolitics/transcripts/bushtext_012803.html.

42. "President Bush's Address on the Iraqi Invasion," March 18, 2003, http://blogs.wsj.com/dispatch/2013/03/18/full-text-of-president-george-w-bushs-speech-march-19-2003/.

43. While some NATO allies, primarily Great Britain, Poland, and Spain, did support the United States and send troops to fight in Iraq, others, most notably Germany and France, were vocal in their opposition. After a major bombing in Madrid in March 2004, elections brought a socialist government to power in Spain. One of the first acts of newly elected Prime Minister Zapatero was to authorize the withdrawal of Spanish troops from Iraq.

44. Leslie Gelb, a former reporter for the *New York Times* as well as former president of the Council of Foreign Relations, wrote a very insightful piece in the *Wall Street Journal* in which he proposed some solutions to the situation in Iraq. He concluded: "Even the wisest of strategies will confront the odds in making Iraq a better place. . . . A good strategy fashioned with Iraqis, fitted to Iraq's political realities plus a U.S. withdrawal plan, can tap that volcano." Leslie H. Gelb, "Tap the Volcano," *Wall Street Journal*, August 2, 2005.

45. See, for example, Thomas Ricks, *Fiasco: The American Military Adventure in Iraq* (New York: Penguin Press, 2006); Andrew Bacevich, *The Limits of Power: The End of American Exceptionalism* (New York: Metropolitan Books, 2008); and Philip H. Gordon, *Winning the Right War: The Path to Security for America and the World* (New York: Times Books, 2007). Even as I am revising this book more than ten years after the initial invasion, the situation in Iraq remains unstable.

46. See "Global Public Opinion in the Bush Years (2001–2008)," Pew Global Attitudes Project, December 18, 2008, http://www.pewglobal.org/2008/12/18/global-public-opinion-in-the-bush-years-2001-2008. The results of these polls, which were administered in fifty-four countries, show unambiguously that "The U.S. image abroad is suffering almost everywhere. . . . Opposition to key elements of American foreign policy is widespread in Western Europe, and positive views of the U.S. have declined steeply among many of America's longtime European allies. In Muslim nations, the wars in Afghanistan and particularly Iraq have driven negative ratings off the charts."

47. George W. Bush, "State of the Union Address," January 29, 2002, http://georgewbush-whitehouse.archives.gov/news/releases/2002/01/20020129-11.html. A video of the address is available at the same site.

48. Amy Belasco, "The Cost of Iraq, Afghanistan, and Other Global War on Terror Operations Since 9/11," Congressional Research Service, March 29, 2011, http://www.fas.org/sgp/crs/natsec/RL33110.pdf.

49. Mike Dorning, "Iraq War Lives on as Second-Costliest U.S. Conflict Fuels Debt," *Bloomberg News*, January 3, 2012, http://www.bloomberg.com/news/articles/2011-12-27/iraq-war-lives-on-as-u-s-conflict-fuels-debt. The only conflict that has been costlier for the United States is World War II, according to this article.

50. Dorning, "Iraq War Lives on as Second-Costliest U.S. Conflict Fuels Debt."

51. "Bush and Public Opinion: Reviewing the Bush Years and the Public's Final Verdict: Bush and Public Opinion," Pew Research Center for the People & the Press, December 18, 2008, http://www.people-press.org/2008/12/18/bush-and-public-opinion/.

52. George W. Bush, second inaugural address, January 20, 2005, http://www.npr.org/templates/story/story.php?storyId=4460172.

53. See chapters 9 and 10 in Judis, *The Folly of Empire*, 165–212.

54. Tyler Marshall, "Bush's Foreign Policy Shifting," *Los Angeles Times*, June 5, 2005, http://articles.latimes.com/2005/jun/05/world/fg-democracy5.

55. Philip H. Gordon, *Winning the Right War: The Path to Security for America and the World* (New York: Times Books, 2007), 96.

56. Steven Lee Myers, "Question of Bush's Legacy Lingers over His Farewell Visits to European Capitals," *New York Times*, June 14, 2008, http://www.nytimes.com/2008/06/14/world/europe/14prexy.html.

57. "Reviewing the Bush Years and the Public's Final Verdict: Bush and Public Opinion," Pew Research Center for the People & the Press, December 18, 2008, http://www.people-press.org/files/legacy-pdf/478.pdf.

58. Irons, *War Powers*, 231.

59. Peleg, *The Legacy of George W. Bush's Foreign Policy*, 32–33.

60. Judis, *The Folly of Empire*, 5

61. Judis, *The Folly of Empire*, 171.

62. Judis, *The Folly of Empire*, 200.

63. G. John Ikenberry, Thomas J. Knock, Anne-Marie Slaughter, and Tony Smith, *The Crisis of American Foreign Policy: Wilsonianism in the Twenty-first Century* (Princeton, N.J.: Princeton University Press, 2009), 9.

64. Judis, *The Folly of Empire*, 212.

65. "Agreement between the United States of America and the Republic of Iraq on the Withdrawal of United States Forces from Iraq and the Organization of Their Activities during Their Temporary Presence in Iraq," 20, http://www.state.gov/documents/organization/122074.pdf.

66. Steven Lee Myers and Marc Santora, "Premier Casting U.S. Withdrawal as Iraq Victory," *New York Times*, June 26, 2009, http://www.nytimes.com/2009/06/26/world/middleeast/26maliki.html?pagewanted=all.

67. Myers and Santora, "Premier Casting U. S. Withdrawal as Iraq Victory."

68. "Agreement between the United States of America and the Republic of Iraq on the Withdrawal of United States Forces from Iraq and the Organization of Their Activities during Their Temporary Presence in Iraq," 22, http://www.state.gov/documents/organization/122074.pdf.

69. Gordon and Trainor, *The Endgame*, 694–95.

70. Steven Erlanger and David E. Sanger, "Chilcot Report on Iraq War Offers Devastating Critique of Tony Blair," *New York Times*, July 6, 2016, http://www.nytimes.com/2016/07/07/world/europe/chilcot-report.html?_r=0.

71. Erlanger and Sanger, "Chilcot Report on Iraq War Offers Devastating Critique of Tony Blair."

72. Ivo H. Daalder and James M. Lindsay, *America Unbound: The Bush Revolution in Foreign Policy* (Washington, D.C.: Brookings Institution, 2003), 80.

7. OBAMA AND U.S. FOREIGN POLICY

1. Mark Landler, "For Obama, an Unexpected Legacy of Two Full Terms at War," *New York Times*, May 14, 2016, http://www.nytimes.com/2016/05/15/us/politics/obama-as-wartime-president-has-wrestled-with-protecting-nation-and-troops.html?_r=0.

2. For the sake of simplicity, we will use the acronym ISIS here.

3. "The Historic Deal that Will Prevent Iran from Acquiring a Nuclear Weapon," https://www.whitehouse.gov/issues/foreign-policy/iran-deal.

4. Barack Obama, "Renewing American Leadership," *Foreign Affairs*, July/August 2007, https://www.foreignaffairs.com/articles/2007-07-01/renewing-american-leadership, 5.

5. "Obama's Speech in Berlin," full script of Obama's speech, July 24, 2008, Berlin, Germany, http://www.nytimes.com/2008/07/24/us/politics/24text-obama.html?_r=0.

6. "Global Public Opinion in the Bush Years (2001–2008)," Pew Global Attitudes Project, http://www.pewglobal.org/2008/12/18/global-public-opinion-in-the-bush-years-2001-2008/, 1.

7. "Barack Obama's Inaugural Address," January 21, 2009, https://www.whitehouse.gov/blog/2009/01/21/president-barack-obamas-inaugural-address.

8. Philip H. Gordon, *Winning the Right War: The Path to Security for America and the World* (New York: Times Books, 2007), 97.

9. "Global Public Opinion in the Bush Years (2001–2008)," Pew Global Attitudes Project, http://www.pewglobal.org/2008/12/18/global-public-opinion-in-the-bush-years-2001-2008/, 1.

10. "Remarks by the President in Address to the Nation on the Way Forward in Afghanistan and Pakistan," December 2, 2009, http://www.whitehouse.gov/the-press-office/remarks-president-address-nation-way-forward-afghanistan-and-pakistan.

11. David E. Sanger, *The Inheritance: The World Obama Confronts and the Challenges to America's Power* (New York: Three Rivers Press, 2009), 455.

12. All references here are from Leslie H. Gelb, *Power Rules: How Common Sense Can Rescue American Foreign Policy* (New York: HarperCollins, 2009), 156–57.

13. Michael R. Gordon, "In U.S. Exit from Iraq, Failed Efforts and Challenges," *New York Times*, September 22, 2012, http://www.nytimes.com/2012/09/23/world/middleast/failed-efforts-of-americas-last-months-in-iraq.html?pagewanted=all. For a more detailed account of the end of U.S. involvement in Iraq as well as the war itself, see Michael R. Gordon and General Bernard E. Trainor, *The Endgame: The Inside Story of the Struggle for Iraq, From George W. Bush to Barack Obama* (New York: Vintage Books, 2012); Michael Mandelbaum, *Mission Failure: America and the World in the Post-Cold War Era* (New York: Oxford University Press, 2016).

14. Remarks of Senator Barack Obama: "The War We Need to Win," delivered at the Woodrow Wilson Center, Washington, D.C., August 1, 2007, online at Gerhard Peters and John T. Woolley, *The American Presidency Project*, http://www.presidency.ucsb.edu/ws/?pid=77040.

15. "Remarks by the President on a New Strategy for Afghanistan and Pakistan," March 27, 2009, http://www.whitehouse.gov/the_press_office/Remarks-by-the-President-on-a-New-Strategy-for-Afghanistan-and-Pakistan.

16. "Remarks by the President on a New Strategy for Afghanistan and Pakistan," March 27, 2009, http://www.whitehouse.gov/the_press_office/Remarks-by-the-President-on-a-New-Strategy-for-Afghanistan-and-Pakistan.

17. Lander, "For Obama, an Unexpected Legacy of Two Full Terms at War."

18. "Obama's Speech on the Death of Osama bin Laden," May 1, 2011, http://www.usnews.com/news/articles/2011/05/02/obamas-speech-on-the-death-of-osama-bin-laden.

19. "Syria: The Story of the Conflict," BBC News, March 11, 2016, http://www.bbc.com/news/world-middle-east-26116868.

20. For a very detailed account of some of the discussions going on in the White House about how to respond to Syria see Mark Landler, *Alter Egos: Hillary Clinton, Barack Obama, and the Twilight Struggle over American Power* (New York: Random House, 2016), especially pages 204–30.

21. "Remarks by the President on a New Beginning," Cairo University, Cairo, Egypt, June 4, 2009, http://www.whitehouse.gov/the_press_office/Remarks-by-the-President-at-Cairo-University-6-04-09.

22. In his earlier speech in Ankara, President Obama said, "The United States is not, and never will be, at war with Islam. In fact, our partnership with the Muslim world is critical not just in rolling back the violent ideologues that people of all faiths reject, but also to strengthen opportunity for all its people." "Remarks by President Obama to the Turkish Parliament," Ankara, Turkey, April 6, 2009, http://www.whitehouse.gov/the_press_office/Remarks-By-President-Obama-To-The-Turkish-Parliament.

23. "Remarks by the President on a New Beginning," Cairo University, Cairo, Egypt, June 4, 2009, http://www.whitehouse.gov/the_press_office/Remarks-by-the-President-at-Cairo-University-6-04-09.

24. "Remarks by the President on a New Beginning," Cairo University, Cairo, Egypt, June 4, 2009, http://www.whitehouse.gov/the_press_office/Remarks-by-the-President-at-Cairo-University-6-04-09/.

25. "Remarks by the President on a New Beginning," Cairo University, Cairo, Egypt, June 4, 2009, http://www.whitehouse.gov/the_press_office/Remarks-by-the-President-at-Cairo-University-6-04-09/.

26. Steven Lee Myers, "Amid Impasse in Peace Negotiations, America's Chief Middle East Envoy Resigns," *New York Times*, May 13, 2011, http://www.nytimes.com/2011/05/14/world/middleeast/14mitchell.html.

27. Anne Barnard, "Death Toll from the War in Syria Now 470,000, Group Finds," *New York Times,* February 11, 2016, http://www.nytimes.com/2016/02/12/world/middleeast/death-toll-from-war-in-syria-now-470000-group-finds.html.

28. United Nations High Commissioner for Refugees, "Syria Emergency," http://www.unhcr.org/en-us/syria-emergency.html.

29. Karen DeYoung, "Congressional Panels Approve Arms Aid to Syrian Opposition," *Washington Post*, July 22, 2013, http://www.washingtonpost.com/world/national-security/congressional-panels-approve-arms-aid-to-syrian-opposition/2013/07/22/393035ce-f31a-11e2-8505-bf6f231e77b4_story.html.

30. Gerald F. Seib, "Few Good Choices for U.S. in Mideast," *Wall Street Journal*, July 30, 2012, A4.

31. "UN Endorses Syria Peace Plan in Rare Show of Unity Among Big Powers," *New York Times,* December 18, 2015, http://www.reuters.com/article/us-mideast-crisis-syria-un-idUSKBN0U10J020151219.

32. Anne Barnard and Michael R. Gordon, "Aid Convoy Is Hit in Syria as Cease-Fire Falters and Bombings Resume." *New York Times*, September 19, 2016, http://www.nytimes.com/2016/09/20/world/middleeast/syria-aid-john-kerry.html.

33. "Russia and Syria: The withdrawal that wasn't," *The Economist*, May 14, 2016, 43.

34. "Russia and Syria: The withdrawal that wasn't," *The Economist*, May 14, 2016, 43.

35. "Syria: The Story of the Conflict," BBC News, March 11, 2016, http://www.bbc.com/news/world-middle-east-26116868.

36. See "Global Public Opinion in the Bush Years (2001–2008)," Pew Global Attitudes Project, December 18, 2008, http://www.pewglobal.org/2008/12/18/global-public-opinion-in-the-bush-years-2001-2008.

37. Jackie Calmes, "Obama Says Surveillance Helped in Case in Germany," *New York Times*, June 19, 2013, http://www.nytimes.com/2013/06/20/world/europe/obama-in-germany.html?pagewanted=all.

38. Calmes, "Obama Says Surveillance Helped in Case in Germany," http://www.nytimes.com/2013/06/20/world/europe/obama-in-germany.html.

39. "Global Opinion of Obama Slips, International Policies Faulted," Pew Global Attitudes Project, June13, 2012, http://www.pewglobal.org/2012/06/13/global-opinion-of-obama-slips-international-policies-faulted.

40. "Nuclear Posture Review Report," Department of Defense, April 2010, http://www.defense.gov/Portals/1/features/defenseReviews/NPR/2010_Nuclear_Posture_Review_Report.pdf.

41. "Chapter 3: Balance of Power: U.S. vs. China," Pew Global Attitudes Project, July 14, 2014, http://www.pewglobal.org/2014/07/14/chapter-3-balance-of-power-u-s-vs-china/.

42. "The Trans-Pacific Partnership: Leveling the playing field for American workers and American businesses," Office of the United States Trade Representative, https://ustr.gov/tpp/#overall-us-benefits.

43. Nicholas Kulish and Michael D. Shear, "In Tanzania, Obama Calls for a Partnership with Africa to Aid Its Economy," *New York Times*, July 1, 2013, http://www.nytimes.com/2013/07/02/world/africa/obama-tanzania-visit.html.

44. Kulish and Shear, "In Tanzania, Obama Calls for a Partnership with Africa to Aid Its Economy," *New York Times*, July 1, 2013, http://www.nytimes.com/2013/07/02/world/africa/obama-tanzania-visit.html.

45. Peter Baker, "Bush a Fond Presence in Africa for Work During and Since His Presidency," *New York Times*, July 2, 2013, http://www.nytimes.com/2013/07/03/world/africa/bush-a-fond-presence-in-africa-for-work-during-and-since-his-presidency.html.

46. For more information about the changing trade relationship between the United States and Africa see The White House, "Fact Sheet: Deepening the U.S.-Africa Trade Relationship," July 26, 2015, https://www.whitehouse.gov/the-press-office/2015/07/26/fact-sheet-deepening-us-africa-trade-relationship.

47. This information is drawn from Landler, *Alter Egos*, chapter 9, "Red Lines."

48. Anne Barnard, "Death Toll From the War in Syria Now 470,000, Group Finds," *New York Times,* February 11, 2016, http://www.nytimes.com/2016/02/12/world/middleeast/death-toll-from-war-in-syria-now-470000-group-finds.html.

49. "Syria: The Story of the Conflict," BBC News, March 11, 2016, http://www.bbc.com/news/world-middle-east-26116868.

50. "Syria: The Story of the Conflict," BBC News, March 11, 2016, http://www.bbc.com/news/world-middle-east-26116868.

51. "Security Council Unanimously Adopts Resolution 2254 (2015), Endorsing Road Map for Peace Process in Syria, Setting Timetable for Talks," December 18, 2015, http://www.un.org/press/en/2015/sc12171.doc.htm.

52. See Sam Dagher, "As Syria Talks Stall, a Hunt for Alternatives," *Wall Street Journal*, April 28, 2016, http://www.wsj.com/articles/as-syria-talks-stall-a-hunt-for-alternatives-1461794024.

8. THE FUTURE OF U.S. FOREIGN POLICY

1. For example, see John Lewis Gaddis, "Toward the Post–Cold War World," in *The Future of American Foreign Policy*, ed. Charles W. Kegley, Jr., and Eugene R. Wittkopf (New York: St. Martin's Press, 1992), 16–32; and John J. Mearsheimer, "Why We Will Soon Miss the Cold War," in Kegley and Wittkopf, *The Future of American Foreign Policy*, 48–62. Also see John Lewis Gaddis, *Strategies of Containment: A Critical Appraisal of American National Security Policy during the Cold War* (New York: Oxford University Press, 2005); and John Lewis Gaddis, *The Cold War: A New History* (New York: Penguin, 2005).

2. Joseph S. Nye, Jr., *The Paradox of American Power: Why the World's Only Superpower Can't Go It Alone* (New York: Oxford University Press, 2002), 8–9.

3. Nye, *The Paradox of American Power*, 9.

4. Walter Russell Mead, *Power, Terror, Peace, and War: America's Grand Strategy in a World at Risk* (New York: Alfred A. Knopf, 2004), 42.

5. Mead, *Power, Terror, Peace, and War*, 62.

6. "Inaugural address by George W. Bush," January 20, 2005, http://www.nytimes.com/2005/01/20/politics/20BUSH-TEXT.html.

7. Mead, *Power, Terror, Peace, and War*, 60.

8. "Remarks by the President on a New Beginning," Cairo University, Cairo, Egypt, June 4, 2009, http://www.whitehouse.gov/the_press_office/Remarks-by-the-President-at-Cairo-University-6-04-09.

9. Jeffrey Goldberg, "The Obama Doctrine: The President Explains His Hardest Decisions about America's Role in the World," *The Atlantic*, April 2016, 72–73.

10. For more detail about Obama and Clinton's perspectives see Mark Landler*, Alter Egos: Hillary Clinton, Barack Obama, and the Twilight Struggle over American Power* (New York: Random House, 2016).

11. Charlie Savage, "Manning Is Acquitted of Aiding the Enemy," *New York Times*, July 30, 2013, http://www.nytimes.com/2013/07/31/us/bradley-manning-verdict.html.

12. Geoffrey A. Fowler, "Converting the Masses: Starbucks in China," *Far Eastern Economic Review*, July 17, 2003, 34–36; and Jason Singer and Martin Fackler, "In Japan, Adding Beer, Wine to the Latte List," *Wall Street Journal*, July 14, 2003, http://www.wsj.com/articles/SB105813294922279100. I was in Guangzhou, China, in 1993 when the first McDonald's was opening in that city. There were major traffic jams and huge lines as everyone wanted to experience this phenomenon.

13. SARS (Severe Acute Respiratory Syndrome) is believed to have originated in the city of Guangzhou, in southern China, in late 2002 or early 2003. From there, it was spread unknowingly by a doctor to Hong Kong, where it spread globally as people who were unaware that they were contaminated started to travel, infecting others. Cases were diagnosed as far away as Canada, and tourism to and within Asia came to a virtual halt. It took months to bring the

situation under control, although no new cases of the disease have been diagnosed since. But in order to control the situation, governments quarantined anyone who appeared to have the disease; responses included stopping air flights coming from areas that were known to have outbreaks of SARS and examining passengers who appeared to be ill. While some saw this as an infringement on basic human rights and freedoms, few objected if it meant stopping the spread of the disease. This is one example of how quickly dangerous diseases can spread globally.

14. George W. Bush, "The President's State of the Union Address," January 29, 2002, https://georgewbush-whitehouse.archives.gov/news/releases/2002/01/20020129-11.html.

15. In an interview with *National Journal* in October 2010, Mitch McConnell was quoted as saying, "The single most important thing we want to achieve is for President Obama to be a one-term president." Quoted in David M. Herszenhorn, "Hold On to Your Seat: McConnell Wants Obama Out," *New York Times*, October 26, 2010, http://thecaucus.blogs.nytimes.com/2010/10/26/hold-on-to-your-seat-mcconnell-wants-obama-out/?_r=0.

16. For a detailed analysis of how Obama has used executive authority to circumvent a recalcitrant Congress see Binyamin Applebaum and Michael D. Shear, "Once Skeptical of Executive Power, Obama Has Come to Embrace It," *New York Times*, August 13, 2016, http://www.nytimes.com/2016/08/14/us/politics/obama-era-legacy-regulation.html?_r=0.

Index

Abbas, Mahmoud, 173

Abraham Lincoln (USS), 152

Acheson, Dean, 94

Adams, John, 16, 33

Adams, John Quincy, 38

Affordable Care Act (Obamacare), 163

Afghanistan war: Bush, G. W., in, 146–148; NATO in, 147; Obama in, 168–171; War Powers Resolution in, 146

Afghan Transitional Authority, 147

Africa, 181–182

African Americans, 24

Aidid, Mohammed Farah, 130

Airborne Early Warning Aircraft (AWACS), 145

Alawite, Shia, 171

Albright, Madeleine, 13

allies: early entanglement with, 33–35; Europe as, 25; on Iraq War, 25; through trade, 35; in World War II, 67. *See also* North Atlantic Treaty Organization

Al Qaeda, 9, 145, 146, 147, 151, 159, 160, 168, 169, 170. *See also* September 11, 2001 terrorist attack

Alsop, Stewart, 95

Annan, Kofi, 152

Anti-Ballistic Missile Treaty, 144

anti-Muslim sentiment, 165

Arab Spring: in Egypt, 171, 173; Syrian civil war and, 174–176; technology in, 174

Aristede, Jean-Bertrand, 131

armed forces, and Afghanistan War, 146–147, 168–170, 224n27; as "force for good", 137; and Haiti, 131; and humanitarian intervention, 133, 138–140; and Iraq War, 148, 149–152, 168–169; Korean War, 94; and National Security Act of 1947, 88–89; in Persian Gulf war, 124–125; in Somalia, 129–130; and Vietnam War, 104, 106, 107

arms control, 120

Article 5, 145

Articles of Confederation, 32

Asia, 40, 58, 180–181; domino theory and, 95; immigration from, 59; Open Door Policy and, 44

Assad, Bashar, 176, 177

Atlantic Charter, 65, 70, 211n34

atomic bomb, 211n32; creation of, 69, 76; foreign policy decisions of, 74–77; on Japan, 69–70; Manhattan Project for, 69, 77; on Nagasaki, 75, 78; Obama on, 75; Soviet Union on, 70, 92; Truman on, 69–70, 77. *See also* Hiroshima atomic bombing

AWACS. *See* Airborne Early Warning Aircraft

Axis of evil, 148, 194

Aziz, Tariq, 124

War Powers Resolution, 22, 108, 114, 124, 217n69–217n70; in Afghanistan war, 146
Washington, George, 16, 33; Farewell Address of, 35; on unilateralism, 35
Washington Conference, 210n7
Watergate scandal, 108, 111
weapons of mass destruction, 7, 22. *See also* nuclear weapons
WikiLeaks, 193
Wilkie, Wendell, 64
Williams, T. Harry, 38
Wilson, Woodrow, 8, 21, 208n33, 208n35; Bush, G. W., and, 156; on dominance, 58; Fourteen Points of, 49–50, 61; idealism of, 46, 47–49, 52; on League of Nations, 51; liberal perspective of, 11–12; values of, 47; on World War I outbreak, 48–49
Winning the Right War (Gordon, P.), 154
women: in foreign policy decision making, 13, 204n14; in World War II, 66–67. *See also* feminist perspective, foreign policy decisions
women's suffrage, 59
World Industrial Output, 47

World Trade Center, 145
World War I, 6, 8, 21, 208n35; end of, 49–50; involvement in, 53, 73; lead up to, 46; unilateralism after, 53; Wilson on, 48–49. *See also* interwar period
World War II, 28; allies in, 67; on domestic issues, 66, 74; economic depression before, 62; escalation to, 61–63; future impact of, 66; legacy of, 66–68; military leader of, 76; neutrality acts in, 63–64; outcomes of, 73–74; power after, 79; Roosevelt, F., on, 65; Roosevelt, F., on end of, 67–68; technology in, 68–69; women in, 66–67. *See also* interwar period; Pearl Harbor attack

X Article, 83, 85–86

Yeltsin, Boris, 125
Yugoslavia, 126, 220n26
Yugoslav-Slovene War, 126

Zimmermann, Arthur, 48
Zimmermann Telegram, 48–49

About the Author

Joyce P. Kaufman is professor of political science and director of the Center for Engagement with Communities at Whittier College. She is the author of *NATO and the Former Yugoslavia: Crisis, Conflict, and the Atlantic Alliance* (2002) and numerous articles and papers on U.S. foreign and security policy. She is also the author of *Introduction to International Relations: Theory and Practice* (2013). With Kristen Williams, she is coauthor of *Women at War, Women Building Peace: Challenging Gender Norms* (2013), *Women and War: Gender Identity and Activism in Times of Conflict* (2010), and *Women, the State, and War: A Comparative Perspective on Citizenship and Nationalism* (2007). As a faculty member at an institution that focuses on undergraduate education, she regularly teaches a political science class on American foreign policy. Joyce P. Kaufman received her B.A. and M.A. from New York University and her Ph.D. from the University of Maryland.